COME SHARE MY FOXHOLE

I think it's Nov. 7
1944
Day of the Election

Dear Evelyn & Larry:
Just a few lines darling to let you know that I love you both with all my heart & darling I will forever & ever. It sure will be a great day when we can all be back together again & darling I'm sure hoping that it won't be long.
I got three letters from you & one from Mom yes —

COME SHARE MY FOXHOLE

Richard D. Floyd, M.D.

Copyright © 2019 Richard D. Floyd

All rights reserved. No part of this book may be reproduced, distributed, or transmitted in any form by any means, or stored in any information or retrieval system without the prior written permission of the copyright owner, except in the case of a reviewer who may quote brief passages in a book review. For permission requests, e-mail the copyright owner/author at the e-mail address below.

The events and conversations in this book have been set down to the best of the author's ability, although some names and details have been changed to protect the privacy of individuals. All quotations remain the intellectual property of their respective originators. All use of quotations is done under the fair use copyright principal.

ISBN: 9781796924602

Bookcover images provided by the copyright owner
Bookcover Brandi Doane McCann (eBook Cover Designs)

Printed in the United States of America

Copyright owner/author e-mail: sfloyd3252@aol.com

DEDICATION

Sixteen million, five hundred thousand Americans served in the United States military during World War Two. Those soldiers, their families, friends, and communities said NO to an evil that threatened to destroy not only their freedom but the freedom we enjoy to this very day. Each participant in this evil war had life changing experiences but most, including my parents, have gone to their grave with their story untold. This book is my parent's story. I dedicate this book in memory of Karl and Evelyn Floyd. They were good people.

COME SHARE MY FOXHOLE

Author's Note

The goal was to clean out the house that my parents raised me and my siblings in. Dad had died over twenty years earlier, my brother had recently died, and Mom was in a nursing home.

We found that day the letters contained in this book in an old metal bread box. It was tucked deep in my parent's bedroom closet. The old box was then moved to a closet in my home along with some other treasures Mom had saved over the years. A few years later, I opened the bread box and discovered the best gift my mom ever gave to me. There were letters that spanned the years from 1940 to 1945. I started reading. After the first letter, I could not resist the urge to keep reading until I had devoured them all. I have to confess that I felt, at times, like an intruder as my parents expressed eternal love and desire for each other.

The letters tweaked my interest of World War Two. I read anything I thought would increase my knowledge and understanding on what my parents experienced. I spent many hours at the library reading microfilm from that era. I kept thinking there was a story that could be told, so I copied the letters into my computer. I edited out the amorous portions and the innocent chitchat. The story became more powerful.

I asked myself many, many times if I should share their story with others. It is, after all, very personal. I also knew Dad never turned away the opportunity to spin a good yarn. I concluded that the story deserves to be told. I decided to be the narrator while Mom and Dad told the story. *Come Share My Foxhole* is that story. My hope is you enjoy reading it half as much as I have enjoyed preparing it.

Acknowledgements

I could not have completed this book without the Rushville Public Library. Whenever I appeared to use the microfilm in the Indiana Room at the library, the librarians happily unlocked the door and let me spend hours doing my research. The library is a jewel. Thank you, ladies.

The book cover was created by Brandi McCann (eBook Cover Designs). She tolerated my ignorance on book cover design and was able to help turn my dream into reality. Thank you, Brandi.

I needed someone to transcribe the letters into a Word document. I asked my son, Mark, if he could accomplish such a feat. He did a great job. Without his work, I could never have put this story into book form. Thanks, Mark. I love you.

I started the manuscript for this book ten years ago. Four of the best dogs to ever grace this planet lovingly and faithfully spent long hours near me while I wrote. Two of them have crossed the Rainbow Bridge. Thanks, Stuart, Duffy, Ribsey, and Lucky.

I trust that my parents would be proud of this book. Without their wisdom in saving their letters, I could never have understood what they went through to give me the freedom that I enjoy. They were good people.

One of my goals was to pass my parents' story on to my kids, grandkids, and future descendants. They have a good family history. I hope they know how much I love them.

My greatest gratitude goes to my wife, Sue. My first drafts were too complex and rambling. She lovingly explained to this hardheaded Floyd that my grammar could be better. She gently prodded me to improve my sentence structure. She reminded me to remember the readers I was writing this book for. She encouraged me to not give up. Without her, this book simply would not have been completed. I still don't know why she chose me to spend her life with. I love you, Beautiful Lady.

Contents

LEAVING HOME 1
RUSH COUNTY, INDIANA 7
KARL 15
EVIE 23
POLITICS 31
FALLING IN LOVE 35
1940 PRESIDENTIAL ELECTION 41
THE MILITARY DRAFT 45
ESCALATION TOWARD WAR 49
YOUNG FAMILY 57
WORLD WAR TWO BEGINS 61
YOU HAVE BEEN SELECTED 65
YOU'RE IN THE ARMY NOW 71
CALIFORNIA HERE I COME 95
FURLOUGH 123
GOING OVERSEAS 129
SOMEWHERE IN ENGLAND 135
FINAL PREPARATIONS FOR THE INVASION 163
INVASION 187
SOMEWHERE IN FRANCE 193
SOMEWHERE IN EUROPE 211
THE BULGE 223
THE FINAL PUSH TO BERLIN 229
VICTORY IN EUROPE 239

THE HORRIBLE END OF WORLD WAR TWO	249
DARKNESS BEFORE THE LIGHT	265
I'M ON MY WAY HOME	281
LIFE AFTER THE WAR	291
About the author	301

"Us boys that actually have seen it can't believe how brutal it was. Thousands on top of thousands of American boys will never see home again, yet we have to face another enemy in the Pacific. I don't know if I'll go there or not, but if I do, I at least want to spend a few days with you and Larry and the folks at home."

Corporal Karl Floyd
May 19, 1945

LEAVING HOME

Karl hated goodbyes. He did not want visitors. Madge kept the baby so he and Evie could spend their last night alone. He played his guitar and sang songs for her. He placed the guitar in the corner of the little living room of their four room house. He told Evie to not move it until he got back. It was well past midnight when they went to bed.

Karl woke before the sun. Evie was still sleeping. She knew what happened next. Here today, gone tomorrow, maybe forever. She had spent most of the night watching him sleep, listening to him breathe, enjoying his scent and the warmth of his body.

The Old Man's young rooster started crowing at the first flicker of sunlight. Now wide awake from the cock's banter, Karl decided he had to see Flatrock River one more time. He got out of bed hoping he wouldn't wake Evie. He hung his hatchet inside his belt like he had done thousands of times over his twenty-three years. He walked down the road to the old Indian trail that led to the river. When he reached his goal, he stood on the bank of his favorite fishing hole for a few minutes. A young sycamore tree on the bank caught his eye. He used his hatchet to hack the letters KRF into the trunk of the tree.

When he returned, Evie was making a breakfast of toast, bacon, and fried eggs sunny side up, just the way he liked them. She didn't ask where he had been. She figured he had gone to his mom's for a cup of coffee.

The moment he dreaded was upon him after breakfast. Uncomfortable thoughts threatened to overwhelm him. The next time he came home, if there was a next time, he might be another dead soldier in a wooden casket. Worse yet, maybe Evie would get a Western Union telegram like his cousin Walter's family had. Would he end up like Walter, buried in a foreign country under a white cross telling no one in particular that Private Karl Floyd lay there? Other fears rolled around in his mind. Would he come back with his head held high or as a coward? He would always love Evie, but would she still love him? What if he returned with an injury so bad that he couldn't work at the factory to support his family? Would their six month old son, Larry, recognize him?

He fought back tears. He thought to himself "Goddammit, I'm a Floyd. Floyds don't cry." He forced himself to think of the exciting adventure he was about to start.

Karl didn't feel like driving, so Evie drove across town to the train station. She put the car in first gear after she backed onto Benjamin Street. As she often did, she killed the engine when she let out the clutch. Karl usually kidded her when she did that. Not this time. He reached over and touched her knee. He told her they would work on letting out the clutch when he got back.

On the way, memories of happier times were everywhere. As always, the Courthouse came into view when they went down the hill that led downtown. Its clock tower, visible in all directions, had chimed every hour on the hour for his entire life. It seemed to be standing at attention for him. The Greek's homemade ice cream shop with the wooden booths where he had spent many evenings flew by. He wanted to stop to say goodbye, but he knew to do so would make leaving more painful. He smiled when the car crossed Main Street. He thought of all the times he and Tom had cruised up and down that street on Saturday nights. He then saw the Courthouse curb where the Courthouse Curbside Court convened on warm Saturday nights while their wives shopped and gossiped. He wondered what profound problems they would solve while he was gone. The beautiful public library came and went quickly. The sun's shadow on the sundial over the door said it was nine o'clock. The Courthouse clocked chimed nine times in agreement. He couldn't resist. He turned around for one more glance at downtown.

Evie pulled into the train station parking lot. It was where two Aprils earlier, eight months before the United States entered the war that Rushville and over 1,000 citizens gave 51 draftees a grand sendoff. The *Rushville Republican* described the events of the day, "A member of the local American Legion post presided at this program with music being supplied by the Rushville high school and Rush County Farm Bureau bands. Miss Betty Belle Campbell sang *God Bless America*. Short talks were given by the local judge, city officials, a pastor of a local church, city attorney, and county Selective Service board members. Pocket bibles were given to each draftee. Each young man also received four packages of cigarettes form the American Legion, V.F.W., and Eagles lodge. Photographs were taken of the entire group. A color guard of ex-servicemen and the local high school band headed the parade from the post office to the train station. Final goodbyes were said and Rush County's latest contribution to the rapidly growing citizen army departed." For Karl's departure on April 14, 1943, only the families of the boys who were leaving were present.

Karl didn't say a word. Evie started crying.

Karl had asked his mom and dad to stay home. They didn't listen. They had walked the mile from their home to the station. He saw them right away. Karl looked at his mom, all five feet tall of her. He tried to ignore the tears in her eyes. He looked to see if she was wearing her apron. Yep. She was, like always. He took a mental snapshot of her lovely, but worn out, face. No doubt she was thinking of her five brothers and step-brothers. They had gone to Europe during World War One. They came back quieter and angrier than before they left. All she could manage was to reach up to straighten her baby boy's collar and say, "Come home, my dearest son." Karl bit his lip.

Karl looked his dad in the eye. He was a man Karl and his brothers feared as much as loved. He reached out and shook Ott's hand. He felt a bit silly. He had never done that before. Adhering to the unwritten rule that Floyd men didn't show emotion, but surprised at his son's gesture, all the Old Man could muster up was, "I'll look after Evie and Larry. You keep your goddam head down and your ammo dry. Now go and get this sonsabitchin' war over and get your ass back home." Karl smiled. The Old Man had just told Karl that he loved him.

Karl told Evie's folks that they didn't need to see him off when they picked up Larry the night before. Madge answered "Over my dead body. We're coming in as soon as Dory has the cows milked and the hogs fed." She already had her son Ronald, an army paratrooper, fighting somewhere in the Pacific. A few weeks earlier, Dory's son left for the army. Now Karl, her only daughter's husband, was leaving. She knew this might be the last time she would lay her eyes upon him. She clutched her bible. She took Karl's hand and said a prayer. Karl felt she had just put a blanket of protection over him. He felt strong.

Dory was a man of few words. He had received a letter from his son the day before Karl was to leave about how hard the army life was. He clasped Karl's arm with his callused hands and quietly uttered, "May God protect you. I'll watch out for Evie and the baby." Karl grinned.

A draft board member read the list of names. When Karl's name was called, he held his nineteen year old wife and six month old son one more time. He then lit up a Lucky Strike cigarette and boarded the train. He found a seat by a window. He could see the people who meant everything to him. He wanted to get off, but knew he couldn't. He had to go. His lips mouthed, "Everything will be okay. I'll be back."

The train station was soon out of sight. Farewell family. Farewell Rushville. Goodbye to his youth.

Alone on the train with the other selectees, he felt relief that the goodbyes were over. He reminded himself he was now a man. The sooner he got started, the sooner he could come home. He promised himself he would become a good soldier so he could have a decent chance of coming home proud, healthy, and intact. He found himself wishing the train would slow down. He had been to Indianapolis so many times he knew every bridge, creek, and town on the way. He had never before paid much attention to the details. Thoughts of his innocent, but sometimes reckless childhood overwhelmed him.

The train passed fields and woods where he, Tom, and the Old Man hunted rabbits, treed raccoons, and trapped for muskrat and mink. He thought of his beloved 12 gauge shotgun he had bought with his own money when he was sixteen. Dammit, he had forgotten to clean it! He made a mental note to ask Evie to have the Old Man clean it.

He got a twinge of homesickness two miles out of Rushville. The train crossed the road that led to Madge and Dory's farmhouse. A smile crossed his face. He remembered one night he and Evie parked on that road next to the train track so they could make out. They fell asleep until four in the morning. Knowing Dory's dog Pepper would bark and wake Madge and Dory, he drove into the barnyard with the auto's lights off. Closing his eyes, he could see Evie throwing a kiss as she sneaked in the back door.

The train slowed as it entered Arlington. It passed the canning factory which sprang to life every summer when the sweet corn was ready. He had visited Evie there when she shucked corn to earn some money. The train then rolled into Morristown. Despite the odor of the sweaty, smoking, and nervous guys packed in the train, he thought he could smell fried chicken from the Kopper Kettle Inn Restaurant. He always said nobody made fried chicken and gravy like Madge. He wondered if the army served fried chicken. He bet himself they didn't.

The train crossed the trestle over Brandywine Creek. This creek was immortalized into Hoosier folklore when storyteller James Whitcomb Riley wrote about it in *The Old Swimmin' Hole*. Karl found himself reciting some words from another Riley classic, *Little Orphan Annie*.

The trestle reminded him of another childhood experience. He and a couple of his brothers were walking across the train trestle that crossed over Flatrock River. His meaner than hell brother, Big Guy, dared Karl, "I bet you're too much of a chickenshit to jump." Seconds later, about halfway down, Karl remembered the water wasn't very deep where he was about to land. When he hit the bottom, a rusty can buried in the mud sliced a huge gash in one foot. He bled like the dickens, so much that his brothers bragged that Karl turned the river red all the way to East Hill Cemetery. Later, as his mom poured mercurochrome over the gash, she said two things he never forgot, "Your brothers are going to be the death of you. Why didn't you think before you jumped?" He chuckled. A shrapnel wound in the war couldn't hurt any more than that mercurochrome did. He reminded himself to not take any dares in the army. Returning to the moment, he noticed that Brandywine Creek's water was muddy. It would be a good day for catfishing.

The rest of the fifty mile trip to Union Station in downtown Indianapolis flew by. After leaving the train, the selectees were herded onto a bus. It transported them to Fort Benjamin Harrison. When the bus pulled into Fort Ben, a mean looking sonofabitch in a Sergeant's uniform bounded on board. He told the selectees to get their sorry asses off the bus and line up. Scanning the group, Karl saw many anxious boys. Some of those faces still had peach fuzz instead of whiskers. He wondered which ones he would get to know. Who in the group would get injured? Who would die? He touched his shirt pocket to feel the picture Evie gave him of her and Larry. He packed his past into a small corner of his mind for safekeeping. Now he wished the goddam time would speed up.

RUSH COUNTY, INDIANA

Rush County Courthouse

Spring in Indiana is proof there is a God. The spring of 1940 was one of the best ever. Hesitant at first, winter released its cold, gray grip and surrendered to warm days.

Central Indiana is flat as a pancake. It was created to produce food and hardwood trees. Fiercely independent, rugged men and women, frustrated with the poor farming conditions in the east, traveled west down the Ohio River. When they arrived at the river towns of Cincinnati or Louisville, they walked and settled near water when the nectar of Indiana dirt intoxicated them. There was no need to travel further. The black dirt contained riches for those with the will, strength, and patience to use it. Those independent, plain, stoic folks didn't want much. They dreamed of owning their own piece of land. A fertile piece of land and an honest day's work would do. They were stubborn and strong as mules. They harvested the virgin hardwood forests that had nurtured and protected the dirt for eons using simple tools, rugged animals, and determination. They turned the young state of Indiana into farmland.

Each Indiana season offered something essential for human survival. Settlers could not alter the laws of nature, but following the gifts of each season offered them a chance for success. They also experienced the viciousness of the seasons by trial, error, and a great deal of pain. There were many one armed men in the state who had learned the folly of haste or careless actions. Graveyards contained other poor souls who had met death from accidents or illness. For the early settlers, a Sunday outfit to thank God for his kindness and protection was often the only luxury of their rough lives.

Surveyors mapped out the land into square mile grids. The grids were framed by roads on which farmers and loggers lived and traveled to their fields or to town. Piles of rocks outlined the boundaries of farms. Fences kept cows or foraging hogs from wandering onto a neighbor's farm. After all, there were limits to neighborliness.

A system of ditches created by Mother Nature meandered over the terrain. They drained the land and provided drinking water for humans and wildlife. The ditches were obstacles for farmers but the dirt would have been nothing but a muddy swamp without them. The ditches merged in low spots to form small ponds which filtered the sediment from the fields. The ponds housed sunfish, bluegill, crappie, and bass near the surface. Catfish and carp lived near the bottom where they could eat organic material. The pond water spilled over to form larger creeks. The creeks merged to form Flatrock River. Flatrock's water flowed south toward the Ohio River.

A traveler through Rush County in 1940 struggled with boredom from the never ending cornfields. Every few miles, a small settlement built around the intersection of two roads broke the monotony. These communities at one time had provided rest and supplies for weary humans and horses. They were so small the only commerce was a general store, a grain elevator, and maybe a train depot. A traveler had to be alert or a settlement could disappear before its name could be read on a sign along the road.

Other towns were large enough to be visible on the horizon. Church steeples, standing tall above the trees, seemed to be pointing to heaven. Some of these towns were the capital of its county and were called the "county seat". They had a dominating Courthouse in the center of town which often resembled a European castle or fortress. A haze of smoke from factories of coal burning power plants usually clouded the sky. Railroads for hauling grain, coal, and humans ran parallel to the roads leading into those towns. The railroad tracks offered an escape to the world beyond. Few residents desired to leave.

Vast amounts of natural gas in the bedrock beneath the Indiana soil offered manufacturers an inexpensive source of energy. Factories flourished in many Indiana towns in 1940. A factory job provided a regular paycheck. Many young people raised on farms chose to seek a life different than their parents. They abandoned the farm to move to town. As a result, towns grew to accommodate the new working class.

Rushville was one such town, the county seat of Rush County. It was the birthplace and burial ground to four generations of Karl's family. It was the adopted hometown for Evie.

The rules, values, and ethics of the early settlers still existed in March of 1940. As winter gave way to spring, it was time for the farmers to get to work. The barren fields were a patchwork of cornstalks, soybean stubble, weeds, and puddles. There were only a few frosty nights left. The soil began to thaw and to offer the nutrients necessary to sustain life. Animals started shedding their winter coats. Crocuses and daffodils chiseled through the warming dirt. Sap started to run up the tree trunks to swell buds on the branches. The sweet smell of pollen would soon remind honeybees to pollinate fruit trees and berry plants. It was impossible to escape the freshness of new life.

Indiana's spring sky was a gift in so many ways. The spectacular sunrises arrived in the eastern sky earlier every morning. As the sun rose above the horizon, cloudlike patches of fog evaporated to reveal a scene of serene beauty. Roosters responded by providing an alarm clock at the crack of dawn. Songbirds greeted the daylight with their cheerful spring melodies. The sun's journey across the sky took longer every day as if it feared missing something. Before setting in the evening, it hesitated in the western sky to paint a beautiful picture of pink, red, white, and blue before it slipped away.

Farmers were ready to resume their love/hate relationship with nature. They had oiled and repaired their farm equipment over the winter. They made certain their plow horses or tractors were ready for the planting season. Their plows would soon be turning over the remnants of last year's crops to create a new canvas in the fields. Farm wives removed debris from last year's garden. They bought baby chicks that would supply eggs and fried chicken for the family. Farmers welcomed the new calves and pigs who were conceived the previous fall. The sweet aroma of fresh dirt, an aphrodisiac to farm families, soon would permeate the air.

Houses were no longer prisons shut tight from the winter weather. Open windows permitted fresh air into homes which had a dirty, sooty odor from the coal burning stoves used for heat during the winter. In Rushville, people reacquainted with their neighbors. Most houses had a porch as big as any indoor room. Families sat on the porch after supper on warm evenings to listen to birds, watch kids play, and eavesdrop on arguing neighbors. The city park came alive with family picnics, baseball games, and children swinging and playing games. Young and old sat on park benches. Teenagers and young adults went downtown to window shop or take in a movie. They spent time at the Greek's ice cream shop where they talked about their plans for the future. The Courthouse Curbside Court re-convened.

Rush County prospered from its mixture of agricultural and manufacturing economies. Rushville was home to 5,900 of the county's 19,000 residents. All roads led downtown. Downtown contained department stores, shoe stores, jewelers, barbers, and clothing stores. One drugstore emitted a distinctive odor from the various medicines it housed. There were two banks which held all the money for the entire county. Two movie theaters played Hollywood movies well into the night. There were a variety of eateries. The smell from one, a joint that sold greasy hamburgers, permeated the entire downtown. The Greek's sold homemade ice cream and candy. On the edge of downtown were several bars and pool halls. One lonely church with a stately spire occupied a remote corner near the library. Downtown was busiest on Saturday nights because everyone and their brother went downtown to show off, spend some money, and visit with friends. It was the night for people to let their hair down.

The Courthouse was the pride of Rush County. Its construction almost bankrupted the county when it was built in 1896. It was the biggest and tallest building in the county. It occupied an entire block smack dab in the center of downtown. Its clock tower was easily visible when a traveler from any direction approached Rushville. The Courthouse square was framed by a curb which was high enough for grown men to perch themselves on for hours. Men from all over the county sat on the curb on warm Saturday nights. Like a flock of crows, they watched life go by while they spread gossip, told lies, and debated local, national, and world news. It was the place where friendships began, and sometimes ended. The only break a member of the Courthouse Curbside Court took was to buy a soda or visit the toilet.

Rush County Courthouse Curb

Entire families traveled to Rushville on Saturday night. Everyone had an assigned position in the auto. Older children sat next to windows while younger kids squeezed in wherever they could find space. It was not unusual to see the littlest sprawled on the back window ledge. The best parking spots to see and be seen were on Main Street. Those lucky enough to get one of the prime spaces lounged inside or on top of the family machine while they enjoyed an ice cream cone or soda. They watched the endless parade of vehicles cruise back and forth from one end of Main Street to the other.

Girls would not be alone for fear of something bad happening. Each girl wore her favorite dress. Their white anklets folded down right above the ankle. The more adventurous wore bright red lipstick. Fearful of being left out, they wandered around like a school of fish. They swam from store to store, never more than an arm's length from the collective mass. Each girl hoped a guy would single her out for attention. They couldn't approach the guy, but it was fine to send encouragement. They pretended disgust at unsolicited catcalls from guys who were hanging out. Though outwardly looking upset, such swooning was answered with a subtle smile and a wink.

Guys acted confident, carefree, and aloof. They did not have the social constraints the girls had. They wore overalls or work clothes during the work week. They dressed in their best duds on Saturday night. Shirts were neatly ironed. They wore their neatly ironed slacks high on their hips. Their wing tip shoes were spit polished. They combed their hair straight back. A liberal amount of hair cream made their hair slick and shiny. The tougher guys let a small strand of hair dangle onto their foreheads. Even those who didn't need to shave smelled like after shave lotion. They did everything in their power to charm the girls. A few ventured out alone. The cool ones hung out in small groups while they strutted down Main Street. Those with decent paying jobs cruised down Main Street in their own car. All guys had girls on their mind.

The bleak and terrible Great Depression of the 1930s robbed the kids from Rush County of their childhood innocence. It hardened them. Harsh lessons of life were taught and learned during those difficult years. They knew the value of hard work. They learned to obey rules. They assumed adult responsibilities instead of spending their adolescent years having fun and challenging their parents. They worried about paying bills and having a roof overhead. They learned any obstacle could be defeated if everyone pitched in. These young people were cocky. They grew into young adults confident they could adjust to and trounce any adversity. One thing was certain. They knew how to survive. They exited the Great Depression knowing that bad times, no matter how despairing, always come to an end. They never, however, fully recovered from the scars engraved into their generational consciousness.

The economy by 1940 was rapidly improving. People found jobs. Money was coming in, thanks in no small degree to the government's increased demand for military goods and materials because of a war in Europe. President Roosevelt assured the country the increased economic activity was only to help America's friends in Europe. He stressed that America was not preparing for war. Most citizens wanted to believe him.

KARL

Karl Floyd was a slim, six foot tall, olive skinned man with coal black, wavy hair. He was the thirteenth of the fourteen children born to Ott and Clara. Only eight lived to adulthood. Four died before Karl was born. Five month old twins died from chronic diarrhea. Two died in 1918 during a flu epidemic. One sister died when Karl was an infant in an industrial accident at eighteen years of age. The fourteenth, an infant, died from whooping cough in 1922.

Karl enjoyed perfect health as a child. His mom and sisters pampered, tutored, and doted on him. They developed him into the one son who would be there for them when they needed help. He learned women would support him when times were difficult. He, in return, developed a need to protect the women in his life.

His dad and brothers badgered, teased, and protected him when the need arose. He learned to confront challenges with the assurance he had plenty of backup if he needed it. His self-assurance bordered on cockiness. He was known to sign his name in school after the famous depression era bank robber "Pretty Boy" Floyd. He became a confident young man. He felt himself to be unbeatable.

Karl's place at the large, chaotic dinner table was next to his mother. He never went hungry. Clara made sure he received more than his share of the greasy, fried food she prepared daily for the family. He seldom felt threatened while in her presence. She defended him whenever the older children picked on him. She turned a deaf ear when the other kids complained. She had lost several children. Karl was her baby. She wasn't about to lose him.

Ott was, behind his back, called the Old Man by his sons. He earned his living as a manual laborer. The 1930 census described him as a brick mason. He worked at a lumber yard in 1940. He had a reputation for being tough and having a quick temper. There was one story that Karl liked to tell about the Old Man, "Dad had an older brother, Ed, who was missing a thumb. Dad told us he lost it one day when he and Ed went rabbit hunting. They had only one shotgun so they had to take turns carrying the gun. Uncle Ed carried first. After a lapse of considerable time, Dad decided it was his time to carry the gun. Instead of giving up the gun, Uncle Ed took off running with Dad hot on his trail. They started fighting when Dad finally caught him. Low and behold, the gun fired and took off Uncle Ed's thumb." After a short hesitation, Karl finished the story, "Whether or not they quit hunting that day, I do not know." Ott's reputation was forever sealed and delivered for his family.

Ott and Clara were schooled on the cruelties and harshness of life. They had limited formal education. They were a physically and mentally tough couple. They faced huge burdens in providing for their large family. They were forty years old when Karl was born. They felt another mouth to feed at the dinner table was a blessing. The more kids they had, the wealthier they felt. They knew how to put food on the table, clothes on their kids' backs, and a roof over their heads. While they struggled to make ends meet, their kids in essence raised themselves. They did not tolerate laziness. They taught by example that failure was a sign of weakness and laziness. They never allowed their kids to use their economic disadvantage as an excuse.

The Floyd family lived by Ott's rules. The honor of the family was not to be violated. Respect and support for each other was vital. The family's good name was all that mattered. No person was better than a Floyd. There was one corollary to the family's rule book: most anything was acceptable as long as the Old Man didn't find out. If he did find the family name tarnished by one of his offspring, punishment was swift and painful.

Clara and Ott Floyd

Clara and Ott believed in God, but they did not attend church. None of their kids attended church, either. They felt churches were where people complained and fought with each other. To depend on God was a sign of weakness. They knew the difference between good and bad, but Ott had a tendency to muddy the difference of the two. A *Republican* article in 1938 gave an example, "Ott Floyd has quit trapping fish, which is against the law, since Blanchard Ketchum, our efficient game warden, came to town." When one of the boys asked Ott about the article, he answered that he was just putting food on the table.

Ott built their house with his bare hands. It consisted of a living room, four bedrooms, a large kitchen, and one bathroom. The kitchen, the heart of the family's life because Clara was always in it, was next to the coal shed behind the house. One of the kitchen walls had a three inch wide circular hole near the ceiling. Ott loved to tell the story about the hole, "When Karl was a wet behind the ears teenager, he decided to clean his shotgun before rabbit hunting season started. Being a young buck without a lick of good sense, he forgot to check if the goddam gun was unloaded. Like any boy would do to admire his work, he raised the gun. He pulled the trigger to discover the gun contained a live shell. The blast made that there hole in the kitchen wall." Ott didn't repair the hole. He knew a good lesson when he saw it.

Karl had four tough, strong, and bullheaded older brothers. They were proud guys and they certainly didn't run from trouble. They never made apologies for who they were. Growing up on the wrong side of town, they protected and supported each other when necessary. They fought among themselves to prove their toughness, but that privilege was not for outsiders to test. Though they envied Karl's "Dearest Son" status, they taught him how to fight. They teased, tested, and tormented him until he proved he could hold his own. They taught him to do whatever was necessary to win. They hardened him with their stubborn mischievous ways. They protected and supported each other when necessary. Their gang of brothers gave Karl the confidence to accept challenges. He knew, no matter how dismal things looked, his brothers would always back him up. If someone outside the family teased or harassed a Floyd, especially the little one, the wrath of the Floyd boys would follow. The Old Man never punished them for sticking up for each other.

Clara often said it was a miracle Karl survived childhood. One prank occurred when Karl was still too young to go to school. Like all good jokes, it taught Karl about naiveté, trust, and winning even when scared out of one's wits. Legend was that a frightening visit occurred every year at a tombstone in the cemetery next to the Floyd house. The person under the stone had been murdered. His ghost would rise from the grave on the anniversary of his death. The ghost sat on top of the stone. His raspy voice begged for the head of his murderer. On a night so black the moon didn't dare come out and the wind and falling leaves created a chaotic, frightening chorus of ghoulish sounds, a night made for whistling in the dark, Karl's brothers decided it was the perfect night to visit the cemetery to see if the legend was true. They urged Karl to go with them, telling him that he was a coward if he didn't join them. They promised they would not let him out of their sight. Karl was young enough to have a colorful imagination, but his young mind lacked the sense to smell a rat. He agreed to go.

They snuck into the graveyard, made the trek to the stone, but no ghost appeared. A whispered discussion followed. The older boys decided the ghost was staying away because there were too many boys in the cemetery. Big Guy suggested if all but one of them left, the ghost might appear. A quick vote followed. Karl was elected to stay. He protested, but his objection fell on deaf ears. To help him muster courage, the older brothers tied their baby brother to the tombstone. With a wink and a nod, they assured him they would return in the morning to release him from the clutches of the haunted stone. They left Karl with nothing more than his imagination for a companion.

The boys arrived home expecting a spanking when the Old Man discovered what they had done. Karl was sitting at the kitchen table with Clara! He had beaten them home. As Karl told the story, the ghost felt sorry and untied him. There was a moral of the story for the older boys. Tie the knots real tight when you're leaving your youngest brother alone in a cemetery. Karl also learned two lessons. Don't volunteer for something you don't understand and avoid situations where you are outnumbered.

The town dump, a putrid, disgusting hole near their house was a source of entertainment for the Floyd boys. They discovered the joy of scrounging. Ott taught them early in life that one man's trash could be another man's treasure. They learned to how to shoot at the dump. The boys liked to sneak the Old Man's 22 caliber pistol out of the house. They would take it to the dump then sit quietly in the rubble. When rats came to the surface in the evening to look for food, the boys took turns shooting the rodents. Karl became the best rat shooter of the bunch. He could shoot a rat thirty feet away by the time he was sixteen.

Karl learned how to survive. He respected and enjoyed nature. He knew how to get what his family needed for food. All he needed was a knife, gun, or fishing pole. The Floyd house was an easy walk to Flatrock River. Ott and Clara couldn't afford butcher shop meat to feed their herd of kids, so Ott taught the boys to fish and to kill their own meat. They hunted rabbits, squirrels, opossum, ground hogs, and raccoons. They trapped for muskrat and mink in the winter for extra money. On summer evenings, they snared frogs on the banks of Flatrock.

Like a sponge, Karl soaked up everything. He skipped second grade, going straight from first to third grade. Ott and Clara didn't argue when seventeen year old Karl dropped out of school. They felt learning more than basic reading, writing, and arithmetic was of no value for a family that barely scraped by. After Karl dropped out of school, he immediately found a job at International Furniture. He felt he had a promising future as he learned how to upholster furniture. He dreamed of someday owning his own upholstery shop, but he spent his entire working life at the factory. By spring of 1940, Karl, a twenty year old high school dropout, had a decent job despite an unemployment rate of ten percent in Rushville.

When he had his own family, Karl followed the same routine every evening after work. Before going into his own house, he walked across the street on a well-worn foot path to Ott and Clara's house. He poured himself a cup of coffee. He often ate supper with them if Clara made something he liked. He sat on the same chair next to his mom that he sat in as a child, the chair that faced the gunshot hole in the wall.

The Floyd family resembled an oak tree. Both grew a taproot for stability when young to create a strong, immovable base. That stability made Karl's life bearable. When Ott's family grew too large for the house Karl was born in, he built a bigger house fifty feet away. Karl never left the neighborhood he grew up in. His idea of adventure was the fifty mile trip to Indianapolis.

When Karl married, Ott built a four room stucco house across the street. Karl lived there until he died. Except for the war years, he lived his entire life within one hundred yards of the house in which Clara gave birth to him.

EVIE

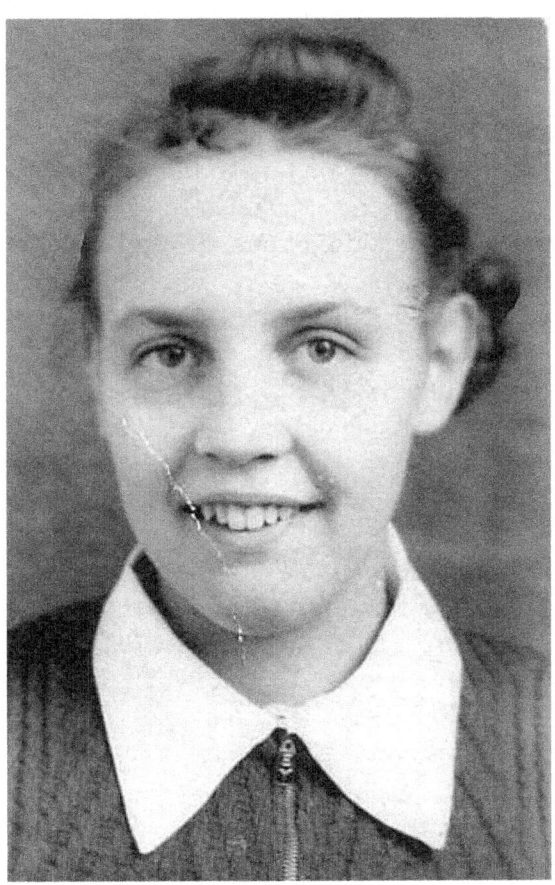

Evelyn Mabel Yoder was called Evie by family and friends. She lived in a rented farmhouse on an eighty acre farm a few miles outside Rushville with her mom Madge, stepdad Dory, a brother Ronald, a stepbrother, and a young half-brother. Madge and Dory, their dream of a farm of their own long abandoned, were hardworking tenant farmers. They were never more than one bad growing season from the poor farm. Besides growing corn, to make ends meet they had a small apple orchard and huge vegetable garden.

They kept an assortment of milk cows, horses, hogs, chickens, and ducks.

Madge held the family together. Her mother died when she was nine years old leaving her father to raise six children alone. Her only sister died four years later. At age thirteen Madge had full responsibility for cooking, cleaning, washing clothes, ironing, gardening and canning, and attending school. She was eighteen when she married Evie's dad. Madge barely survived that disastrous marriage. She never talked about how hard her life had been. She liked to say, "Complaining won't make things better, so don't." She refused to give up on anyone. She often threatened to "shake a knot in your tail" if one of the kids got out of line. No matter the severity of the transgression, she forgave easily. She always had a hug to give and knew the right words of encouragement for a pouting child. Her kids knew she had their back.

Dory wasn't anything like Madge's first husband. He had lost his first wife from complications of pregnancy. He hired Madge to care for his son and second wife, who was dying from consumption, so he could farm. Dory and Madge married two years after his second wife died. He treated Evie like she was his own flesh. He gave her his time after a tiring day's work to listen to her chatter about her life. He seldom gave an opinion and didn't judge. He just listened. Not a large man, he was surprisingly strong. He had a weakness for desert, especially pumpkin pie. He liked to put two or three pats of butter on his piece then smother it with molasses. He was a quiet, hardworking, steadfast, and reliable man of faith. Dory was a good man.

Evie never knew her real dad, Claude. He moved the family to Dallas, Texas before she was born. He deserted the family when she was a toddler. Haunted by his absence, Evie thought she was the reason he left. She wondered why he could hurt her so much. She had a constant feeling of emptiness in her heart. She cried herself to sleep many nights. Madge went to such great lengths to remove all evidence of Claude that she cut his face out of family pictures. If Evie asked about her dad, Madge answered that he was a gambler and loser. She never divulged that he spent time in prison for check forgery. Madge said as long as Evie and her brother, Ronald, lived in her house, they were forbidden to have any contact with him. Evie couldn't send him letters to ask how he was or if he loved her. She never received birthday cards or Christmas gifts. Once, Evie thought he came to visit her when a man knocked on the front door. After seeing who was knocking, Madge told Evie to go upstairs. From her bedroom window, Evie peered down to see the man but she didn't get a good look at his face. Madge didn't answer the door. After a few minutes he got in an automobile and drove away. Claude deserted her one more time. Claude moved to Nebraska. He committed suicide when Evie was fifteen.

Madge and Dory Brown

Madge and Dory were devout Christians. Religion was their answer to the miseries of life. They were present whenever the church doors opened. They believed Christians spent eternity in Heaven while sinners went to Hell. The kids went to church with their parents, but Evie was the most devout of the bunch. She studied the Bible and tried to live a Christian life. She enjoyed the services and listened attentively to the preaching, unlike her brothers who liked to sneak out during the sermon and reappear before the closing prayer. She wanted her future husband to be a Christian. There was a problem. None of the bashful and boring boys who attended her church interested her.

The farm was home to many animals. There were always six milking cows, each with a name and treated like pets. The cows never missed the chance to be petted or eat an apple from the orchard. They spent their days munching grass in the pasture. Twice a day when their internal alarm rang, they formed a line behind their leader and walked to the barn to be milked singing a loud song that they needed relief or they were going to burst. The mooing intensified when they arrived at the barn door. They waited impatiently at the door. They entered, oldest first, youngest last, when Dory let them enter. The cows were milked by hand. Everyone in the family knew how to milk a cow. They could milk a cow in their sleep which they often did since the cows came to the barn for the morning milking at 5 am. The milk truck picked up the milk and cream every morning.

A bull roamed the pasture but was never given a name. He was just referred to as The Bull. He weighed close to a ton and possessed frightening strength. His behavior was unpredictable. Every human and animal was always aware of his location. Preferring to be alone, The Bull was content to meander about the pasture. A female in season made him almost unmanageable, capable of tearing down all but the strongest fence, barn door, or gate. Nothing prevented The Bull from fulfilling his duty.

Female calves were valuable as future milking cows. Only one bull was needed on the farm. Most male calves were sold at the livestock yard, except for the one chosen to supply the family with meat. This calf was castrated, given a name, and treated like royalty. He spent his days in a stall in the barn eating all the hay and corn he wanted until butchering time. The family enjoyed him while he lived, but they ate him anyway. His loss was not regretted. His meat fulfilled a need.

Not able to afford a tractor big enough to work the fields, Dory owned two stout horses. The horses worked very hard during planting and harvest. They spent the rest of their time in the pasture co-existing with the cows.

The barn was ruled by a slew of cats. Their job was to keep the rodents under control. Dory rewarded them for their efforts. At milking time, they mysteriously appeared in the barn singing a pitiful song. They circled Dory as he entered the barn nearly tripping him as they rubbed against his legs. Their high pitched meows and the bellowing of the milking cows sounded pitiful when Dory sat on his stool to start milking. When the milk started to flow, Dory expertly directed a squirt to each cat's mouth for a small drink. After the snack, the cats disappeared to resume their hunting.

Chickens were everywhere on the farm. Madge bought a hundred baby chicks every spring. She kept them in an old hog house using a light bulb to keep the chicks warm. The chicks became "layers" who were expected to produce one egg daily. A fence surrounded the henhouse, but it did not keep the hens confined. There were always chickens in the barnyard eating insects and plucking at grass. They dodged automobiles when they ventured onto the road. They rested on the front porch during the heat of the day. Instinctively, they went to the henhouse when it was time to lay an egg. They laid their eggs in the small wooden box nests padded with straw. The sound of cackling hens was constant until sunset when they roosted for the night in the henhouse. The family consumed some of the eggs. Madge sold the rest to people in Rushville. The rule of the henhouse was simple. Lay eggs or become fried chicken. Every Saturday, Madge sacrificed a couple of unproductive hens. She twisted off their heads, plucked the feathers then cut the carcasses into pieces. Other hens didn't notice. All seemed to know everything had a purpose on the farm.

Two or three roosters, ornery as the devil, strutted about the yard. They were almost as feared as The Bull. Their contribution to life on the farm, besides keeping the hens productive, was to awaken the family with annoying crows at dawn. They lived up to their nickname: cocks. They didn't think they were in charge. They knew it. Paranoid by nature, the roosters kept to themselves. They stalked the barnyard looking for an opportunity to molest any living creature. Everyone but Madge had a rooster encounter. She didn't tolerate their nonsense. If one tried to attack her, he became the main ingredient in her chicken stew.

Any respectable farm in Rush County had hogs and pigs. Dory usually kept three or four females and one boar. The hog houses were located at the back of the farm because the smell of manure and the hog wallow was overwhelming. The wallow was muddy pit that the hogs laid in to keep cool. Its odor could become over bearing during the summer months. When a female sow was ready to bear pigs, Dory led her to the barn. She lived a life of luxury until her pigs no longer needed her milk. She was then sent back to the wallow. Every year, Dory butchered a neutered male pig for the family to eat. He sold the rest at the hog barn located a block from the Courthouse in Rushville.

The farmhouse did not have indoor plumbing. Water came from the well in a musty smelling room at the back of the house. To get water, the well was primed by pouring water down the casing. Someone cranked the pump handle, over and over, until metallic tasting well water poured out. To take a bath, Madge heated water from the well to a boil in large pans on the stove. The scalding water was carried to a small room next to the kitchen. It was poured into a bathtub barely big enough to sit down in. The water temperature was adjusted by pouring cold well water into the tub. Dirty water was dipped out of the tub after the bath, carried outside, and thrown onto the ground. Washing clothes in warm water required a similar process.

The outhouse, with a small circle cut near the top of the door for light, was a few feet from the back door of the house. A trip to the outhouse meant foul odors and uncomfortable heat or cold. One didn't waste any time when visiting it. Dory brought the chamber pot to their bedroom to eliminate the inconvenience of venturing to the outhouse at night. He emptied the pot into the outhouse hole every morning.

Evie had her own bedroom. She loved that room. Not much bigger than a closet, it had one window and an electrical outlet for a lamp so she could read at night. She hung her clothes on hooks on the wall and kept her books and treasures under her bed. Her room was the hottest room in the house during the summer and coldest in the winter. She loved to lay on her bed while she wrote in her diary and dream of life when she was old enough to move to Rushville. She fantasized about the man she would marry. Where was he at that moment? What would he look like? Would he have a good job? How many children would they have? Would he be faithful? Would he desert her like her father if times got tough?

School was a relief from the routine and chores of farm life for Evie. She rode a school bus to Rushville where there were many exciting things to do and see. She was bright and she studied hard. She was determined to escape the hardships and poverty she watched Madge endure. She didn't fancy the life of a farm wife. Instead, she wanted to be a secretary. No one in either Madge or Dory's family had ever finished high school. Madge, hoping Evie would be the first, pushed her to do well in school. She was not satisfied unless Evie brought home all A's on her report card.

POLITICS

RUSHVILLE REPUBLICAN

GERMANY ATTACKS POLAND

A war was destroying Europe, and Japan was spreading evil through other parts of the world in 1940. Japan didn't appear to threaten American interests because Asia seemed so far away, but all Americans realized the stakes in Europe were high. Politicians argued among themselves while ordinary Americans deliberated the upcoming presidential election. Everyone knew the next president would either continue America's neutrality or lead the country to war.

President Franklin Roosevelt was a father figure for many Americans. He was at the end of his second presidential term in 1940. He wanted something never before attempted in America, a third term. Precedence hampered his desires. President Washington had refused a third term despite pleas that he continue to be president beyond two terms. He feared the irresistible allure of presidential power would tempt a man to become a king. Following Washington's example, no president had ever sought a third term. Many urged Roosevelt to disregard Washington's precedent. A skilled politician, he told colleagues he would not seek a third term. He would, however, accept a third term if his party called upon him to do so.

The *Rushville Republican* linked Rushville to the outside world. It carried front page stories daily about the wars. The evening radio news provided news and comments on the political debate. Movie theaters played newsreels of the growing threat of German and Japanese aggression. Rush County's Courthouse Curbside Court deliberated world events and politics constantly.

Politicians in Washington differed on the direction America should follow. Republicans supported an anti-isolationistic agenda. They wanted America to join western European countries in fighting the Nazis. Most Democrats countered that such an alliance would force America into a war. They felt Germany had no plans to expand outside its borders, but if Germany did continue its aggression, its bitter rival, Russia, would respond. Roosevelt said he was against entering the war. He emphasized that he had followed an isolationist policy throughout his second term. In fact, he had encouraged Congress to pass legislation to prevent America from entering Europe's problems "for the cause of peace and in the interest of American neutrality and security."

Roosevelt's isolationist argument started to unravel in 1939. Germany and Russia agreed to not intervene if either occupied other European countries.

Soon after signing the agreement, German troops assembled on Poland's western border. Germany invaded Poland on September 1, 1939. British Prime Minister Neville Chamberlain lamented the Polish invasion. He said, "The responsibility for this terrible catastrophe rests on the shoulders of one man, the German chancellor. Adolph Hitler has not hesitated to plunge the world into misery in order to serve his own senseless ambitions. Such acts of brazen, preemptive aggression obligated resistance. If not, Germany would become so powerful that it could control not only Europe, but the entire world." After his forceful words, Chamberlain appeased the Germans. He vowed to not intervene on the continent as long as the Nazis did not invade other countries. Despite Chamberlain's words, England and France declared war on Germany on September 3, 1939.

No combat followed the war declaration for months. Troops from both sides faced off each other at the border between Germany and France. The press branded the inaction as the Phony War. The Phony War gave hope to many that the stalemate meant that Nazi Germany's hunger for conquest was over.

On October 13, 1939, Hitler aided Roosevelt's desire for a third term. He challenged America in response to a British rejection of a German peace proposal. Hitler requested the Americans mediate between the Germans and British to prevent "the most gruesome bloodbath in history. Those peoples and their leaders must now speak up who are of a similar mind. Those who reject my hand must believe they see war as a better solution."

The outmanned, outgunned British and French attempted to convince America of the gravity of the German threat while the Phony War continued. There was no satisfactory response in return. America was waging its own political debate to elect the next president. The Rush County Courthouse Curbside Court passed a verdict. America didn't have a hound in this hunt.

Roosevelt faced overwhelming anti-war sentiment. The Neutrality Act prohibited him from becoming involved in foreign conflicts. Besides, America had inadequate supply routes to Europe or the Pacific. He had less than 350,000 personnel in ALL branches of the military. The American Navy had a meager 396 commissioned ships in its fleet. America had no conscription/draft laws which meant the American military could not to assemble the necessary personnel to fight a war.

Aware of the problems he faced politically, Roosevelt continued to state America would remain neutral unless provoked. Though fatigued and secretly wheelchair bound from the rages of polio, he desperately wanted that third term. He was very popular among most Democrats. Those folks insisted he accept the nomination "whether he likes it or not." There were, however, some in his own party who desired to be president. He was bitterly, almost unanimously, disliked by Republicans.

Roosevelt started the debate regarding the war on September 21, 1939. He proclaimed he wanted peace, but he offered no hope, "The shadow over the world might pass swiftly. I conceive that regardless of party or section, the mantle of peace and patriotism is wide enough to cover us all." Republicans favored a collective alliance of resistance. They agreed the future of the world depended on nations living in peace with guaranteed freedom for all. A neutral America was nonsense, morally wrong, and doomed to fail. They predicted that once Germany conquered Europe, it would turn its sights to America.

Roosevelt continued preparing for war despite his statements to the contrary. He wanted America to join the European Allies as soon as it was domestically and politically possible. He began dismantling the Neutrality Act. He urged Congress to repeal sections which prevented America from shipping arms to foreign combatants. He argued such restrictions on arms shipments were "most vitally dangerous to American neutrality, American security, and American peace." He warned to continue such restrictions would increase the chance America would someday be invaded. On January 1, 1940, the President emphasized the German danger to a joint session of Congress, saying, "What we face is a set of worldwide forces of disintegration, vicious, ruthless, destructive of all moral, religious and political standards which mankind, after centuries of struggle has come to cherish." He asked Congress to approve new taxes to finance a "common sense" national defense.

Hitler gave the President another assist on January 31, 1940 saying "We have grown so strong that nothing any longer will be able to defeat us." The threat Hitler presented was becoming obvious to the American people. America might have to enter the fight.

The Nazis gave Roosevelt another gift in March, 1940. They said sensational documents had been discovered which proved "American diplomats had helped hasten the outbreak of hostilities" of September, 1939. The Nazis then accused Roosevelt of "conjuring up a war psychosis."

Wendell Willkie was an Indiana born New York lawyer and business man. Willkie was well known in Rush County. His wife was from Rushville. They owned several local farms. They frequently visited his wife's mother in Rushville. Rushville's citizens, even those who disagreed with his politics, enjoyed the publicity Willkie brought to the town.

Willkie had gained national attention as an outspoken critic of Roosevelt. He switched from the Democrat Party to the Republican Party in 1939 because of concerns over deteriorating conditions in Europe, Roosevelt's isolationist leanings, and Roosevelt's desire for a third term. Willkie praised George Washington's wisdom that no one should be president for more than two terms saying, "If no man is indispensable, then none of us is free." Willkie argued against American military involvement on foreign soil. He blamed Roosevelt for America's lack of military preparedness. Willkie also felt America should supply aid to friendly forces in Europe. This position disagreed with Republican Party isolationists who argued America should maintain a "tight rein on our emotions" with "scrupulous neutrality."

By the spring of 1940, Willkie's criticism of Roosevelt was gaining support. Many Republicans considered him a viable presidential candidate.

FALLING IN LOVE

The weather on Saturday, March 30, 1940 was partly cloudy and warm. After the cows were milked, Evie's family traveled to Rushville in their black 1933 Chrysler. The prime downtown parking spots were taken, so Dory parked a couple blocks from Main Street. The boys disappeared into the crowd. Evie, hoping to see the movie *Stars and Stripes* at the Princess Theater, searched for her giggling friends. Madge went window shopping. Dory sought out the wisdom and gossip of the Courthouse Curbside Court.

The court's main topics were the upcoming presidential election and the war in Europe. The *Republican* contained two volatile articles which primed the evening's debate. The European combatants were still stalemated and Roosevelt warned of "scant immediate prospect for the establishment of any just, stable and lasting peace in Europe." The court also debated a rumor that was spreading like wildfire. Willkie was so frustrated with Roosevelt that he was thinking of running for president. Word was he might visit Rushville soon.

Something wonderful happened that evening. It had nothing to do with the economy, politics, war, or the weather. Sixteen year old Evie left the safety of her friends to spend the evening with a cocky, carefree guy who played a guitar and sang songs.

Karl made her feel like she ever felt before. When she finally reappeared, she begged her friends to say nothing about the guy. She knew he was so different from her family she didn't dare let Madge know about him.

She got back to the automobile to find Dory, Madge, and the boys waiting for her. She was late because she had taken time to buy a small notebook to use as a diary. Back home, she wrote in her diary the first lines of her love story. Writing in beautiful cursive diligently practiced in hopes of someday becoming a secretary, she wrote: *I met Karl Floyd on March 30, 1940.*

At first glance, Karl and Evie were as different as night and day. Closer inspection revealed they were made for each other. She was insecure. He was proud of who he was. She had trouble making decisions. He had plans for the future. She was so devoutly religious that she felt constant guilt. He didn't give a rat's ass about religion. Instead, he worshipped his guitar. She craved security and protection. He took risks, but only if the odds were in his favor. Haunted by her childhood, she didn't trust men. Karl, from a tight close knit family, was secure to a fault. Evie despised tobacco. He smoked a pack of cigarettes a day. She wouldn't utter a swear word. He cussed like a sailor. She needed a stable man to rescue and never abandon her. He needed someone care for who would paddle down the river of life with him.

News traveled fast in Rush County. Parents learned from friends the events of the day before the kids got home. Madge quickly got wind of Karl. She gave Evie permission to continue seeing Karl, but only after Dory had consulted with the Courthouse Curbside Court. The verdict on Karl was positive. Freed from hiding the relationship, Tom started driving Karl the four miles out to the farm on Sunday afternoons. They went to the movies on Saturday nights. They didn't talk on the telephone. Homes with a phone line shared a party line with their neighbors. This made it impossible to talk for more than a few minutes before a neighbor started listening to their conversation. Instead of eating lunch at the factory cafeteria, Karl often walked several blocks to the high school to see her on his lunch break. Evie packed an extra sandwich so they ate together on the school playground. Evie and Karl wrote letters when they couldn't be together. They told each other everything. Their letters were like they were sitting next to each other. Never could they have dreamed that in a few years, letters would be the only way they had to communicate.

Karl started going to church to be with Evie. Like the snakes he shot on the banks of Flatrock River, he slithered next to Evie in the back row after the singing began. He didn't sit too close or hold her hand because Madge had eyes in the back of her head. He preferred cowboy songs but enjoyed singing the hymns. He didn't hesitate to let his tenor voice impress everyone in attendance. Evie had a high pitched, squeaky soprano voice. She preferred to be seen, not heard. She was embarrassed when other worshipers turned around to check out the kid with the nice singing voice. Karl lost interest when the preacher started to preach to his flock. He preferred to scribble notes while the preacher talked about salvation. He disappeared like a magician before the preacher reminded the sinners in attendance to repent of their sins or go to Hell.

While Karl and Evie courted, they could not have imagined the horrors the next five and a half years would bring. Though the stalemate at the French border gave hope for a peaceful solution, Congress continued to debate what role America should have. Roosevelt continued to increase the military's readiness. Congress did amend the Neutrality Act to allow the president to provide aid if such help remained short of war. Poor political leadership in England and France stymied efforts to get adequate equipment and supplies across the Atlantic.

Hitler made a terrifying announcement on April 3, 1940. He was going to end the war. He said, "The decisive blow must be struck and for this decisive blow the Fuehrer has mobilized all resources." In the next two months, Hitler altered the European landscape. First, Germany invaded Norway and occupied Denmark. Hitler said those countries needed German protection because England and France were planning to occupy them. The Nazis invaded the lowland countries of Holland, Belgium, and Luxembourg on May 10.

Seventy-one year old British Prime Minister Neville Chamberlain was disgraced by his miscalculation of Hitler's intentions. He resigned on May 10.

France was next. German troops entered Paris on June 6. France surrendered sixteen days later. Italy sided with Germany. It declared war on France and England on June 10. England was spared of a German invasion only because the English Channel made a German supply line difficult to maintain. England was the last remaining hope to resist complete Nazi occupation of Europe.

The Phony War was over.

Winston Churchill replaced Chamberlain as British Prime Minister. He immediately started to rally his nation for all-out war. He augmented his navy's presence in the English Channel. He increased spending on the Royal Air Force. He dispatched British soldiers to the continent. He also knew Britain could not win a war against Germany without the Americans. He gambled his country could stand firm until the Americans finished their debate. He increased his efforts to lure America into the war.

Karl and Evie feasted on each other while Hitler devoured Europe. Karl wrote: **I'll miss you tonight so I may take in the dance to forget my troubles, but don't worry about me.** The day Churchill pleaded to America for desperately needed supplies, a swarming horde of Nazi planes bombed Paris. The same day, Karl wrote: **How about getting a date for Sandy with that girl you were with Sunday night when we saw you? We came up by the church last night and saw you girls in there. You were doing everything but listening to the preacher. Let's go somewhere on Saturday night and have some fun, that is, the four of us. I was lonesome last night and that is what made us come up by the church, so I guess to keep from being lonesome I had better go to church too.**

Karl wrote on the day Paris surrendered to the Nazis: **Some orchestra is playing *Little Brown Jug* on the radio and it makes me feel at home. You were far from napping Sunday night when Sandy and I saw you girls in there. I'm going fishing Saturday again. I wish you could go with me. By the way, you are supposed to teach me how to swim this summer, so don't forget it. I have to get another bathing suit before we go though. They must like that song because they're playing it again. It sounds like me and my brother playing together, so you know it's good. I'll bring the guitar sometime and show you how well I can play after 7 or 8 years at it. Tell your grandpa Lewis that Roosevelt is going to run again and there's no use of any Republicans running against him. They won't have a chance. Spread that around to your neighbors too! I can hardly wait from one Saturday to the other and I hope you feel the same way. Have you been a good girl all week? If you haven't I'll get even Saturday night. Anyway, I have been good this week and been out only one night and was home by 10.** Though he was attending church to spend time with Evie, Karl needed to work on the commandment about lying. He could swim like a fish.

Hitler made a mistake when France fell. He stopped his army's advance a few miles short of the French coast where over 330,000 British, French, and Belgian troops were stranded. Churchill organized a makeshift armada of naval vessels, ferries, tugs, pleasure boats, yachts, fishing boats and about 700 privately owned lifeboats to rescue 190,000 British and 140,000 French and Belgian troops from the beach at Dunkirk, France.

Churchill realized England would be a vital staging area and supply depot if and when America joined the fight. He frantically scrambled to rebuild his armed forces after Dunkirk. He prepared his nation for invasion on June 18, 1940 saying, "The Battle of France is over. I expect the battle of England is about to begin."

Churchill then spit in Hitler's face. England started aerial bombing raids into Germany.

While Churchill and Hitler rattled their cages, Karl wrote on June 18: **Yes, I caught some fish, but not Saturday night because you never got me home till 1 am. I went as soon as I could change to my fishing clothes. I sure wish that you were there with me. It took nerve to go out in the dark all by myself. I been thinking about you all week and wouldn't know what to do if you didn't write. I can be working over at the factory and all I can do is think of you and that is bad business when I'm tacking all around my fingers.** (A furniture upholsterer's routine was to put a handful of upholstering tacks in his mouth. Using a hammer with a magnetized tip, he placed the hammer tip in his mouth to get a tack. Karl was a fast tacker.) **Tell your mother I won't let that happen again because I really didn't pay much attention to the time. Tell her I will be more careful about it.** (He was referring to when he and Evie fell asleep while making out.) **Good night and pleasant dreams.**

Karl still had a problem with that lying commandment. Running alongside the bank of Flatrock River were foot paths imprinted over the centuries by animals, Indians, trappers, hunters, and boys. Karl had walked those paths all his life. He knew every dip, rock, and protruding root. He could walk those old paths on the darkest nights without the aid of a flashlight.

Hitler was infuriated at England's defiance and the bombing attacks on his motherland, Hitler offered a laughable peace proposal. He demanded that England surrender and to accept a German occupation. Churchill summarily refused the offer. In response, Hitler ordered his military to prepare for an invasion of England, Operation Sea Lion. He then announced on July 16, "I have decided to prepare a landing operation against England and, if necessary, to carry it out."

Hitler's plan was to weaken England's military and demoralize the resolve of the British civilians. Operation Sea Lion's initial goal was to bomb only British military targets. On September 15, 1940, Hitler ordered day and night bombing raids, not just on military targets, but also on random targets in London. The *Rushville Republican* reported, "Uncounted Toll of Dead Left in London Streets as Nazis Strike Heavily". Churchill's leadership and the King of England's decision to not leave London invigorated the British people. The bombing of London didn't weaken the British. To the contrary, it united and fortified their resolve.

Operation Sea Lion shifted Americans' attitude about war against Hitler. Patriotic fever escalated to frenzied levels. The mood of the Courthouse Curbside Court changed. They discussed doing one's duty. They knew America had moral duty to help the Brits. Some members of the court fretted about a possible invasion of America if England fell. They concluded America needed to fight the Germans. Throughout Rushville, American flags hung on front porches. *God Bless America* was sung at sporting events and school functions. Movies started to romanticize war. Evie wrote that she and Karl watched *Three Men from Texas*, *Buck Private*, and *Flight to Destiny*. Movies like those filled her with fear and anxiety. War movies excited Karl.

Luckily, Hitler did not realize how ripe England was for defeat. To the contrary, his generals told him Germany lacked sufficient naval and air power to invade an impregnable island like the British Isles. He gave in. He did know the strategic threat England posed to his western border. He ordered bombing of England to continue. He cancelled his plan for a British invasion on September 17.

Hitler chose instead to concentrate on his bitter enemy, Russia. His army wouldn't need to cross a body of water. Russia possessed desperately needed commodities: labor, agriculture, and energy. Hitler invaded Russia with 4,500,000 troops on June 22, 1941 in an operation named Operation Barbarossa. Barbarossa's four year battle ultimately claimed the lives of nearly 27 million Russians and 5 million Germans.

Hitler's decision to redirect his military might toward Russia gave the British the time needed to increase its defense. His miscalculation allowed America to continue its military buildup. He also gave Roosevelt the time he needed to win a third term.

1940 PRESIDENTIAL ELECTION

Wendell Willkie made his decision. He announced his candidacy for President of the United States in June, 1940. The Republicans gathered in Philadelphia to pick their presidential nominee two days after France surrendered to the Nazis. Willkie ran on what he called "some kind of major trend going on that I'm the head of." The Republicans settled on Willkie as their nominee on the sixth vote. He immediately focused on the war, "Our very way of life, our democratic system, is at one of those testing points in our history. We are facing the most ferocious assault, physically, psychologically, and ideologically that we have ever faced."

Willkie's nomination thrilled Rushville. The Chamber of Commerce met to "discuss various angles that may bring publicity to this city." The Chamber sent Willkie a telegram which said, "Every person in Rushville shares your happiness in being chosen. We offer you Rushville in its entirety to use as you deem best. You are cordially invited to make your campaign headquarters here." Billboards touting Willkie's land ownership and other business interests in the county appeared on the main roads into the town.

The carefully controlled Democratic Convention in Chicago prohibited any criticism of Roosevelt or his policies. He won the nomination with no opposition. He immediately abandoned his policy of isolation and neutrality once he had the nomination. He rebuked some in his party who urged him to support a Democratic Party statement that America would not participate in foreign wars or send troops overseas. He fired a clear warning to the Axis Powers when he implied America needed to enter the war soon. Roosevelt, whose legs were unable to support his weight without braces, proclaimed he was ready to lead the nation toward its destiny after he defeated Wendell Willkie. Barely concealing its bias, the *Republican* ran a brief second page story on Roosevelt's re-nomination.

Evie had other things on her mind. She wrote in her notebook diary on July 2nd: *Karl got his driver's permit.*

Rush County held its annual agricultural fair as the presidential campaign heated up. The fair was the most anticipated event of summer. It was a time to have some fun. It was held the first week in August, a time when the crops needed no attention, the hay was in the barns, and animals were unwilling to do anything but rest in the shade. Kids saved money all summer in anticipation of the rides, games, and freak shows. The livestock building was full of animals brought in from the county farms. Both farm and city kids displayed vegetables, flowers, and 4-H projects in the high school gym. Everyone and his brother enjoyed the bright lights, carnival rides, car races, socializing, and food. It was such a big event the Courthouse Curbside Court didn't meet downtown on the Saturday night of the fair. They assembled instead at a tent that served Hoosier breaded pork tenderloin sandwiches.

The fair was the perfect place to discuss current events. At the fair of 1940, presidential politics was THE topic of conversation. As usual, people were full of opinions. Partisan bickering was everywhere. Most was good natured, but some bordered on hostile. The Republicans and Democrats passed out buttons and yard sticks with the candidates' names on them.

Both presidential candidates were well known in Rush County. Their differences created controversy. Willkie had family ties to Rushville. His detractors said he had no political experience. Roosevelt, loved by a few but hated by many in Rush County, wanted an unprecedented third term. Those against him said he was itching for a war. There were a few fistfights. Evie and Karl avoided the talk at the fair. She only wrote in her diary: *We went to the Rushville fair. Karl and Tom won baby ducks at a Ping Pong Ball Toss game. Karl named his duck Buck Rogers. Tom named his Flash Gordon.* Karl and Tom gave the ducks to Evie. They became pets in Dory and Madge's barnyard menagerie.

Willkie gave his nomination acceptance speech several weeks after the Republican Convention. The *Republican* headlined a front page story that announced he would spend the night before his speech in Rushville. The candidate said, "Why should I go anywhere else when we always stay with Mrs. Willkie's mother when we are in Indiana?"

EDITH AND WENDELL COME HOME

Mr. and Mrs. Wendell L. Willkie

Willkie's visit brought extreme excitement to Rush County. Willkie, who could be the next president, made it his adopted home. His picture was everywhere. The excitement peaked on August 16, 1940 when Wendell and Edith Willkie arrived in town. An estimated crowd of ten thousand lined the streets to see the candidate. Willkie's caravan drove around the courthouse square before traveling to the home of Mrs. Willkie's mother. The next morning another rousing crowd gathered to watch Willkie board a train headed for his boyhood hometown. He gave his acceptance speech in front of thousands of citizens on that hot, sweltering afternoon.

Willkie then returned to Rushville to work on plans for his campaign. Before retiring for the night, he gave a rousing speech to another large crowd of supporters at Rushville's city park. To the consternation of Willkie's supporters in Rushville, Roosevelt ridiculed Willkie's acceptance speech. The President coined a slogan he used throughout the campaign, "Better a third term than a third rater."

Karl wrote to Evie the next day: **We got off from the factory this afternoon to hear Mr. Willkie's talk, but I went hunting instead. We'll have to make the time up we lost this afternoon so that will mean 12 1/2 hours tomorrow. While you're having a good time at the prayer service at your house, you can think of me working my head off at the factory. Did Willkie give a talk this afternoon! He is a fine man.**

Maybe you're right about him so I'll back you up on anything you say from now on. We had a nice week at the factory. I made $24.76. Is that right what the woman told you about getting married? If it is, I'm aiming to be the lucky man.

Willkie, a born and bred Hoosier, had become a New York lawyer and business man. He needed a grassroots campaign to negate that issue. He put Rushville in the national spotlight when he selected a Rushville hotel to be his campaign headquarters. His campaign staff and national media reporters stayed at the hotel. They ate at local restaurants. They discussed politics with the local residents. Some reporters even sought the counsel of the Curbside Court.

For himself, Willkie rented a private office owned by his mother-in-law on Main Street. It was within spitting distance of where the Courthouse Curbside Court gathered. He never sought the court's counsel. He stayed in Rushville until September 12 when his eleven car campaign train left to begin his presidential campaign. In a parade led by a live elephant, Willkie's caravan was escorted to the train station. Before boarding and relying on torches for light, Willkie told a large, noisy crowd he was "unafraid" of what lay ahead of him. He even joked that he faced "the worst gang of buccaneers ever organized in American political history."

Indiana was one of ten states to vote for Willkie. Roosevelt won the popular vote 54.7% to 44.8%. His Electoral College landslide was 449 to 82. In his concession speech, Willkie thanked his supporters. He assured Roosevelt he would support the President in dealing with the challenges the country was likely to face. In appreciation, Roosevelt appointed Willkie to be a special envoy for his administration. With that assignment, Willkie traveled all over the world. He gained great international stature, but he remained loyal to Rushville. He kept his office in Rushville for his use when he and Edith visited her mother and their farms.

Roosevelt saw his reelection as the American people's support of his policies. His speeches moved the country closer to war. His efforts to prepare the military escalated. 18,633 men were drafted into the military in 1940. 923,842 men were drafted in 1941. Nearly 700 were from Rush County.

THE MILITARY DRAFT

Times were tough. The Battle of Britain was raging. America was not capable of defending itself.

There had not been a military conscription since the end of World War I. Congress debated the issue through the early months of the presidential campaign. Congress passed the Selective Training and Service Act on September 14, 1940. It authorized the implementation of a military draft during peacetime for the first time in American history. The new law mandated:

- All men ages 21 to 36 years must register for military service in the county of their residence.
- Each "selectee" would serve for 12 months.
- No more than 900,000 men could be in training at any one time.
- No "selectees" could be sent to foreign possessions overseas.
- Local communities were to establish draft boards comprised of local residents to administer the process.
- Local boards were required to fill their quota ordered by the government.
- ALL eligible men were required to register on "R" day, October 16, 1940.

During the Congressional draft debate and presidential campaign, Karl and Evie were falling in love. He wrote her letters expressing his love for her: **Darling, some night when we're together I'll get the guitar and sing you all the songs I know or even heard tell of. So remember I love you and would do anything in the world for you and you only.**

Evie was not too concerned about the upcoming draft registration. Karl was too young to register. While other girlfriends worried themselves sick about their guys, she wrote in her diary: *The car caught on fire. Karl gave me a small picture of himself. We went to a Sunday school party. Karl sang Tumbling Tumbleweeds and Sierra Sue.* On the night before "R" day, she only wrote: *We went to choir practice.*

That same night, Karl wrote: **Honey, I didn't sleep at all Sunday night. I was thinking of you all the time. I love you more each day and wish I was near you all the time or at least see you more often. I have been listening to a love story on the radio and it kinda reminded me of you and me. I brought me a song book and now I know a few of the latest songs.** ***The Old Plantation Party*** **is coming on the radio now and I wish you were here to enjoy it with me. I hope you still love me. I could never get along without you anymore**.

In anticipation of the draft registration, The *Republican* provided information about what registrants would do on "R" day. The Courthouse Curbside Court held special sessions at local eating establishments. They debated how the process would go. Some members predicted mass turmoil. Others worried whether all eligible men would register. What would happen if a man didn't register?

Roughly sixteen million men registered with the Selective Service on Wednesday, October 16, 1940. Registrants answered eleven questions "to put them on record as being of draft age." Each Registrant received a draft certificate because the law required each registrant to always carry the certificate on his person as proof that he had registered.

The next day was a busy day for the local draft boards. Using information the registrant had furnished, each man was assigned a classification:
- Class 1: Fit for military service.
- Class 2: Deferred because of occupation.
- Class 3: Deferred because of dependency.
- Class 4: Unacceptable for military service.

Each registrant's name was then written on a card. The cards were shuffled then scattered face down on a table. A member of the draft board drew the cards one at a time. When drawn, the board assigned the name on the card a number, starting with the number 1. The process continued until all registrants had a number. The draft board posted the assigned classification and each registrant's number on a bulletin board. Needless to say, a lot of folks visited their draft board that day.

Rush County's local board gave 1,925 Rush County men, about ten percent of the county's population, a number. The largest number of numbers in any one county across the country was 7,836. Local draft boards sent the name of every man and his assigned number to Washington.

The Selective Service held a national lottery in Washington, D.C. on October 29, 1940. The lottery determined the order in which each registrant would be evaluated for military duty. The lottery was broadcast live on the radio for the nation to hear. Families gathered around their radios to learn the fate of their eligible men. President Roosevelt attended the event. He spoke to the nation before the lottery started, "We are mustering all our resources, manhood and industry to make our nation strong in defense. We are well aware of the circumstances, the tragic circumstances in lands across the seas, which have forced upon our nation the need to take measures for total defense. The young men of America have thought this thing through. They know simply that ours is a great country, great in perpetual devotion to the cause of liberty and justice, great in faith that always there can be and must be a will to a better future. To the young men themselves, I should like to speak as Commander-in-Chief of the United States Army: You who will enter this peacetime army will be the inheritors of a proud history and an honorable tradition. You will be members of an army which first came together to achieve independence and to establish certain fundamental rights for all men. Ever since that first muster, our democratic army has existed for one purpose only: the defense of our freedom. You have answered that call, as Americans always have, and as Americans always will, until the day when war is forever banished from this earth."

The same bowl used for the draft lottery during World War One was brought back into service. 7,836 blue capsules, each containing a number from 1 to 7,836 which represented the registrants' assigned numbers, were dumped into the bowl. A ladle stirred the capsules. The Secretary of War was blindfolded. He then drew capsules out of the bowl one at a time. Each capsule was opened after being drawn. An official announced and recorded the number that was inside the capsule until all 7,836 numbers had been recorded. If a registrant's number was 13 and 13 was the first number drawn, he became the first selected by his local for military service.

President Roosevelt read the first number drawn. 158. The Rush County registrant who held number 158 was William Hollis Fulton. Of interest for the Floyd family, Tom's number was 1660. It would be a quite a while before his number was up.

The lottery went on for seventeen hours.

The Selective Service Act contained options for registered men to ponder. A handful of registrants chose to declare conscientious objection on religious grounds. This deferred them from combative military service. They were often ridiculed and called cowards. Registrants with dependents (a wife) received a Class 3 deferral. Not surprisingly, many couples got married. The government promised to provide for families of soldiers killed during a war. Many couples took advantage of this. They married just before a drafted man left home. Several volunteered before being drafted. They got to choose which branch of the military to join. Millions of others decided to serve when selected. They waited until their number came up.

After the lottery, the *Republican* reported "Rush County will have 141 young men in military camps under the Selective Service Act" by July, 1941.

The first physical exams of the draft were given to 13 Rush County men on November 14, 1940.

ESCALATION TOWARD WAR

America was no longer a neutral observer. In his inaugural address for his third term as President of the United States on January 20, 1941, Roosevelt told America, "If we lose that sacred fire, if we let it be smothered with doubt and fear, then we shall reject the destiny which Washington strove so valiantly and triumphantly to establish. The preservation of the spirit and faith of the Nation does, and will furnish the highest justification for every sacrifice that we may make in the cause of national defense. In the face of great perils never before encountered, our strong purpose is to protect and to perpetuate the integrity of democracy. For this we muster the spirit of America, and the faith of America. We do not retreat. We are not content to stand still. As Americans, we go forward, in the service of our country, by the will of God."

Rush County was sending its young men to war. Selectees were leaving most every week. Few families were unaffected. The largest group yet, fifty men, left on April 3, 1941 for an induction center evaluation. Nine of the fifty did not pass the physical or mental assessment. They were sent home. The next nine men on the list received notice to report. The *Republican* printed the rejected boys' names on the front page. The procedure continued until the quota was filled.

Meanwhile, Karl and Evie's romance took the next step. Evie wrote in her diary on April 12: *Karl gave me an engagement ring*.

Any hope England had of winning the war rested upon receiving supplies from America. Congress responded to Roosevelt's call to assist the Brits. It passed the Lend-Lease Act. This Act gave the President the power to sell, transfer title, exchange, lease, lend, or otherwise dispose of, to any government he deemed vital to the defense of the United States. Soon thereafter, a steady convoy of unarmed American merchant ships crisscrossed the Atlantic. The

British Navy protected the shipping routes since America was not a combatant. Nonetheless, German submarines sunk several merchant ships with great loss of American lives. Roosevelt and Churchill denounced such acts of war on the unarmed ships. Neither side backed down. Germany ignored the complaints. The shipments to Britain continued.

Germany's most powerful warship, the Bismarck, torpedoed and sunk the HMS Hood, one of England's most prized ships, on May 24, 1941. Only three of the Hood's 1,421 crewmen survived. In retaliation, Churchill issued an order to sink the Bismarck. The British navy torpedoed and sunk the Bismarck three days later. This event gave England a much needed psychological lift. Churchill told his countrymen, "Let us hope that the destruction of the Bismarck, Germany's latest and greatest ship, marks the beginning of the end."

President Roosevelt continued to emphasize the gravity of the German threat to Americans. He also assured his country of his resolve to continue transporting goods to England. He stated in a radio address on May 27, 1941, "We will not hesitate to use our armed forces to repel attack. An unlimited national emergency exists and requires the strengthening of our defense to the extreme limit of our national power and authority. Your government has the right to expect of all citizens that they take part in the common work of our common defense, take part from this moment forward. All will have opportunities. All will have responsibilities to fulfill."

After the Presidential address, the army announced that 50,000 men would be drafted every month. To increase the number of registrants available, the Selective Service announced there would be a second R Day on July 1, 1941 for the one million boys who had turned twenty-one years old since October, 1940. The military announced that those from the second registration would make up a large percentage of new draftees since those younger men were "ideal soldiering material."

Karl was one of those required to register on the second R-Day. He took the morning off from work. He walked to the Post Office where the draft board had its office. He descended the stairs and got in line. Karl along with Evie's brother, Ronald, and 98 other Rush County boys registered for the draft that day. The Registrar's Report listed him as six feet tall, 152 pounds, brown eyes, black hair, and dark complexion. He was given a draft card.

The following day, the draft board drew cards to assign numbers to the registrants. Karl's card was the thirty-eighth drawn.

He became number S-38.

Karl and Evie had a disagreement that evening. It started with her saying she couldn't understand why he would want to go. She was afraid he might get drafted. He declared excitement that he might get drafted. She couldn't appreciate his talk about duty. He couldn't see why she was making such a fuss. There was no winner. He finally told her, "There's no use talking about it. I'm going if I get drafted." All she wrote in her diary that night was: *We went out home.* (Madge and Dory's farm)

After Karl left, Evie cried herself to sleep.

Karl's draft card. He carried it in his wallet for many years.

The second lottery was held on Thursday, July 17, 1941 with little ceremony. President Roosevelt did not attend. There were no patriotic speeches. 750,000 men across America registered on the second R-Day, so only 800 pink capsules were needed this time. Karl's fate rested on the capsule that contained the number 38. He and Evie listened to the lottery on the radio with Madge and Dory. Their hearts sank when Ronald's number was the 11th drawn. He would be drafted soon. Finally, the 93rd capsule picked was number 38. They now knew Karl's place in line. Of 100 Rush County boys who had registered on the second R-Day, Karl would be the 93rd registrant called.

The Rush County Draft Board kept a Classification Record. It contained all information about every registrant. Karl completed his data questionnaire on August 22. He wasn't given a classification until after he and Evie married in October.

His classification was: III-A, a man "with dependents (a wife) not engaged in work essential to national defense."

Roosevelt requested Congress to change the Selective Training and Service Act before the second registration day. He wanted to:

- Lengthen the term of duty from twelve months to thirty months but for defensive purposes only.
- Grant Presidential authority to send draftees out of the hemisphere.
- Eliminate the limit on how many draftees could be in the military.
- Defer all men over twenty-eight years of age from being drafted.

Congress debated the proposed changes. Roosevelt prevailed in the end. The House of Representatives approved the changes by only one vote (203-202). The Senate passed it by a larger majority (77-19). Roosevelt signed the new provisions into law a month and a day after the second R-Day.

Roosevelt had completed his legislative preparations. The American public was ready to fight. Factories were producing vast amounts of war materials. A functional supply route was moving supplies across the Atlantic. The Selective Service was conscripting large numbers of men. Congress had voted to repeal more of the 1939 Neutrality Act. He then placed the final pieces of the puzzle. He assumed authority to commandeer or shut down radios stations. He granted himself the power to seize control of utilities. He ordered that movement of troops and war materials supersede all transportation priorities.

To all but the most naïve, it was obvious America was going to join the war.

Roosevelt had all his ducks in order. He sought a fuse to light so America could enter the war. He concentrated on the Atlantic Ocean. Germany's warships and submarines were sinking unarmed American cargo ships. He ordered the Navy to attack Italian and

German warships if they were in waters deemed necessary for America's defense. He also encouraged American merchant vessels to arm and to defend themselves if attacked.

While Roosevelt directed his attention to the tinderbox in Europe, something unexpected happened in the Pacific. American and Japanese diplomats had been conducting talks to keep the Pacific calm. Without forewarning, Japanese diplomats rejected an American proposal of conciliation. The talks ended as a result. The Japanese diplomats went back to Japan. Japan, shortly after their departure, staged an attack on Sunday, December 7, 1941. It was "an unprovoked and dastardly attack" on the American Naval Fleet in Pearl Harbor, Hawaii. Over 3000 Americans were killed or wounded. It was only luck that prevented the total annihilation of the American Naval Fleet.

Karl and Evie traveled to Madge and Dory's for Sunday dinner on that fateful day. Madge served the usual Sunday dinner: fried chicken, mashed potatoes, dumplings, and gravy. With the dishes washed and put away, the family sat around the coal burning stove in the small parlor. Madge and Evie embroidered pillow cases. Dory and Karl listened to a football playoff game on the radio. The talk was mostly about the draft. Tom had just left for Army basic training six days earlier on December 1st. Evie's brother, Ronald, thanks to his low draft number in the second lottery, had left in October. The talk was quieter than normal. Madge's dad, Grandpa Lewis, with whom Karl liked to play Checkers, was very ill. He was sleeping in the front room.

Suddenly a bulletin broke in, "We interrupt this program to bring you a special news bulletin. The Japanese have attacked Pearl Harbor, Hawaii by air. The details are not available. They will be in a few minutes. A Japanese attack upon Pearl Harbor naturally would mean war. Such an attack would naturally bring a counterattack, and hostilities of this kind would naturally mean that the president would ask Congress for a declaration of war. There is no doubt from the temper of Congress that such a declaration would be granted..."

The entire world shuddered!

No one sitting around the stove said a word. They were all lost in stunned disbelief. The only sound in the house was Grandpa Lewis' snoring. He died two days later.

On the way home, sensing what was ahead, Karl told Evie a story. When he was about fourteen, he walked over to Flatrock River like he did most days. He saw a muskrat making its way across the cornfield Karl was crossing. He told her muskrats swim like fish, but on land they're awkward and slow. Instinctively, Karl ran down the animal. He had caught and killed many muskrats for their fur during trapping season, but it wasn't trapping season on that particular day. He couldn't resist the urge for an easy kill. Before he hit the muskrat on the head with the hatchet he always carried when he went to the river, the animal stopped and froze. Its eyes looked directly into Karl's. The look of fear haunted Karl ever since. He killed the animal for no reason. He didn't take the dead animal home. He buried it instead. He told Evie he could still see that animal in his head, but it wasn't only the animal's frightened look that bothered him. He had violated two of the Old Man's rules. It is okay to kill for food or if an animal is dangerous. It is not okay to kill an animal for pleasure, except for shooting rats with a pistol at the city dump. Karl ended his story with a declaration. He could kill the sonsabitching Japs and Jerries because they wanted to harm his family and country. Evie knew he was itching to go.

Any hope for peace was gone. One member of the Axis powers had attacked America. Roosevelt no longer needed to pretend the United States was only defending itself. The next day, he addressed a joint session of Congress and the nation. Still in a state of shock, the scared, anxious, and angry public gathered around radios to listen to the President say, "December 7, 1941, a date which will live in infamy, the United States of America was suddenly and deliberately attacked by naval and air forces of the Empire of Japan…Hostilities exist, there is no blinking at the fact that our people, our territory and our interests are in grave danger…I believe that I interpret the will of the Congress and of the People when I assert that we will not only defend ourselves to the uttermost, but will make it very certain that this form of treachery shall never again endanger us…With confidence in our armed forces, with the unbounding determination of our people, we will gain the inevitable triumph, so help us God…I ask that the Congress declare that since the unprovoked and dastardly attack by

Japan on Sunday, December 7, 1941 a state of War has existed between the United States and the Japanese empire."

Congress declared war on Japan that same day.

Roosevelt did not mention one important fact in his speech. Japan, Germany, and Italy had agreed to defend each other when they signed the Tripartite Act. War with one of the Axis countries meant war with all three.

Roosevelt waited for Germany and Italy to honor their Tripartite Act obligation. He didn't have to wait long. Both countries declared war on the United States of America on December 11, 1941. Hitler, eager to help his Japanese ally said, "After victory has been achieved, Germany, Italy, and Japan will continue in closest cooperation with a view to establishing a new and just order."

In return, Roosevelt immediately requested Congress to declare war on Germany and Italy. He wrote, "The long-known and long-awaited has thus taken place. The forces endeavoring to enslave the entire world now are moving towards this hemisphere. Rapid and united efforts by all peoples of the world who are determined to remain free will ensure world victory for the forces of justice and righteousness over the forces of savagery and barbarism."

Congress agreed. Only a Congresswoman from Montana voted against declaring war on Germany and Italy.

The war had come to America.

Congress then amended the Selective Service Act to:
- Give the President authority to send draftees anywhere in the world.
- Change the age of eligibility to eighteen.
- Make previously deferred 28-35 year old men available for the draft.
- Eliminate the limit on how many men could be drafted.
- Extend the required length of time a draftee would serve to the length of the war plus six months.

The incensed citizenry was eager to fight. Overnight, America converted to a war mentality. Suspicion and paranoia gripped the country. Newspapers reported possible danger on both American coasts. The December 9, 1941 *Republican* reported sightings of

Japanese planes in California. New York City had two air raid alerts because of reports of imminent German bombing attacks.

YOUNG FAMILY

Larry Thomas Floyd

Twenty-one year old Karl and seventeen year old Evelyn became husband and wife on October 11, 1941. The ceremony took place in the living room of Evie's minister.

Evie wore a plain royal blue dress of rayon crepe fabric and a pink carnation corsage from Madge and Dory. The pocket over her heart had six rows of alternating red and gold studs. The dress resembled a military uniform with battle ribbons. She never parted with that dress. It hung beside Karl's army uniform in their bedroom closet for over sixty years.

Karl was the essence of the style of the day. He wore a gray suit with a wide lapel and broad padded shoulders. His pleated pants were so baggy he looked heavy. His tie was dark blue with bold images of red flowers. A white handkerchief tucked into his coat pocket completed his ensemble. His slicked back, coal black hair reflected the light of the room. He stood tall with his chest puffed out. He left no room to doubt he was ready to take a wife to share his future.

Dory, Madge, Ott, Clara, the minister, and his wife attended the simple ceremony. Madge played *Here Comes the Bride* in the small room on an upright, out of tune piano. Evie was five feet, two inches tall. She weighted about one hundred pounds. She clutched Karl's arm as the minister read from the Bible. They pledged to love and honor each other for the rest of their lives. Karl gave her a wedding ring he had bought on credit from a local jeweler. Evie didn't give Karl a ring. She had recently dropped out of school and had no money for such a luxury. The minister said a prayer. He pronounced them man and wife. They kissed, and became Mr. and Mrs. Karl Floyd. They signed the marriage license then took a quick ride down Main Street. They spent their first night as man and wife at Ott and Clara's house. A couple of Karl's brothers harassed them late into the night with off key songs and dirty jokes.

Evie was pregnant within a few months. As fate would have it, they became parents on their first wedding anniversary date. Evie gave birth to a five pound, two ounce boy at Rushville City Hospital. They named their son Larry Thomas.

Larry's birth gave Karl and Evie reason to look forward to the future. They dreamed of the opportunities he would have. They bragged about how he would excel in sports. They wanted him to get the high school diploma they only dreamed of. One night, while in bed with Larry lying between them, they came up with a motto for their family. It wasn't fancy, but they liked it. They pledged to each other: You're mine, I'm yours, Larry's ours, and we're Larry's.

Like those moments when the darkness of night swallows the daylight, their joy was soon replaced by fear and anxiety. Somehow Larry had suffered damage to his brain. He did not have the ability to accomplish the hopes and dreams they anticipated he would achieve. His life became an endless stream of challenges and setbacks. He didn't sit up without support until he was over one year old. He didn't walk unassisted until he was five. He didn't learn words like other kids. He jabbered sounds others could not recognize.

He did have two things in his favor, a great big smile and parents that loved him. After Karl and Evie accepted that something was wrong, they didn't ask why God burdened them with a handicapped child. They pulled up their bootstraps and chose instead to move on to the next challenge. They dedicated themselves to help Larry become the best person he could be.

Their battles were many. Evie sought advice where ever she could get it during the two and a half years Karl was away from home during the war. The medical experts told her Larry would never live independently. They said it wouldn't be fair to future children to have Larry around. They advised her to place him in an institution for "retarded" people.

During an era focused on earning the American dream, children gave couples a sense of wealth. For years, Evie got down on her knees and prayed every night. She prayed to God that Larry would be healed. Karl worked hard to provide for his family. Over time, they realized Larry was a special person. They learned to ignore the nasty, unsolicited and unwelcome comments. Instead, they bragged of Larry's achievements. They relied upon family for help through the difficult times. Larry never doubted Karl and Evie loved him. They cared for him the rest of their lives.

Larry Thomas Floyd's birth sealed the three of them together for eternity.

WORLD WAR TWO BEGINS

Vast Hordes Of Japanese Troops Attempt Invasion Of Luzon, North Of Manila

The War didn't start well for America. The Japanese attacked the Philippines ten hours after the Pearl Harbor attack. Vicious fighting followed. The American military evacuated a large naval base on December 12, 1941. The Japs occupied Manila, the capital of the Philippines, on January 2, 1942. Japanese military leaders publicly boasted that America was in its last stand. They appeared to be correct. American General Douglas MacArthur and his staff evacuated to Australia on March 11. They left behind 76,000 sick and starving American soldiers and Philippine defenders. As he left, MacArthur made a promise that finally rallied America's spirits, "I came out of Bataan and I shall return."

It became a way of life to have Rush County's boys leave for war. A new group left for evaluation every Wednesday. There were no longer parades or speeches to send them off.

The *Republican* devoted more print to the county's soldiers. A daily column told where individual soldiers were stationed, who had received promotions, and who was home on furlough. There was also a regular column telling how soldiers' families were doing. The men sitting around the Courthouse curb didn't talk much about the boys who were gone. It was as if mentioning their names might bring bad luck.

There were no reports of Rush County casualties during the first several months of the war. That changed on the September 29, 1942 when the *Republican* reported that Rush County had suffered its "first known casualty of the war." A twenty-one year old pilot had died in a training accident. His death was the county's first exposure to the cold manner the wartime military operated when a soldier died. No comforting chaplain visited the family with the bad news. Instead, his folks received a Western Union telegram. Its message informed them "the youth had died in an airplane crash… and the body was being shipped home."

The Selective Service deferred men who worked in industries essential to the war, such as farming, from the military. Roosevelt called those civilian war related workers the Arsenal of Democracy. This policy left few workers for nonessential industries like furniture manufacturing. Those industries became desperate for workers. Men with deferrals from military service or those not yet called up had their choice of good jobs and lots of overtime hours. They had some extra money to spend.

Karl's employer, International Furniture Company, flourished from the demand for furniture. In September, 1942, it leased a factory building eighty miles from its Rushville factory. Karl was one of the few eligible men not yet drafted from the second registration. The furniture company transferred him to that factory which was, because of the 35 mph speed limit, about a three hour drive from Rushville. For several weeks he lived in a hotel. He and his buddies traveled home on weekends if they didn't have to work. In his absence, Evie had difficulty living alone with the burdens of a new baby. She moved back to Madge and Dory's home on the farm.

Karl and Evie wrote letters to pass the lonely nights. He mentioned the war for the first time on December 10: **Buck got a letter from his wife and she said Walter Floyd** (Walter was Karl's cousin) **was killed in that Commando raid on France's coast. Well, he's one in thousands, I guess. God bless him. He was really a fine guy and always full of life and would do anything for you.** Karl realized his words probably scared Evie, so he changed the subject. **So Larry has been talking a whole lot? Boy, I sure will be glad when I get back home so we can be together again.** He ended the letter with words he would use in most of his war letters. **Darling, take good care of Larry till I get home. Love More Than Ever For You both, Karl.**

The war required everyone at home to sacrifice. The government declared the choice was between "discomfort or defeat." Rationing became a way of life.

- A Food Rationing Program was created to control certain commodities and prevent class struggle. Karl and Evie felt themselves lucky. They were issued a special Sugar Purchase Certificate which allowed them seventeen pounds of sugar a year because they had a baby.
- Car manufacturing was stopped in January, 1942.
- No new vehicles could be brought by citizens after February 22, 1942. Automobile factories were converted to make jeeps, tanks, and bombers. New car manufacturing was not resumed until July, 1945.
- A national Victory Speed Limit of 35 mph was established in May, 1942.
- Rubber was vital to the war effort. Gasoline rationing started on December 1, 1942 in order to limit tire wear. Every motorist was issued a windshield sticker with a letter on it. Most motorists were given an "A" sticker. They could buy three gallons of gasoline per week. This was reduced to two gallons/week in March, 1944. Farmers like Dory were given a sticker with the letter "R" in which unlimited gasoline for non-highway farm vehicles could be purchased. Christian man that he was, Dory was known to siphon gas from his tractors so he could drive Evie to doctor appointments for Larry in Indianapolis.
- The maximum miles a car could be driven in an entire year were 5000 miles.
- Pleasure driving was banned. Citizens were encouraged to vacation at home.

Within months of America's entry into the war, the country had troops in Africa and the Pacific. Invasions of Italy and Western Europe were being planned. The military's hunger for soldiers continued. The government announced the military would need seven and a half million men in uniform by the end of 1943.

The huge demands for more soldiers made it difficult for the Selective Service. In response, Congress amended the Selective Service Act once again:
- The least disagreeable change lowered the draft age. The Selective Service Act had originally set the age of eligibility at twenty-one. The law was now amended to lower the age to eighteen.
- More stringent standards were instituted on which industries were essential to the war effort. Managers of "essential" industries had to specifically name the workers who were vital.
- Communities were required to create committees of local citizens to decide as one congressman put it, "who shall go to war and who shall work at home." Those determined not essential to an industry became eligible for selection.
- The most controversial section of the amendment ended automatic deferments for married men. Married men became eligible for selection as of December 5, 1942. A married soldier's wife would receive a $50 monthly stipend. The government would pay $28. The other $22 would come from the soldier husband's military income.

Karl continued to work for the furniture company. He was not one of the 3,033,361 men drafted in 1942. His "3- A" classification did, however, change in December, 1942.

He became 1-A: Available; fit for general military service.

YOU HAVE BEEN SELECTED

(form image: Order to Report for Induction, dated MAR 27 1943, addressed to Karl Richard Floyd, Order No. S-1908, reporting at 9:25 a.m. on the Seventh day of April, 1943)

Nature ignores man's nonsense. It follows a comforting routine. The spring of 1943 arrived with the usual fanfare despite a war that was devastating the planet. Birds chirped their merry songs as they mated and made nests. Beautiful flowers once again painted color onto the landscape. Dandelions resumed their conquest of the earth. Farmers prepared for the next growing season. People escaped the confines of their houses.

The mood, though, was eerie. It was like walking through a cemetery at night and wondering, "What am I doing here?" No one was happy. The boys had gone to war. Many had seen combat. Some had been injured. A few had died. The Courthouse Curbside Court did re-convene. Its members' jokes were fewer, but the gossip was rampant. The court's only topic open for discussion was the war. Farmers didn't feel the usual excitement of the upcoming planting season. Saturday nights weren't graced with excited young people. To top it off, rationing made life miserable. If people needed to shop, they bought only what their ration coupons allowed. The only thing anyone wanted to do was to listen to the war news on the radio.

Young men not yet selected were anxious. They were pre-occupied about their future. The boys who failed the induction evaluation or had received a deferment felt guilt. They tolerated cruel comments about not doing their part. Those who avoided the military on religious grounds, faking medical problems, or giving false information, were shamed.

Moms and dads still did their work and made it through the day. War worry chiseled itself onto mothers' faces. Cursed to experience fear and agony with silence, fathers displayed a stiff upper lip. Young women were lonesome. Wives worried having enough money to pay the bills. They had nightmares about what would happen if their man did not come home.

In the meantime, the military's need for soldiers intensified.

The January 29, 1943 *Republican* reported the Selective Service changed from an army only draft to an all service draft. From now on, every branch of the service would secure its manpower through the general induction centers. Selective Service officials did say every effort would be made to fit men into whichever branch of the service they preferred.

Soon thereafter, the Selective Service ordered local draft boards to not, until further notice, draft men with dependent children. The director of the draft added that he was confident those men would soon be eligible for service, some by May 1. When the dust settled, men who were fathers before September 15, 1942 maintained their deferral. Those who became fathers after that date were eligible. Larry had been born four weeks too late.

Karl and Evie knew it was now only a matter of time. Only two questions remained. When would he get the selection letter? Which branch of the military would he join?

One answer came on March 5, 1943. The draft board mailed a postcard to Karl. It said, "You are directed to report for physical examination by the local board examiner at the time and place designated below at 6:30 pm on March 10, 1943. This examination will be of a preliminary nature, for the purpose of disclosing only obvious physical defects, and will not finally determine your acceptance or rejection by the armed forces. Failure to comply with this notice will result in your being declared a delinquent and subjected to the penalties provided by law." Karl reported as directed. He passed the exam, and then he went home to wait for the next shoe to drop.

The draft board met on March 27 to determine which boys were next to go.

The board mailed Karl an envelope containing two typewritten pages two days later. The first page read, "NOTICE OF SELECTION to Karl Richard Floyd, Order No. S1908. You have been selected for training and service under the Selective Training and Service Act of 1940. You will receive an Order to Report for Induction – such induction to take place on April 7, 1943 when adequate facilities are expected to be available. This notice is given you in advance for your convenience, and is not an order to report. Persons reporting to the induction station in some instances may be rejected for physical or other reasons. It is well to keep this in mind in arranging your affairs, to prevent any undue hardship if you are rejected at the induction station. If you are employed, you should advise your employer of this notice and of the possibility that you may not be accepted at the induction station. Your employer can then be prepared to replace you if you are accepted, or to continue your employment if you are rejected. The Order to Report for Induction will specify a definite time and place for you to report."

The second page read, "ORDER TO REPORT FOR INDUCTION. The President of the United States to Karl Richard Floyd, GREETINGS: Having submitted yourself to a local board composed of your neighbors for the purpose of determining your availability for training and service in the land or naval forces of the United States, you are hereby notified that you have now been selected for training and service therein. You will, therefore, report to the local board named above at The Local Board Office at 9:35 am, on the seventh day of April, 1943. The local board will furnish transportation to an induction station. You will there be examined, and, if accepted for training and service, you will then be inducted into the land or naval forces. Willful failure to report promptly to this local board at the hour and on the day named in this notice is a violation of the Selective Training and Service Act of 1940, as amended, and subjects the violator to fine and imprisonment."

Karl and Evie were now in World War Two's grip. They were down to two weeks. He was likely going to leave for "the length of the war plus six months." She was going to raise Larry alone, maybe for the rest of her life. They told each other what needed to be said. They got their affairs in order. Karl said goodbye to family and friends. It wasn't enough time, but the war didn't care and wouldn't wait. A young couple from Rush County, Indiana, didn't matter one iota in the grand scheme.

They wasted some of the time arguing. Evie told Karl she prayed he would fail the military evaluation. That made him mad. Didn't she understand? Rejection was an intolerable thought for him. In no uncertain terms, he told her he was fit, strong, and willing. It was his duty to go. When her persistent pouting got to him, he told her he wanted to go. He asked her, "How could I look myself in the mirror every morning if I didn't go?"

They weren't prepared for how fast Wednesday, April 7, 1943 arrived. The draft board provided transportation to the induction center in Indianapolis. Twenty-nine of the men sent that day, Karl included, passed the exams. Karl was one of the twenty-five assigned to the Army. Each man was given a serial number. A train brought the group back to Rushville. He walked home from the train station. The military permitted him one week at home before he was to report for active duty.

What a two years it had been. Karl met a girl. The country conducted a contentious national election. A military draft was instituted. The government stopped its neutrality policy. Karl and Evie married. Japan bombed Pearl Harbor. The country declared war. Evie's grandpa Lewis died. They became parents of a handicapped child. Karl joined the army.

Things were now about to get interesting for Karl and Evie.

Karl's group left Rushville on a train for Indianapolis on April 14, 1943. It was a day like all others in Rushville. The sun came up in the east. The factory whistle blew on time at seven o'clock. The Courthouse clock tower was visible from all directions. The Princess Theater played movies. The *Republican* published the names of the boys who were leaving that day.

Karl knew the army was going to strip away his individuality. He felt letters could keep him connected to home and family. His letters would make it seem he was no further away from Evie than when he had written letters to her as they were dating. He promised her he would write whenever he could. He would tell her what was going on, like he always did every night after work. He would remind her how much he loved Larry and her. He vowed to be faithful. He would assure her he would come home as soon as the war was over.

Out of the blue, something occurred to Karl. He didn't know what was ahead for him but, Hell, he might enjoy some of this adventure. He was going to see the world. He would help rid the world of evil. He felt pride that the army selected him. A phrase came to his mind. He learned it when he was a child playing a game of Hide and Seek with his brothers. Here I come, ready or not.

YOU'RE IN THE ARMY NOW

Karl and the other boys got off the bus as ordered. A sergeant immediately yelled at them to line up. He told them to raise their right hand. They repeated the oath of enlistment after him.

I,_____, do solemnly swear that I will support the constitution of the United States. I,_____, do solemnly swear to bear true allegiance to the United States of America, and to serve them honestly and faithfully, against all their enemies or opposers whatsoever, and to observe and obey the orders of the President of the United States of America, and the orders of the officers appointed over me.

That done, the Sergeant lectured the new inductees in a loud voice. The length of duty was "for the duration of the War or other emergency, plus six months, subject to the discretion of the President or otherwise according to law." Each inductee received a copy of the United States Articles of War. He asked if anyone had questions. No one did.

Karl Floyd from Rushville, Indiana ceased to exist. He was now on the lowest rung of the totem pole. He was a buck private in the United States Army.

The Army began the process of turning Private Floyd into a soldier. He became serial number 35140696. He filled out more forms than you could shake a stick at. He felt satisfaction that he was caring for his family when he agreed to buy life insurance. He moaned when he realized the premium came out his pay. He took aptitude tests to see if he possessed any special skills though he wasn't sure what aptitude meant.

Karl noticed a mistake as he read his enlistment papers. It made him wonder if the local draft board was either, at best incompetent, or at worst dishonest. The board had him recorded as "Single, without dependents." He knew it wouldn't do any good to make a fuss over the mistake. He did utter a few choice swear words under his breath.

The sergeant ordered the greenhorns to line up after they completed the paperwork. He spent several minutes lecturing them about army life. One important item was the identification tags, better known as dog tags. Each soldier wore two chains around his neck at all times. One chain was one twenty-eight inches long. The other six was inches long. Each chain had an oval shaped tag on it. The soldier's name, serial number, tetanus immunization status, blood type, next of kin's name and address, and religion were stamped on each tag. He again told them to wear their tags at all times, including when off duty or on furlough.

The sergeant then told the raw recruits the simple reason why soldiers wear dog tags. The dog tag on the long chain stayed with the body for identification if a soldier was injured or killed. The dog tag on the short chain would be removed and used for recording the soldier's name and notifying next of kin. He now had the buck privates' full attention. He re-emphasized, "Never ever be without your dog tags." He hesitated for a few seconds before relieving some of his audience's tension, "Even if you are with your woman." That did get a small chuckle from the new recruits.

Karl had to forget civilian life to become a soldier. Ralph Ingersoll described in his book, *The Battle Is The Payoff,* how a civilian learned to be a soldier, "The time when a soldier learns what an army is and how and why, is during the months he is in training. There he learns faster than he ever thought he could learn anything, not only because of the pace of training, but because the life is so different from what he has left. Everything is new and vivid to him and he is wholly preoccupied with learning, and must learn a great deal in order to survive at all. But during this time, the soldier is out of touch with his old world. He is too tired to write. When he tries to talk he finds that, anxious as his listeners are to know, there is too much to explain, too many terms to translate."

Private Floyd got a bunk at the end of his long first day in the army. Partly to hide his anxiety and exhaustion, he observed his fellow privates. Many bitched and moaned about the hardness of the bunks. Some fell asleep as soon as their heads hit the pillow. One guy a few bunks away snored as loud as the Old Man. A few cried. Several, like Karl, wrote letters.

Lying in his bunk, Karl thought of the first day of one rabbit season when he was a little boy. He was too young to shoot a shotgun. He begged his older brothers to let him go hunting with them. Needing someone to kick up rabbits, they agreed to let him come along if he would carry all the rabbits they shot. He also had to agree to skin and gut the rabbit carcasses. Karl agreed with no hesitation. His big brother, Big Guy, gave Karl a hunting coat. The coat was way too big on him, but he wore it with pride.

The hunt went well. Karl kicked up a lot of rabbits that day for his brothers to shoot. When they headed home, there were so many rabbits in the pockets of the coat that it almost dragged on the ground. He grumbled about the weight of his load, but was too proud to ask for help. None was offered, either. He fell behind his older brothers by several minutes but somehow made it home. He then spent most of the afternoon skinning the rabbits. Clara was proud that he lived up to his end of the bargain. She didn't offer one word of sympathy to her darling boy. She did take the opportunity to remind

Karl, "You got what you asked for. They took you with them. Stop the belly aching." The family enjoyed a mess of fried rabbit and gravy. He fell asleep immediately after eating himself silly.

Without warning, the barracks door suddenly flew open. The sergeant's piercing voice brought Karl back to reality. He yelled, "Lights out in thirty minutes." He then disappeared. Karl reached into his duffel bag to get a pen and paper. Sitting on the edge of his bunk, he wrote his first letter as a soldier to Evie.

April 14, 1943
About 8:00 pm
Honey, well I'm in the Army now but haven't got my uniform yet. I will get it tomorrow. I get my three shots then too. We got up here about noon today and ate chow then we went to some place up here and took three tests. Boy, they were something. I'm not kidding. Evelyn, how is Larry making it? I can see him now as he rolls over and blows and then he gives you a big laugh. Boy, I'll sure miss you two but I can't help it so we will have to buck up and take it on the chin. Talk about grub, well, we sure have it up here. The 2 meals I've had weren't fit for a dog to eat. Boy, I'm counting the hours already till you get up here tomorrow. Honey, this war won't be on forever and when it's over I'll come back and we'll be sitting on top of the world. We'll have our furniture and we'll have Larry and home and our own happiness. Sweetheart, there is something I want you to remember. I Love you and will all my living days and longer if possible. I think Larry is the grandest child and only child in the world. God Bless you both as long as you live, so honey, with lots of love I'll close for this time. Kiss Larry for me and then let him kiss you on the cheek. Please take care of yourself and Larry.

Home was too close. He wanted to get out of Indiana, but buck privates always were the last to know anything. He didn't have a clue what happened next, where he was going, or what he was going to do. He knew the army would ship him to basic training when it was ready, not when he was ready. He was still in Indiana five days later.

April 19, 1943
Just a few lines to let you know we weren't shipped today for some unknown reason. I don't know why. I've been thinking of you and Larry all day and night. I sure have had a hard time marking my

clothes. I never saw so many clothes in all my life. Evelyn, I don't know when I'll be shipped out now. Maybe tomorrow and maybe not, but the sooner the better. Boy, I'd like to see Larry, but if I see him now it would be that much harder to get away from him again. I borrowed this paper from a guy that came up with us because mine was down at the bottom of my bag and I didn't want to get it out. Evelyn, there isn't much to write since there isn't anything that goes on here. We're all being called at our barracks tonight at 7:00 for some unknown reason. We all would like to know why. So I'll be seeing you sometime. I don't know when so I'll hope for the best. Darling, take good care of Larry and yourself. When I get located at my regular camp I'll send you my address.

Karl got some good news at the meeting that night. He had scored well on the aptitude tests. Most of the boys in his barracks left the next day for infantry training. Private Floyd and a few others boarded a train headed for Fort F.E. Warren near Cheyenne, Wyoming. It was the training center for men assigned to the Quartermaster Corps. The Quartermaster Corps had responsibility for general supplies, mortuary affairs, food service, fuel, water, field services plus material and distribution management. Karl was one of 20,000 troops who occupied its 280 buildings. He wrote a postcard to let Evie know where he was.

Basic training site near Cheyenne, Wyoming

April 23, 1943

We just arrived at Fort Francis E. Warren near Cheyenne, Wyo. It's so hot here that you can hardly breath. Honey, I'll give you my address after they assign us to some barracks. They say two weeks ago it was 25 below zero. I miss you and Larry but someday it will be different and I'll be home with you all.

April 24, 1943

Just a few lines to let you know that I got in Cheyenne, Wyoming about 8:30 yesterday morning. Honey, I'm between 1100 and 1200 miles from home. I guess I'll get back there someday but I don't know when. We came through lots of states to get out here but it didn't take long. I guess we will be here for about 6 weeks to get our basic training. This place where we're at is in the middle of the desert and not a tree for miles around. Boy is it hot here in the day time and chilly at night. We went out to drill a little while this afternoon and I got so hot I almost felt like passing out, but I didn't. Honey, I forgot to tell you. I'm in Quarter Master Division and at Fort Warren. Darling, some of the boys and I are going to church Sunday. Sweetheart, I'll have to close for this time but will write again when I can. I would love to see Larry but I guess that is out of the question. The lights are ready to go out so I'll close. I will love you forever and ever.

Private Floyd made the adjustment to army life without as much as a burp. The Old Man had taught him to obey orders from above without questioning why, where, who, or what. Civilian life became a distant memory at Boot Camp. The GIs (Short for General Issue) had no control over their lives. They needed permission to do or say anything. They had to salute anyone with a higher rank. That meant saluting almost anyone a buck private encountered.

Evie went through her own basic training. She had to adjust to being a single mother who had lots to worry about. She knew something was wrong with Larry. He was over six months old but didn't roll over, push with his legs, or track with his eyes. She had tried to tell Karl before he left, but he didn't grasp what she said. He thought Larry's activities were cute. Evie didn't want her soldier husband to worry. She knew lying was a sin, but she decided to tell Karl little white lies about Larry. She prayed to God for forgiveness.

The letters Karl and Evie wrote to each other continued. It was like they were talking across the table from each other. She tried to keep a stiff upper lip, but she couldn't hide her lonesomeness, anguish, and insecurity. She told him what happened in her life, the latest Rushville gossip, and what she knew of other boys in the military.

April 25, 1943
I'm trying to write you most every day. I hope you enjoy my letters. We started drilling yesterday and it wasn't bad. I don't know whether I sent you my address or not but it is: Pvt. Karl Floyd 35140696, Co. B. 1st regt. Bks. 230, Q.M.R.T.C., Fort F.E. Warren, Wyo. Us boys out here have to ask one another how to address our letters. There are about 21,000 men out here in this fort. Honey, this is Easter morning. The whole camp got up at 4:30 and went to sunrise service. It's now about 9:30 and I suppose you're going to Sunday school about this time or getting ready to. The weather is pretty hot out here but is cooled off some today so far. The weather can change out here in one minute or even sooner if it wants to. Is Larry still laughing? Has he been sick? Does he still blow like he used to? Does he turn over yet? How is your health, honey? Now be sure and take care of yourself! How are my brothers getting along? Boy, I'm sure glad they're not in here because it will make an old man out of you if you're not careful. So with lots of Love, I bid you goodbye till I get a furlough or the war is over. Now sweetheart, don't forget my address and that is important. This Fort is right outside of Cheyenne Wyo. You can't imagine how hot it is in this place and it's better than 7000 feet above sea level.

April 26, 1943
I sure was glad to hear from you and to read you are going to church. I hope you continue going. Did that Bradfield get sent the same place you did? Omer Stephens and Robert Smith and also Hardie Copple were sent to North Carolina. Your red headed sister and I went to church Sunday night but had to come home before it started. Some woman brought her children to church with the whooping cough. I hope and pray Larry doesn't take it. They sure have a good chance for it because those kids whooped. Larry is getting along just fine. He has been awful cross today. He doesn't blow much anymore, but he sure does jabber. I think I will go out home next week and stay till I get my first check. I sure do miss you. Sometimes it seems as though I can't go on but then I know I have to. I told Mom I could laugh and try to have a good time but that ache is always in my breast. I'm not satisfied anywhere I go. I

sure hope this war doesn't last much longer so we can soon be together again. Aren't you in the same kind of division Cuttie (a good friend from Rushville) *is in? What do you have to do? Do you like what you're doing? Coleman wanted to take your guitar over home with him but I didn't let him. Do you want me to let him have it? I like to see it sitting where you always kept it. Are you very close to a town where you're at? How do you like it out there? Are you going to apply for a furlough when you get your training done? I'm living for the day when you come home again. Please write everyday if you can. P.S. Larry is asleep now. What does Q-M-R-T-C stand for?*

April 26, 1943
Honey, my mind has been worrying about you and Larry. I can hardly wait till I know whether you got home alright the day I left. The day is almost ended and the weather is so windy and cold you can hardly breathe. Another reason is the air is so thin out here. I started taking out bonds again today and you will start getting them in about three months. We been drilling pretty hard today and we're supposed to take some Commando training before we end our training here. I'd love to see you both, but can wait till I get my furlough because they say out here they would rather not for your wives to come to see you. We're not here very long and we would have no time to be with our wives. There isn't much to say since nothing goes on here except drilling. Honey, do you want to know a big secret, well that is I love you and Larry so much I can almost taste it. When this war is over we will be happier than anyone in the world. The only thing I can think of is I love you and Larry so much it makes me feel good all over and when I get back I will prove it to you by loving you night and day.

April 27, 1943
I've got time to write you a letter so will try and make it as interesting as I can. I haven't received any mail yet but I can wait as it's a long ways for a letter to travel. Are you staying out at the farm more than at home or are you dividing the time up? I got my second round of shots this afternoon and my arms are already beginning to hurt. We drilled some this afternoon. I like it an awful lot, but it would be a whole lot better to be back home. We got our gas masks this afternoon and we're learning how to use them. It does not seem to be so hard. After we have 5 weeks of drilling we take about 8 weeks of schooling. I should like that a lot better than I do drilling.

Darling, I got a big surprise for you. I got a G-I haircut! It is no longer than 1 inch at the very longest on top. As soon as I get my drills done I will have a picture made and send it to you. I bet Larry sure keeps you good company, doesn't he? I sure will be happy when this conflict is over so we can be together again. And we can go places together and do whatever we want to. Honey, things like that a person doesn't realize till after it's too late. Remember I told you the weather up here was hot? Well, I take that back. It's cold up here now and at night you almost freeze. All you can see is sand blowing. I bet you within 1½ years this war will be almost over. Do you want to take that or not?

April 28, 1943
I received your letter this morning. How did you like going to church so early? I didn't go to Sunday school because it was not pretty enough. It has been rather cold here today. It's a wonder people don't take pneumonia. It is hot one day and cold the next. Have you had any passes since you've been there? Do they have any dances out there? How do you like the looks of the women out there? I dreamed about you all night long last night. I wonder if you miss us as bad as we miss you. Larry Thomas is sitting on my lap watching me write this letter. He sure has been a good boy today. He laughs a lot anymore. I don't know what I would do if it wasn't for him. I called all the stores in Rushville and New Salem trying to get Karo (Karo was a corn syrup that mothers used to make baby formula.) *and they didn't have any. Larry has enough to last him for three or four days. I don't know what I will do. Dorothy* (She was the wife of one of Karl's brothers.) *told me today she was expecting a baby. She said she didn't come sick this month. She said she craved certain things and when she didn't get them it made her sick. I don't think she knows what she is talking about! Larry just told me to tell you he said "Hello." I think I've started getting fat again. My jaw is still sore where that wisdom tooth is trying to come through. I am going to send you the Republican paper as soon as I can get down to the office. Dory had another spell last Friday. He got a letter from my step-brother* (He had left for basic training a few weeks before Karl) *and he said he was homesick, which of course is natural. I wrote him a letter and told him Dory was in a serious condition and he would have to write more cheerful letters. I guess I will start going to Sunday school and church now. I wanted to go all the time but you wouldn't go. I hope and pray you are different when you come home. You know it never hurt anybody by going to church. You said something about the army making an old man out of you. I hope it doesn't make one out*

of you. If it does I'll make you get young again when you come home. I can hardly wait till that day comes. Two other happy days were when I got married and when Larry was born. I sure have had a bit of sad days though. I bet you get tired of reading my letters because I write and write but never say anything. I hope and pray it won't be long till we can all be together again. P.S. What time do the lights go out there and what time do you have to be in bed? How come you have your number after your name? I didn't think you needed that unless you were overseas.

April 28, 1943
Just a few lines to let you know that I'm getting bigger every day. That is, I'm gaining weight. Our barracks won 1st in the bond drive and we were treated to a big T-bone steak supper and was it fine. We had so much to eat we couldn't eat it all. There's one thing about this camp. They feed you good. This weather up here is terrible. One day it's so hot you can't breathe the next day it's cold and windy and the sand blows and you can't even see where you're going. You've heard of sandstorms well, I've been in them now and I know what they're like, but so much for that. I think Army life is fine. If anyone tells you that in the Army you get plenty of sleep, tell them they're nuts. You go to bed at 9:00 and you don't go to sleep till about 11:00 because some of the guys talk till about then and you get up between 4:00 and 5:00. We cleaned rifles tonight awhile. It sure was good to get hold of a gun. By the way Evelyn, have someone clean my shotgun up. I forgot to do it before I left. Have them to take it apart and clean the inside and oil it and clean all the rust off of it because I can't do it myself now and I hope to use it again someday. Honey, do you and Larry miss me much? I bet you do and I miss you both an awful lot but there's a job to do and we can't do it at home. If you ever get lonesome, just remember I'm away to the Army so we can be free and happy. I must close. It's about time for the lights to go out.

April 30, 1943
Well, I will finally get your letter wrote for today. I went downtown this afternoon and I just got back from a pitch-in supper at church. I suppose you're in bed by now. I had the paper sent to you for three months. It cost a dollar and fifteen cents for three months. You mentioned in your letter about it being cold. Well, it isn't much better here. The wind has been blowing awful hard today and it has been pretty chilly here. It tried to storm last night, and of course it woke me up. You said you bet the war would be over

in a year and a half. Well, I bet it will be over before then. Or at least I hope and pray so. It sure is awful to have to go any place without you. It seems like I'm just half there, which of course is true because you've got my heart with you. I am aiming to go out home Sunday night and stay for a week or two. I cashed in two bonds today. I hope it is the last I have to cash in. I think I can make it on what I've got now without having to draw any out of the bank. I've got $10.05 left. Larry takes his formula pretty good now. He sure is getting fat. He looks so much like you. He has been sleeping pretty late of a morning. He sure was glad to get to bed tonight. I sure would like to see you with that G-I haircut. How do you like your hair cut like that? I wish you were here so I could curl your hair again. I guess Ruth, (Ruth was a neighbor. She was known as a "Rounder") *the old rip or worse than that, is going to go to Bob when he gets stationed. I think that's an awful way for Bob to treat Della. I hope you'll never treat me that way. If I was Della I'd rip that old thing from end to end. I still love you with all my heart and will forever. And little Larry does too.*

May 1, 1943
I can't understand why you haven't got any mail yet. I sent you a letter and a card Monday afternoon. Larry is in bed sleeping. He has been kind of cross today. He sure does laugh a lot anyway. You asked me if Larry and I miss you much. I miss you so much I can hardly stand it. I hope and pray I won't have to miss you much longer. I bet that T-bone steak supper did taste good. I wish I'd of been there to help you eat. I went to the show this evening. It was pretty good but, it would have been a hundred percent better if you'd of been with me. Talking about the weather up there being awful, so is this down here! It still is pretty cold out. Your dad said he would clean your gun for you. I write at night before going to bed. I love you so much. I would rather sit at home and think of you than go anyplace.

May 1, 1943
We get up at 4:30 or 5:00 and the lights go out at 9:00. Honey, you asked me about the girls out here. Well, there are no girls here. I haven't even been off the post and we're not liable to be for a few weeks, at least till our basic training is over. The dances out here are none because this camp is for work, not pleasure. Instead of going to Sunday school tomorrow we have to drill. Sometimes we get to go to the show if nothing else is taking place. You said it was cold one day and warm the next. Well, you can't imagine what this weather out here is like. You've heard of dust storms. I'm in the state

where they start at. So Dory had another spell because his son said he is homesick? Well, if he pays attention to his drilling or schooling he won't have any time to get homesick. Tell Dory to forget and keep his mind off of his son. Worrying about him like he does is not necessary, that is if he is able to take care of himself. Of course, I miss you all back home more than you can think but I don't aim to let it get me down. Tell our boy his dad will be back as soon as this conflict is over. Why don't I get homesick? There's no use because it won't do any good. The things I can look forward to are after this war is over. Keep your chin up. Tell all the folks back home "hello" and to be good while I'm gone. When I get through my training, I won't be scared to take on a wild cat in a fight or anything because they tough you up out here. I must ring off now and go and shave and take a shower before I go to bed.

May 3, 1943

It sure has been cold here today. Tommy's duck and your duck got in a big fight today and we had to separate them. Just think, those ducks are three years old this summer. Larry is in bed sleeping. He sure has been cross today. He didn't sleep hardly any last night and he got up early this morning. He was just getting over one cold and now he is taking another. Larry sure does like to be romped with. I suppose you're in bed by now and sleeping as it's almost 10:30. Do you ever dream about Larry and me? You said something about having to go overseas. Do you think you'll get to come home before you do? Yes, when your dad held Larry for the first time he held him real still. Larry started to go to sleep for him. He has held Larry several times since then. Larry weighs about fourteen pounds now. I hope the next one is a girl. Larry just woke up and I am holding him now. Do you have a recreation hall and places to buy eats out there? What do you do to pass the time anyway? I heard over the radio today that men who are supposed to know what they're talking about said the war would be over in 1944. I hope and pray so, don't you. Do you have a radio out there to listen to?

May 5, 1943

I saw one of the U.S. secret weapons the other day. I can't tell you what it was but it will do the trick. Don't think it won't. Honey, you asked me how much I took out in bonds. Well I take $6.25 a month and that gives you a bond every three months. If I get any money ahead I will send it to you. By the way, when you receive the five dollars I sent you, let me know you got it. I had some more drilling today. We also took a three hour hike with field packs, gas masks,

and gun belts, canteen, medicine packs, and rain coats. They were just an extra load because it never rains out here. I sure like basic training but I will be glad when it's over with and we can get our schooling in so we can get this war over in a hurry. Have you got any money left? If you haven't, write and tell me so I can send some home to you. I've got $10.00 left and payday isn't far off. Honey, has Larry got any Karo syrup left? If he hasn't, be sure and consult a Dr. about it. So he is taking his Pablum (a processed cereal for children with rickets) **pretty good now. I hope he likes it and it makes him better. Be sure and be careful of Larry because he might get some disease, but I know you will be careful. Tell the others to write if they have time but don't cramp their recreation any. By the way, we go to the gas chamber Friday. I imagine it will be fun, don't you think so? P.S. You asked me if any mountains are around here. Well, we can see them about 40 or 50 miles away and they always got snow on them.**

Evie's Army wife war training continued. As if women weren't suffering enough, the Red Cross ignorantly reminded them, "This is everyone's war." It scolded women for shirking their responsibility to make surgical dressings. The *Republican* printed an article on Evie's first ever Mother's Day. It encouraged mothers to pray because, "Victory will serve us little if brave men fighting abroad for us return to a Godless nation."

The Civilian Defense conducted the first of many blackout drills in case of an enemy raid. Rushville's citizens were instructed to recognize the sirens and whistles that warned of a possible attack. When the sirens sounded, street lights went black. Citizens turned off all lights and sought cover until the all clear signal sounded. Evie followed the instructions. Ott refused to turn his lights off. He figured the war was the same as lost if the sonsabitching Krauts made it to Indiana. He declared he would go down shooting, not hiding in the goddam basement.

May 10, 1943
I got a letter and a Mother's Day card from you this morning. It's the prettiest card I believe I ever saw. That was my first Mother's Day card I ever got. It won't be long till Father's Day. Then is when you'll come in the picture. Larry and I love and miss you every minute of the day. I get so tired of cold damp weather but there is nothing I can do about it. Have you ever

been on guard duty yet? Do you still have to be on fire patrol in the barracks? Please answer some of my questions. You don't answer more than half of them. Larry has been pretty good today. He sure can make faces now. He got mad at me today and you ought to have seen the faces he made at me. He gets cuter every day, I think. I wish you could be with us to see the different things he picks up. I skated a little bit on the front porch this afternoon. Do you get tired while you are on those hikes? Talking about not knowing what girls look like, you better know me when you come home. Nobody around here has started to plant corn yet. If this weather keeps on, it looks like they won't get to plant it. I sure miss you at night when a storm comes up. I get to wanting you so bad sometimes it seems like I ache all over. Don't forget to be good and don't start drinking, which I know you won't. Don't cuss too much. Try to go to church if you can. I can't on account of the weather and the whooping cough. I told you I thought Larry was taking the whooping cough, but I don't think he is.

May 10, 1943
I received your letter today stating you got the five dollars. When you get the next ten I sent you, please write me. If this barracks keeps on there won't be anyone here to go to war overseas. Everybody is getting the scarlet fever, pneumonia, or the flu. The reason is the altitude is high and the air is so dry and thin it brings on the sore throat. They just took the guy out that I came from Indianapolis with. I've been drilling all day and up till 7:00 tonight. Boy, I tell you they're really putting us through the ropes. We got a lot to do in four weeks instead of five and we haven't got much time to do it in. You said I didn't answer all your questions. Well, I try to but there are some I don't know the answers to. Such as I don't know when I'll get a furlough. We don't know from one day to another what we're going to do. I start to take up rifle shooting tomorrow. I bet that will be fun. After our basic training is over we go to school for eight weeks and from there I don't know where I'll go. I don't care as long as we get this conflict over. I think I might get off to go to town this weekend. You keep asking me about women. Well, there are only a few out here and a guy wouldn't take a second look at them. Boy, they really are feeding us salt peter out here. You don't even care if you ever see a woman. Darling, tell me when Larry cuts his first teeth. I'd like to know every step he takes like that. Honey, did my red headed sister tell you I wished you'd named Larry after me? (His fiery red headed sister and Big Guy were twins.) **Well, I never said a word like that. Remember the night you and I laid in bed and picked those**

names out? If I wanted us to name him Karl, I would have said so, wouldn't I? I'd love to see you both, but we got bigger things to do and that is getting this war over. It can't be much longer before the war is over. Sweetheart, my motto is: Your Mine, I'm Yours, Larry's ours and We're Larry's. That's the way it's going to stay.

P.S. Darling, remember this is going to be a war which will free other people. When you're blue, remember that.

May 11, 1943

I didn't get a letter today but I never get one on Tuesday. It has been another rainy day. I think all it knows how to do is rain. The water has come up again in the basement. I think I'll go home the latter part of next week if the weather isn't too bad. Do you remember Larry Thomas is seven months old today? I weighed him and he weighed about fourteen pounds and two ounces. You ought to see him make faces and try to patty-cake. It's so lonesome without you. I sometimes wonder how I'm going to get along without you, but then I know it has to be done. When it is all over, it will probably seem like going through a long bad dream. I went to town this afternoon to pay bills. I drove in by myself. Imagine that! I paid $9.28 to the Home Outfitters, $5.00 to Rhodes-Burford, and $2.00 for rent. I also paid a light bill of $3.50. Out of $38.00 and some change I have $8.13 left and I still have Spiegel's to pay. Your mother's house sure looks nice. I have to start house cleaning when the weather gets fit. I think if I have the money I'll get a good rug for the bedroom next fall. Of course, that's a long way off and I want to talk to you about it when you come home on a furlough. Does it seem to you that your heart aches all the time anymore? I love you a whole, whole lot and more than that. Larry is in bed and sleeping. He has been sleeping pretty good the last few nights. P.S. If you need any money, write and tell me and I'll send you some.

The *Republican* featured glimmers of hope in a May 13 article, "Unrest, open defiance is nearing a climax within Nazi ruled countries. Some of the most exciting news of the war came out of occupied Europe today. London hears that open revolt has spread like wildfire across the border into Belgium. London hears that a series of attacks on German troops, military establishments and communications throughout Belgium. Reverberations of the Allied victory in Africa are said to be shaking the whole of Hitler's Europe."

Karl kept learning to be a soldier. Evie kept praying to God for the war to end.

May 15, 1943
I'm thinking about you both all the time. Another boy discovered he had the measles. He is one guy who had a brother killed at Pearl Harbor when the Arizona was sunk. In about one hour I'm going out on the rifle range and right now we're having one of the worse snow blizzard's I've ever seen. There is about 6 to 8 inches of snow. By evening, if it keeps on, there will be a foot on, but we have to march in it just the same. Also, we have to lay down in it to fire our rifles. Some job, eh? But we have to do it before we get out of this place. Is the weather warm there yet? Did you run out of coal or do you still have some left? I can see Larry laying in his crib right now and jumping back and forth. Does he want to stand up on his feet yet? Is his foot still crooked or is he just lazy? I certainly would love to see you both right now but I have to wait till I get my turn. Mom wrote and told me dad caught a big bunch of fish the other night. I certainly wish I could have caught some myself. Did you ever get your ten dollars I sent you? I've still got another $10.00 left plus $2.00 and some change so that will carry me through for a long time. **Has Madge heard from Ronald** (Ronald was Evie's brother. He was a paratrooper somewhere in the Pacific) **lately? The war news certainly sounds good, doesn't it? I heard on the radio the Japs are trying to make some drives in the Pacific. They had better do their best now. It won't be long till they won't be able to do anything.**

May 16, 1943
I still love you both more than anyone can imagine. This is Sunday morning about 9:15 and I just got up. I can't go to church today. We're supposed to stay here on account of we're getting to go out to the range to fix it up for us to start shooting. I don't feel so good today. I've finally got a cold and one of the hardest coughs I've ever had. It causes my head to hurt awful. This weather up here is enough to kill anyone. I'm certainly glad I'll be shipped out of here pretty soon. At least I'm supposed to be. I can get a picture of those warm and rainy days you've been having back there, but no one can imagine the weather they have out here. Yesterday, we had some more snow and it sure was cold. They don't heat these barracks at all. That's why everyone is getting sick. Honey, is Larry still as cute as ever? Does he laugh out loud yet? Is he sitting up any at all? Don't ever worry about me drinking or anything like that. I've still got my common sense. That's one thing I'll never do. Remember before

Larry was born how you and I would go squirrel hunting? Well, all three of us can go after this is all over. I'm going to teach you and Larry to swim too. Remember last summer when we all went swimming and had roasted hotdogs? It doesn't seem possible so many things could happen to anyone in such a short time. P.S. Sweetheart, remember whenever you feel blue or lonely, this war won't last forever and someday we'll all be back. None of us boys will dread it if we don't come back because we all know we're fighting for the ones back home. This war, before it's finished, will take the lives of more men than anyone will ever think of, but a good American isn't scared to die for a reason. Remember to cheer up and keep your chin up high.

May 16, 1943
Another blue and lonely Sunday has passed by. It sure is awful without you. Maybe this war will be over soon and you can be back home with us. Did you get to church today? I didn't because I was afraid those children with the whooping cough might be there. Larry is sleeping good tonight because he is worn out. I've finally found a way to get him to take water. He likes cold water out of a glass. Getting to be quite a man, isn't he? Do you wear your glasses now? Did you have them changed? If so, do they have rims? I suppose you're in bed by now. I wish you could fly home and be here in a few minutes. I'm hoping and praying for this war to end soon.

May 17, 1943
I'm lying in bed writing so my writing isn't very good. You asked me when summer started out here. To tell you the truth, I don't think they have one. I also like making my own bed. I'm really fast and good at it, too. There is a certain way we have to make them out here. I've a rifle of my own and it's a 30-caliber Winfield and its number is 792578 so you can see there are a lot of things I have to remember. I only got $15.13 when I got paid because I wasn't in a full month and my insurance was taken out of it and also my laundry. Yes, it was real tear gas in the gas chamber. It really makes your eyes and skin burn, but it doesn't harm you any at all as long as you don't rub affected parts. If I got Scarlet fever I wouldn't be able to write, but I'm not going to get it if I can help it. The guy that left Indianapolis with me, he's right across the room from me now. He's had pneumonia instead of Scarlet fever. Has Larry's shoes started wearing out yet? If there is anything you need, just tell me. There is nothing else to use the money for that I've got. I usually go to bed

about 8:30 or 9:00. I'm always in bed by 9:00. When I get back home, if I start staying up till 11:00 or 12:00 o'clock I'll nearly die because I'm not use to it. The boys out here say I can go to sleep faster than anyone they ever saw.

May 17, 1943
Just a few lines to let you know I'm still thinking of you. There is a foot of snow on the ground out here and it's starting to melt and it's all slushy. I didn't go out on the rifle range because I've got that sore throat again. I went down to the infirmary a while ago and the doctor told me to go to bed today, then come back and see him tomorrow. He gave me some pills to take every 4 hours. I sure hope I get out tomorrow. If I don't get to go out on the range this week, I have to take my basic all over again. Darling, I had a dream about you last night. I dreamt you, Larry, and I were all home together. I had popped some popcorn and we were sitting around and eating it. It seemed so real. I could hardly believe different when I woke up. But I realized finally it wasn't true. Do you know I've been in the Army now more than a month? The Army is fine if you can get accustomed to military life and forget civilian life. That's what you have to do to get along in the Army. How is Larry getting along darling? Tell me some about yourself when you write me. I bet Larry will be a big boy when I get back. I wrote you two letters today. There wasn't anything else to do so I just sat down and started writing. I'm using Forest Miller's tablet. I run out of paper yesterday and I didn't feel like going down to the P-X to get some more.

May 18, 1943
I miss you terribly. I didn't hear from you today. We're all getting along fine, except I am lonely for you. Maybe I won't have to miss you many more months. Dory's nerves seem to be a lot better. Larry seems to be over his cold now. I sure have a time with him. I think he wants to play most of the time. I went to town this afternoon and drove in by myself. I went up to your folks and stayed most of the afternoon. I sent $5.00 to Spiegel's. That cuts it down to $25.85. By the time summer is over, I'll have most of the debts out of the way. All except the hospital bill from when you had your appendix removed. I also paid another 92 cents to the insurance man. I've got around $6.50 left. I bought some candy, franks for supper, and some embroidery thread. I want to buy some paint for the kitchen chairs and I've still got to get Larry some more medicine. I ought to get my check the first of June, so you see I'll get by pretty good. It rained again today, but I think it will be pretty tomorrow. At

least I hope so because I've got to get Larry some dry clothes. Larry's case of milk is almost gone except a can or two. I suppose I'll have to buy him another case soon. I'm embroidering some vanity sets now. Don't forget to be good and go to church when possible.

May 18, 1943
I'm thinking of you both constantly. I wish I could see you all right now, but I know that's impossible so I can get along without it. Today, we've been having a hard downpour of rain. Of course, I was out in it. The raincoats the Army gives out are a failure as far as keeping anyone dry. They leak or the rain soaks right through them. Tomorrow, we aim to finish our rifle shooting. Of course, I'm upholding the old Hoosier honor with a 179 out of a possible 200. That gives me an expert medal, so you see your old husband isn't too bad with a gun, eh! Well darling, it looks like the Allies have got the Axis on the verge of going nuts waiting for the punch on Europe. The sooner they invade the Germans, the better chance they'll have of catching them off guard. I'll almost bet they'll invade through Italy, but I'll leave it to a source higher up. I certainly hope it comes soon. I counted your letters yesterday. I've received 15 of them so far and 9 from mom. I've been writing to you pretty good this week, but I doubt if I get to write tomorrow night as we will probably get in from the range late. I will if I can as I really enjoy writing to you. I often wonder if Larry will remember me when I get back. I worry he won't. If you keep showing him my picture, I'm sure he won't forget a mug like mine. Is he sitting up yet? How are his teeth getting along? Is he still cross like he always was? Is his hair still brown or has it changed colors? Those sound like silly questions but are some things I've been wondering about. Some questions about you now. Do your eyes still shine as bright as ever? Have you still got that cute smile? Do you still love me? Rub that out. I know you do. If you need any money, write and tell me. I'll send you all you want since there is no place to spend it out here. I love you and Larry and I always will. As I said my motto is: You're mine, I'm yours and Larry is ours. That makes a perfect three doesn't it, honey?

May 21, 1943
I got four letters from you today. I sure was tickled to get them. I think of you all the time and wish for you because it's awful here without you. I am sending you a sample of Larry's hair so you can see what color it is. It's between a blonde and a brown with kind of a reddish cast. Larry is

outgrowing his shoes. I've tried to get sized ones but can't. I don't know what I'll do, but I'll keep trying. He hasn't cut any teeth yet, but they're hurting him pretty bad. I'll let you know as soon as the first one comes through. He still jabbers out loud and has started blowing again. I hope he doesn't forget you, but if he does it won't take him long to know you. He sure is cross at times and he wears me out when he is cross. He is sitting on my lap now because he won't go to sleep. You asked if Larry's and my eyes were as bright as ever. His are, but I don't know about mine. I didn't know they were bright. I do know I've gotten dark circles around them since you went away. I didn't know my smile was cute, but I reckon I've still got it. Larry is kicking my hand and he is doing it deliberately. You bet that's right about you're mine, I'm yours and Larry's ours. I don't know what I'd do if I didn't have that to think of sometimes. It sure does make a perfect three, and I'm sure proud of you and Larry. That is a good shooting record you've got. Be sure and keep the good work up. I hope you take care of yourself and don't take any diseases. I'm glad to hear your throat got all right. Mom got a letter from Ronald today. He said he's made five jumps since he's been in Australia. He's alright but anxious for this war to be over so he can get back home. It has been pretty here today for a change. Your duck and Tommy's have made up. They were roosting side by side this evening. Remember, it probably won't be long till we can be together again. Then we can be really happy and maybe plan for another baby. I hope.

May 21, 1943
It's Sunday morning about 7:15 and I'm still in bed. I wasn't awake a while ago so the boys got together and upset me, in a pleasant way. We got completely through tonight with our rifle marksmanship. That means we're ready for shipment, but I don't know if it will be Illinois or California. I hope Illinois, but they may not ship me to either place. I don't know much to write except we just got through cleaning the barracks up. The Friday night cleanup is really tough. We clean the place up from top to bottom. We ought to win the battalion award again tomorrow. There are a lot of nice fellows out here from Indiana so I got plenty of company. We guys have been comparing wives and you are the tops as far as I'm concerned. I bet Larry really is cute now because he was getting in the cute age when I left. The Army way of saying that is: Keep on the ball! I'll almost bet the next drive will be on Asia or Japan instead over in Europe. I started this letter Friday night but I had to quit. I thought I was going to be in the quartermaster. Well, I'm in the Ordnance (The branch of the Army

that procured, maintained, and issued weapons, ammunition, and combat vehicles) **but I'm going to be a clerk. I bet I'll make a good one don't you? Be sure and take good care of yourselves while I'm gone. Honey, you have to be brave. Try not to get lonesome or worrying. I want something to come home to that is worthwhile. Everything is going to be okay.**

One of Ott and Clara's older daughters was Lucille. She had given birth to a son two years before Karl was born. She named him Thomas. Shortly after Clara gave birth to Karl, Lucille died from an abdominal infection. Though Clara and Ott had a new baby of their own, a house overflowing with kids, and limited resources, they welcomed their two year old grandson into their home after his mother died. They raised him like he was their own son. They became Mom and Dad to Tom. Tom was drafted into the Army in December of 1941. From 1942 to 1945, he was stationed in a desolate area of India helping get arms and supplies to an American wartime ally, China. Tom was a grizzled veteran by the time Karl went in. He thought Karl might need a pick me up, so he wrote his nephew a letter.

Karl's best friend and nephew
Tom Beckner

India, May 22, 1943

Hello Rookie! You're in the army now and not behind the plow! I just got your address from home and I thought you may need a little cheering up. I know just how you feel. I went through practically the same thing. Well Karl, how do you like the old army? I'm a hoping you don't find it too bad. Just take it easy and do everything you're told and do it to the best of your ability. You will make a good soldier. You have all it takes and plenty more. Army life is what you make it. It never has been real bad on me because I've done everything I was told and kept my mouth shut. Always respect your non-Coms as they are the ones who can make it hard for you. I don't mean for you to be a sucker though. I know you wouldn't anyway. Mom is sure proud of you and me. Let's both get in there and pitch with everything we got. If there is anything I can do to help you, don't fail to write me and ask about it. You and I went the opposite way when we left the induction center. I liked the part of the country where I was. The camp was pretty good also. Let me know all about Wyoming. Be a good boy and keep your chin up. This war will be over before you know it and then you can return to your wife and baby. Keep plugging, chin up. Your nephew, Tom

Karl and Evie continued their conversation.

May 24, 1943
How are you, darling? I'm out of paper so I thought I'd write a card. Four of us guys finally got up to town today. I had three pictures made so I'll send them to you. I'm sending you a pillow cover. I hope you like it. I tried to get something, but I couldn't find anything I thought Larry would like. It's raining out here now and it's pretty cold.

Karl had been gone six weeks. Evie couldn't resist letting him know how lonely and jealous she was.

May 27, 1943
I've got the blues so bad I could just cry and cry. I get so lonesome for you sometimes I can hardly stand it. I received a card and a pillow cover this morning. I sure was glad to get the pillow cover. I think it's very pretty (She kept it in her bedroom until she died). *We went to town tonight and Larry and I went up to your folks. I read the letters you wrote to your mother. You told her about going to a broadcast. How come you never said anything about it to me? Did you have a good time when you went? Did you go to Cheyenne or some other town? How did you like the town and is it very big? What day did you go? Why didn't you write me a letter Saturday night? How long of a pass did you have? You never tell me much about what you do of evenings. Larry is sitting on my lap now. He wants to know if his*

daddy thinks of us as often as he used to. I weighed Larry tonight and he weighed almost 15 pounds. He has begun blowing again and he sticks his tongue out at me. He has been kind of cross today and he has me rather tired. I think Dory is aiming to start working in the fields tomorrow. Do you still love me? Be sure and keep your chin up, as you tell me to do, and I'll try and keep mine up although it's awful hard to do sometimes. Be good and don't forget to go to church.
PS. Thanks for the pillowcase.

Headlines and articles about the war continued to dominate the newspaper. On May 24, the *Republican* reported "Seven dogs, Rush County's first shipment of animals under the Dogs for Defense program were enlisted by their owners to the Army. The animals left Rushville for Fort Robinson, Nebraska to be trained in the type of war work for which they are best fitted."

Despite the encouraging and patriotic news, Evie's nightmare worsened. On Karl's last day of basic training, the *Republican* reported that a Rushville soldier died in combat in North Africa. He worked at the International furniture factory with Karl.

CALIFORNIA HERE I COME

The war forced Americans to learn War rule number one: All decisions were made for the benefit of the war effort. The military feared "some loose-lipped soldier" would say something that might benefit the enemy. Karl wasn't told where he was going, when he was leaving, or how long he would stay until he needed to know. He could not discuss what he did know with civilians. An officer read his letters before he could mail them. The censor crossed out anything written that might aid the enemy.

Those at home also learned to live with War rule number two: The military didn't give a rat's ass if a family didn't know the whereabouts of their soldier.

A sense of adventure gripped a soldier after he accepted he had no control over what happened next. It became easy to forget about the worries back home. Karl was visiting places and seeing things he had only heard or read about. His next stop was Los Angeles, California to attend an eight week course to learn typing, filing, nomenclature, and procedures essential to the Quartermaster Corps. The war seemed far removed from California. The thought of getting an education excited him. The postmarks on his letters changed, but the conversation continued.

May 29, 1943
Hotel Willard, Downtown Los Angeles, California
As the days go by, I find myself loving you both more and more. I just arrived here from Fort Warren. Darling, I got my first rating which is a P.F.C and I dressed in my suntans for the first time. (P.F.C. stood for Private first class. He was now one small rung above a buck private in the Army's pecking order.) **They fit me perfectly except the shirt is too big around the collar. I came with a bunch of handpicked men and we start college on Monday morning. The college is Woodbury College which is a pretty good place. I will get through here in about 8 weeks. I sure will be glad to get some college education. I've had a tough time so far in the Army but I'll keep my chin up and take all they can give me. Out here, I stay in the Willard Hotel. We have private rooms. Out in Wyoming I had to write lying down on my bunk and write the best way I could. I have a desk here to write on. We eat chow at a restaurant. It's sure is grand and don't think it's not. When we get out of this camp into another barracks somewhere, we will be sorry. When we left Fort Warren, we came down through Colorado, New Mexico, and Arizona, and then California. When we came though the desert in California, we saw some of the giant cactus. I said some, well, I mean mile after mile of them. I also saw a lot of the flat leaf cactus like your mother has, but much larger than hers. The mountains were beautiful, but I'd give a whole lot to be back east instead of out here on the Pacific coast. It took us about 50 hours of steady traveling. Have you got your first paycheck yet? I missed my pay for this month because I left Fort Warren when it was almost time for pay, but we're supposed to get supplementary pay. I have to do a lot of night studying now, so be sure and think of me at nights because I'll be in my room studying. I bet the weather out there is nice about now. I can picture the sun shining down on the pretty green grass and all the kids going barefooted. That's the things I used to like to do. I'm sure you'll let Larry do the same because going barefooted sure is fun as long as you don't cut your foot. Are Larry's teeth still hurting him? It won't be long before Larry will start crawling, then you'll have to watch him like a chicken hawk. He'll really get dirty when he starts. Honey, speaking of**

churches, there a big church next to our hotel. On the other side is the Los Angeles City Library, so you see we're ranking pretty high.

May 30, 1943
Well, another Sunday has come and gone. I sure missed you today. I miss you so much I can hardly stand it. My heart aches sometimes so bad it hurts. I guess I can try and bear it out till the war is over which I hope and pray won't be long. Larry is in his bed sleeping now. I hope he will sleep there all the time. He sure says do-do a lot. He can really make faces. It won't be long till he'll be 8 months old. We'll soon be married two years. It doesn't seem like it's been that long. I drove Tommy's car once to get some meat for supper. I think I'll get a driver's license one of these days. Maybe I will when you come home on a furlough, if you'll let me. I will close for now. I hope to see you before many more months pass.

May 31, 1943
I received a letter from you and one from mom today. It was pretty good mail service as I only got here Saturday afternoon. I spent my first day at college today. I really thought it was fine. We have two recesses in the morning and two in the afternoon. We have places right in the college for cokes, candy, sandwiches, ice cream, cigarettes, or anything we want to eat, drink, or smoke so you see we have everything we want, but the thing we have to realize is we got a job to do. Our job is to be clerks so we have to learn typing and Army regulations. It's a big job. Those Army regulations are long and tough. We have typing 3 hours a day. I sure like it, but I wish you had taught me something about it. You asked me what I did at the PX till 10:30 at night. I didn't say I stayed at the PX till then. I said a person could stay there if he wanted to. The lights always go out at 9:00 at Fort Warren, but out here in Los Angeles we stay up till 11:00 studying, and I mean studying. Darling, have I told you I saw the Pacific Ocean for my first time? Well I did and I couldn't believe it. It was like a big mad animal of some kind. The waves were about 15 ft. high and the water is as blue as indigo. I have seen several sea going liners or, in civilian life, I'd say the big ships. I also saw some destroyers and one battleship. I've seen several things in this Army that are secret weapons, but I'm not supposed to say anything. The reason is, in case this mail is lost and falls into enemy hands, no secrets would be given out. I never get homesick or anything of that sort, but I do miss you and Larry and the good times we've had together. We have a piano on every floor of our hotel and some boy is

playing "My Old Kentucky Home". He sure knows his music. I'm telling you, this kind of Army life is the best anyone can offer, but I'd give $2,000, if I had it, just to see old Rushville again, but I can wait till my turn comes up. We have the "Church of the Open Doors" right besides our hotel. It sure is big. It holds about 3,000 people. The boy I run around with is a sort of religious guy and we chat now and then about churches. I'm sure glad to hear Larry is laughing out loud now. Tell him to keep laughing because Daddy wants to see him in that kind of mood when I come home. I'm all out of paper, so with lots of love I bid you a lovely goodnight with all the love and kisses in the world. Tell our boy to be good for daddy and mommy and we'll repay him some day.

June 2, 1943

I sure do miss you but I guess I can take it on the chin for the duration. I'm trying to keep my writing up. When I was on the train, I couldn't write. I got my second day of schooling in today, but I've got about 3 hours of studying to do yet. I can tell you I'm in the Ordnance division. The things we have to learn are a whole lot, every branch of service, every gun, all sorts and all parts of them, the ranks of all officers in all branches, all the things needed to run a war, the president and his cabinet, and what each man in the cabinet does. Besides that, each member of the cabinet has about 75 people under him and we have to know who they are and what they do. I also have to learn all the tactics of modern warfare plus the tactics of our allies and our enemies. I have to be able to tear up all kinds of guns and reassemble them in a certain length of time and also identify each and every piece of them. We have 7 books and they're about 2 inches thick, so you can see what I have to learn in 8 weeks. Are you so lonely you don't know what to do with yourself? If you are, darling, be sure and buck up. It's not that bad. Before you know it, this war will be over and everyone will be home. It will seem like a big bad dream except for the ones who won't come back, and there'll be a lot. Darling, I miss the fishing I always did in the spring time and groundhog hunting too, but I guess the longer this war lasts the more fish and game there will be. Did anyone ever clean my shotgun up? If they did, thank them for me. If they didn't, have someone to do it for me. I forgot all about it before I left. PS. I'm getting along fine in typing.

June 3, 1943
Honey, I got another letter from you today which was forwarded from Fort Warren. I sure was surprised to hear about Miles (the Rushville soldier killed in North Africa). **He was one of the boys I worked with at the factory and was the one I got into a fight with for calling me a son of a bitch. I heard him say lots of times no German would ever take him prisoner, so it's possible that's why he was killed. Out here, you can see lots of boys who came back from the war theaters with legs torn off or an arm or maybe both of them. In that case, a person would be just as well off dead. Me and another fellow talked to some Marines the other day. They said the way the men were mangled up was awful. They said those Japs were some tricky fellows but the Americans are a little smarter than the Japs give us credit of being. Some of the boys and I are going to go get paid, so we plan to catch a streetcar and see what it's really like out here. Sometimes we take in a show till our money runs out. I'll tell you something about California. In the first place, it's over rated. In the next place, it's too crowded to suit me. The people out here are pretty good, but there are a lot of them of them who picked this kind of climate to do their loafing in. For example, on Sunday a man about 35 or 40 years old came up to me and asked me for some money. He said. "Soldier, have you got a spare quarter you would give to a man out of work?" The flame got real hot inside of me. I told him, in the first place, I didn't have a quarter. In the second place, there was no reason why he shouldn't have a job and he shouldn't even be classified an American citizen. The last thing I said was a man shouldn't ever ask a soldier for any money. Our whole month's pay isn't enough to last a guy two weeks. Then he told me a line that he was starting to work at the Douglas airplane factory just to smooth things over. The whole place out here is full of men like that. So much for California! A person in the Army can't imagine what it would be like to get back in civilian clothes again. In fact, the civilians we see, and we see all sorts of them here as we're right in the heart of the city, look like some kind of foreigners as we're used to uniforms all the time. The U.S.O.** (The United Service Organization was the soldiers' home away from home. It was a place to relax and have some fun.) **is awfully good to soldiers here. They get us deductions on certain articles we need and if we want to go to the show and have no money, all we have to do is go down there and tell them which one we want to go to and they give us a ticket for it. Myself, I've got too much pride, or not enough nerve, because I'd never do anything like that. I'll be glad**

when I get the pictures of you and Larry. You say he's going to have eyes like mine? I'm proud of it but it would be better if he has blue eyes like yours as mine haven't got any color to them. I can picture how we used to ride around on Saturday and Sunday nights and park down at the tobacco barn. Do you remember the evenings when you and I would go squirrel hunting and how you would spot them and then I'd miss? How about the times when we'd go fishing? Evelyn, I haven't got any stationary. All I have in money is 5 pennies, so until I get paid I can't buy any paper. When I get my pay, I'll get some stationary and then I'll write everyone. Tell mom not to worry about Tommy as the mailing system is pretty tough to get through over there and I know he can take care of himself. There is a big chance that any of us could get killed, but that's a chance we have to take in warfare. If anything ever happens to Tom, you can bet your last cent I'll make up for it or die trying. Tell Mom and Dad 'Hello' and I'll write them at least once a week. Again, tell Mom not to worry about Tom. Things will happen for the best no matter how much worrying she does. PS. This was my third day of college. I sure am beginning to like it although it's plenty tough. We have to study constantly on the subjects we have and there are a lot of them. I had a test today. I made 91, so you see that wasn't bad.

June 4, 1943
Talk about being lonely, I'm that way all the time. It seems like part of me is gone which, of course, is true. Do you still belong to me? Larry has got hold of your letter and he's trying to chew on it. He is sitting on my lap and is barefooted. He sleeps without stockings anymore. You're going to have a man to be proud of. Have you got any letters from any of your "women", as you called them? Do you still write to all the boys in the army? Where will you go after college? I sure hope and pray that they send you closer to home. Will you have to go overseas? After you get stationed, could Larry and me come and live with you? I haven't got a paycheck yet and I had to draw $2.00 out of the bank yesterday. When do you think you'll get a furlough? Do you think it will be very long from now? Are they still feeding you salt peter? Do you go out with any women? Isn't Hollywood a suburb of Los Angeles? You sure are seeing a lot of country. I bet by the time I get to see you again, you will be a Corporal or Sergeant. I will be proud of you whatever you are. Be good and try to go to church.

June 5, 1943
I look forward to your letters. I sure enjoy reading them. I also got Larry's pictures today and I am sending you some. The sun was bothering him and I look awful. Do you have to make your own bed now? What time do you get up of a morning? I've been getting up around seven. I saw Dory tonight and he said he got done planting corn today. Your dad cleaned your gun for you a few weeks ago. He and your brother went groundhog (A groundhog is a woodchuck.) *hunting this afternoon so we had groundhog for supper. Do you get tired studying? I wish I could see the Pacific Ocean, but I suppose I'll never get to. Are there many boys going to college with you? My stepbrother is still in the same camp. I guess he doesn't like it much better. He and 44 other boys went A. W. O. L.* (absent without leave) *and got caught. That will sure go against them when they go to ask for a furlough. Larry is getting cuter and sweeter all the time. Would you have been just as proud if he would have been a girl? Are you sorry we ever had him? He still laughs and jabbers. He sure can say da-da and he says it a lot. Maybe some of these days, we can have a little girl or another little boy. I've never got my check yet, but I'm looking for it any day. Be good and don't worry about Larry and me because we're alright.*

Sunday night, June 6, 1943
This has been an awful long Sunday. You're on my mind all the time. I miss you so much I could cry. How much longer do you think this war is going to last? Larry has been pretty good today. The hot weather makes him fussy. He is broke out with the heat. I sure hope I get my check tomorrow. If I don't get it by Tuesday, I'm going to find out why. If you need any money, write and let me know and I'll send you some. There is still $65 and a few cents in the bank. How do you like going to college? When you get stationed after these eight weeks, I hope Larry and I can come to you. We could wait maybe until you come home on a furlough and then go back with you. All of your folks are fine except your mother. I think her nerves are about shot. Do you ever go to church? PS. You keep telling me to keep my chin up. You be sure and do the same. I know you'll take everything on the chin like a man.

June 11, 1943
I got my check for sixty-two dollars this morning. I put $10 in the bank, so now we have $75.21 in the bank. I also made the last payment on the lounge chair and living room suite. I sent $15 to Spiegel's and $5 to Rhodes-Burford. I got Larry some clothes and paid the gas bill, which was a dollar. I paid the rent too. I have $11.85 left so I'm sending you five dollars. I hope it comes in

handy. I've still got the light bill to pay, which is $2.30. Do you realize Larry is eight months old today? He likes to go to bed early anymore. He is getting so he likes to stand on his feet, but his right leg isn't straight. I expect we'll have to have a brace put on it. His hair is getting darker. I got him a sun-suit, a pair of white anklets, a pair of pants supposed to take the place of rubber pants, and two sleeveless shirts. I tried to get him a pair of size 1 shoes. He has outgrown his others, but I couldn't find any. I suppose I'll have to let him go bare-footed. Everybody talks about Larry being such a cute and sweet baby. He makes the funniest faces with his mouth and he still blows. I showed him your pictures tonight and he acted like he knew who it was. He tried to scratch your face like he did when you were home. I sure hope he doesn't forget you. Yes, I remember how we used to park on Saturday and Sunday nights. We never got so cold because we kept each other warm. I remember about squirrel hunting too. You never could hit a squirrel I showed to you. I also remember going fishing. I sure miss those good times and hope and pray it won't be much longer till we can do them again. Does it seem funny going to school after all these years? I never dreamed about you going to college, did you? What time do you get up of a morning? What time do you go to bed at night? Do you get your meals for free? Larry sleeps by himself anymore, but he's sleeping with me tonight. He sure has got an awful temper. I will close for now and hope you all the success in the world with your college work.

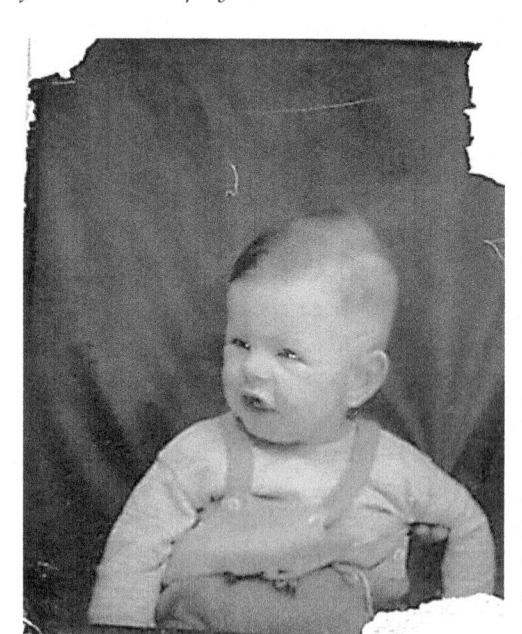

June 12, 1943
I just received your money order for the five dollars and was I glad to get it. It's the first time I've seen money of my own for so long I almost forgot what it looks like. I sure do appreciate those pictures you sent me. I keep them in my left shirt pocket all the time, right next to my heart. Larry sure looks cute in the pictures. Is he still saying da-da? I would like to hear him say that. The only thing I have to look forward to in the Army right now is receiving letters from home. I usually get about 15 to 20 letters a week, so that isn't bad, is it? It

takes four days for your letters to reach me out here, so you see I'm going to read it word for word. Speaking of church, every time one of us boys goes out on the street, some civilian hands us a copy of paper on how to get saved. The people out here really try to help the soldiers out that way. We took our second exam this morning. I think I made pretty good on it, at least I hope I did. I went down to buy some paper. I'm using Navy paper instead of Army, but I guess that's alright, isn't it?

Karl wrote about missing home, but Evie thought he was enjoying himself a little too much. While he was having fun, she kept reading in the *Republican* that things in Europe were out of control. The June 12 headline said, "Aerial Attacks On Western Germany Largest Of War; 2,000 Planes Deal Blows." The June 18 paper talked of what was coming, "Nazis Looking At Two Spots for Allied Invasion; Balkan Front Is Their Main Worry."

Evie didn't attempt to hide her despair in her next letter.

June 13, 1943
Another long and lonesome Sunday has passed by. I miss you awfully bad. I hope and pray this war will end soon so all the boys can get back home. It won't be long until fair time. I wish you could be here and we'd go together. Larry and I went to church with Mom and Dory tonight. Our new pastor at church is going to be the one holding the revival now. That fellow really can preach. He can say some of the funniest things. He will get forty dollars a week. I wish you'd go to church with me when you get back. You said the church was so gossipy. Well, you'll find gossip in all churches. Larry is lying in his crib laughing, kicking, screaming, and saying da-da. He weighs 15 ½ pounds. He still doesn't sit up alone, and he hasn't got any teeth yet. I think he's going to be toothless. I put a little blue sun-suit on him today and he really looked cute. Everybody that sees him says he is his daddy made over. We had fried chicken today and it sure tasted good. I thought of you while I was eating and ate some for you. I wish you could have been here to eat with us. Mom said she got a letter from Ronald this week and he had heard about me staying by myself and keeping our home. He thought it was the right thing to do, but couldn't imagine me staying by myself. I'm glad I kept our home. You'll have your own home to come back to and also Larry and me. Your dad has been using some of your shotgun shells. Be good and keep your chin up and study hard. I'm wishing you all the luck in the world on those tests you took. You'd better pass them or I'll whip you.

June 15, 1943
It sure is lonesome without you. I hope and pray this war ends soon. I'm trying to get my house cleaning done, but Larry is so cross I have to hold him almost all the time. He is sleeping now. I think he hasn't been feeling very well. This heat sure makes him cross. He plays with his toes now and he is always taking his shoes off. He even takes his anklets off. When you do something he doesn't like, he will say dada just like he meant he was going to tell his daddy. He isn't sitting up alone yet (babies typically sit up without assistance by six months of age) *but I think the reason he's not is because he's too lazy. You're doing pretty good in your typing by doing eleven words a minute. When I quit school, I was doing over fifty words a minute. See if you can beat that, which won't be so hard for you to do. Another bunch left Rushville today to be examined. The way things are going now I don't see how this war can last much longer. We sure are cleaning up the Italians. Don't forget to go to church. Christianity is what will win this war. People need to go to church more than they do. That includes me. I wish I'd never got out of the habit but I'm going to try to make it a habit again. Be good and don't study too hard. I will send you five more dollars in a week or two.*

June 16, 1943
I sure hope and pray this war ends soon. I don't know what I'll do if it lasts two more years or longer. I went to the show (movie) *tonight with your mother. Next week there will be fifty dollars given away.* (The Princess theater in Rushville held a drawing every week. The lucky person won $50.) *Larry is in bed sleeping but I think the neighbors might wake him up. He stands on his feet pretty good now. He also drinks a lot of water anymore. He takes it out of a glass. He hits himself in the face and thinks it is funny. He sure does love for people to look at him and he tries to act real cute. You said something about it being an insult to him to look like you. Well it isn't. It's something to be proud of. Talking about Larry stuttering, well, he sure has a good chance to because he's so much like his daddy in every way. Do you ever get the headache studying so hard? Do you really think your gray matter is burned up? That would be awful. I bet school is hard but you'll know a lot more. I don't see why they don't take such low-down men like Raymond R. Instead they take all the good boys and leave the bad. But then I know I've got a lot to be thankful for. Your mother seems to be pretty good but she told me today her and your dad was getting too old to have to*

raise more children. (Three grandsons and a granddaughter were living with Clara and Ott.)

June 17, 1943
I've missed you something awful today. Mom is getting a hundred little chickens so it looks like I might get some fried chicken later this summer. I can't enjoy it so much because I miss you so bad. Dory is plowing and working from daylight till dark. I sure am having a time with my feet. They hurt me so much anymore. The corns ache almost all the time. Our boy is in his bed sleeping. I can hardly get my work done for him. Everybody makes over him and that's why he is so bad. Everybody talks about him being so sweet. He sure does try to talk and looks at you so seriously. He hits himself in the face and makes it smack. He can really pull your hair now and scratch your face. Everything is da-da. I drove Tommy's car down to the store every once in a while. I'm surprised at your mother letting me because she is so particular with the car. I have to get Larry some more medicine and get about five dollars out of the bank. We've got $75.21 in the bank but I've got to pay the light bill, which is $2.30. It's awful lonesome without you. I guess Larry and I will get by some way till you get back.

June 17, 1943
I saw in the paper (*Rushville Republican*) **where Dad found the bones of some kind of animal. Have they found out what animal it was? Boy, for the first time in my life, I missed the opening day of fishing season. I'm looking forward to it in the next couple of years. Did anyone catch any big ones the first day? Of course, I didn't expect you to know, but I thought maybe Dad caught some. I sure would like to be there for some groundhog hunting. That is a very good sport. I found Goodson's address in the paper. He's here in L. A. somewhere and maybe we can see each other. I'm going to write him a letter. It sure would be nice to see a Rushville boy once again. The weather out here is kind of warm, but it's a pleasure compared to Wyoming. Tom wrote and asked me if I would give him the low-down on Wyoming. I didn't say anything when I wrote him because I couldn't think of enough bad names to call the place. I will the next time I write him. We signed the payroll twice since I've been here and haven't got paid yet, but I guess we will Saturday. I hope! One thing, if you haven't got any money, you won't have to spend it. Honey, I want to thank you and Larry again for the cigarettes and candy. They come in mighty handy. A couple of the boys and I went to the show and just got in for bed check. We have passes all the time while**

we're here, but if we're late for bed check we lose them for the remainder of the time here. Is Larry starting to crawl yet? I sure wish he would because that will keep you busy enough so you won't worry about me so much. I remember quite well how he used to scratch our faces, but I sure enjoyed it didn't you. Honey, are you still in tip top shape? I sure hope so. I want a good healthy girl and boy waiting for me after this war.

PS. This is typing period and I thought I'd type to you. This typing sure is fun, isn't it? I can type about 25 words a minute without counting my mistakes. Don't count the mistakes. I was in an awful hurry. When I'm typing I can't think of anything to say other than I love you both more every day and I'm always thinking of you.

June 19, 1943

It sure has been hot out. I guess it stays this way most of the year. We had another exam his afternoon. I think I made about 96 on it. I got five more weeks of college to go and then I don't know where. I sure hope I do go back east, but if I don't I'll have to make the best of the west, I reckon. The West Coast is alright, but this kind of country wasn't made for me. I'm awfully glad you're fixing the house up pretty but if you're fixing it up for me, I think you've got a long time yet to wait. You keep asking me about a furlough. Well honey, it's like this. After I'm in the Army 6 or 7 months, maybe I can get a furlough. As soon as I'm due for one I'll try and get it, but it costs a young fortune to go back and forth from out here. That's why I'm wishing to be shipped back east. Tell Dad when this conflict is over, Tom and I will show him how to kill groundhogs. I guess I'll take in a show tonight and kind of rest my mind a bit. After you go to school six days a week and study till eleven o'clock your brain seems to be in an uproar. No, I don't write to any of the girls back at the factory. I'm glad to hear that Larry will soon be crawling. I sure bet he's sweet, but not any sweeter than his mother. I keep your pictures in my shirt pocket right over my heart, darling, and there is where they'll always be. Something funny happened to me the other night. I keep your letters by themselves and all the rest in another box. When I came in my room, something was missing. Well, to make a long story short, someone swiped all the letters and boxes and everything else. They only left the box with your letters in it. It must have been the maid. I don't know who else it would be. If I ever find out who it was, there sure will be some wool flying for a while. So all the letters I have left are only yours. I'm glad they never took them.

Evie was reminded daily of the horrors of the war while Karl wrote of his adventures in California. The *Republican* reported American casualties total "so far" were 63,958. The numbers broke down to 7,528 killed, 17,128 injured, 22,687 missing, and 16,615 prisoners. She cried as she wrote her next letter.

June 24, 1943
There sure have been a lot of people die around here since you've left. I suppose after tomorrow you'll only have four more weeks of college. I sure do hope they'll send you back east but they might not. Will you be glad to get done with college? I guess I'll have to wait till the army sees fit to let you come home. Do you share your room with anybody? That was too bad about your letters. What would anybody want with them? Have you tried to find out who took them? Larry is trying to cry because he can't go to sleep. It's so hot I think he is miserable. I weighed him today and he weighed sixteen pounds. He sure can drink water out of a glass good now. I think he is going to have curly hair because his hair is curling on top. He's sitting on my lap right now. He said to tell you he still loved you. He still says da-da especially when I do something he doesn't like. I suppose he means he'll tell you all about it. I'm glad you're doing so good on your exams. Will you get another promotion when you get through college? What kind of an office will you work in? I am going to try and clear all the bills up so when you get home we'll have a clean slate to start on again. We've still got $65. 91 in the bank and I'm going to put $10.00 in again next month. It takes a lot of money to keep Larry going. His medicine comes due about every three weeks, and also insurance. I'm glad to hear you carry our pictures over your heart. I'm going to carry your pictures with me in my pocketbook. I can hardly wait till this awful war is over. I think it won't be many months till it will be. The news sure is good right now.

June 24, 1943
Darling, Last night I sent the letters you've written me and the pictures I had taken up at Fort Warren. When you get the pictures, don't laugh. They aren't very good. Mom said in her letter she had fried chicken. I sure would have liked to have been there to gnaw on the bones. The fried chicken you get in the Army isn't worth walking after, although it's a treat when we do get it. I'm awfully sorry about not sending Dad or Dory anything for father's day. I started to one night but it slipped my mind completely somehow. Is Larry still

getting fat? I'm glad to hear he wants to stands up on his feet a lot. Well honey, another test comes up Saturday and it ends my first month at Woodbury College. I sure hope I pass it. If I don't, it isn't because I don't study enough. I study continually. This subject is tough, and it's not in my line, but I'm trying to make the best of it. Do you want to know what we had for chow tonight? Well, we had spaghetti with hamburger cooked in the form of slop. Then we had lettuce with tomatoes and meringue, sour kraut, and ice cream. We have regular rations for every meal during the week. Everyday I'm gone my love for you seems to grow more and more. PS. I opened my last pack of cigarettes this morning.

June 25, 1943
Larry and I went to supper with Mom and Dory at the party given by the Willing Workers (A lady's group at her church). *They put me on the entertaining committee and told me to pick out somebody to help me. I picked out Mom. Larry had his first fall tonight. I think it hurt me worse than it did him. He fell off of your mother's bed while we were doing the supper dishes. He sure did cry and I could have cried right with him. He fell on his forehead and he's got a big bruise there. It didn't take him long to get over it. He rolls so much you can hardly keep him anywhere. He also laughs out loud quite often. He still says da-da and mom-mom. I heard tonight Bob Frittz was killed in action. Did you know him? I did. Do you think this war will last much longer? I sure hope and pray not. I'd kind of like to work in the canning factory this fall but I haven't got anybody to keep Larry. Mom is aiming to work there. I guess my place is with Larry though, as a baby needs its mother. Be good and keep your chin up and I'll try and do the same.*

Karl also received letters from his siblings. His sisters wrote letters of encouragement. His brothers told him all the local dirty news and gossip. One brother was one of two of the Floyd kids to graduate from high school. Like most of the Floyd boys, he was a hard worker and possessed a short fused temper. He was five years older than Karl. He did not get to serve during the War because he was color blind. He wrote Karl a gossipy letter.

June 26, 1943
Dear Karl, I thought was about time I was writing to you. We are all OK. I took Mom and all of them out riding last evening. Mom sure enjoys riding, doesn't she? Larry sure is sweet. I

never knew any baby that has caught my eye like he has. Red (another Floyd brother) is over at Connersville again. I believe he has a 'woman' over there. Ha! There have been two boys drowned here in the last 2 or 3 weeks. I knew one but can't place the other. The latter boy drowned right down behind Reddens house. They found his body down at the cement bridge. I supposed you know that Bob was killed in action. He worked at Hoosier Dairy. Ratekin tells me he's having a hell of a time. He had to go to the hospital on account of a snake bite. He says he's ready to be shipped across. I don't know whether I'll have to go or not but I'm not worrying about it. I get so lonesome for all of the old gang. Nobody left but Chester and me and he won't speak to me because I gave him hell about the way he treated his wife. He's NUTS. Said he didn't trust no man around his wife. I wonder who would want her. Is the country pretty out there? Do you ever get to see the ocean? Can't see across it, can you? Ha. Ha! Well, Karl, that's about all for now. I will write again as soon as there is some news.

June 27, 1943

It's so hot the sweat is running down my face. I've been thinking about you all day and wondering what you were doing. We had fried chicken today. I tried to eat enough for you. Larry and I went to Sunday school this morning, but we didn't go to church tonight. Larry got his second fall today and fell off your mother's bed. He skinned his head a little bit. It sure did scare me. It's a good thing he's got his bed to sleep in or he'd be on the floor all of the time. This hot weather sure is making him cross. He is sure broke out with heat although I powder him good. He really is getting fat and he still hasn't got any teeth. I tell him he's going to be toothless. When I get my check, I'll send you five dollars. What time do you go to school in the morning? What time do you get off of an evening? Be good and go to church. Remember, you're closer to a church than I am and you don't have a baby to get ready. If I can do it, you surely can.

June 28, 1943

I received your letter this morning and also the letters and pictures of you. I set mine on the chest of drawers so I can look at you when I'm in bed. I got Larry's high chair today. It sure is nice. Its maple colored and folds into a chair and table. It cost $8.95. He really looks cute in it although he can't sit up by himself very well yet. His rompers didn't come, so I will have to send and get some others. They sent one pair but they're too big so I'm sending them back. Larry has been laughing at everything today. He also has been hitting himself in the face with his fist. He'll hit himself real hard and then laugh when you tell him not to hit the baby. Are there many boys with you from Indiana? I wish we could drive around like we used to. I'm hoping that day won't be far off. I bet you'll be glad when you get out of college. I sure hope you get moved a lot closer to home. When I get my next check, I'm going to get a roll of film and take some more pictures of Larry. Larry won't open his eyes when he is facing the sun so I can't get as good pictures as I'd like. My wisdom tooth sure is hurting me. I think the skin is growing back over it. It has hurt me all day. I kind of think I'll have to have it taken out but I'm going to wait for a while. I never was in a dentist's chair and I'm rather afraid. I would like to have another baby in about four or five years. How many children do you want? I would like to have two but we may have more.

June 29, 1943
Larry has been kind of cross today. I was just thinking about how much he has cost us, but he's sure worth it. His bed, buggy, and chair have cost us over forty dollars. When we have another one, we won't have all of that to buy. I know our home is fixed nice and will be fixed nicer when you get back. The only things we need are a refrigerator and a washing machine. My wisdom tooth has hurt me all day again. I'm going to have it pulled tomorrow. I sure dread it, but it will be a relief to get it out. I sent you some stationery and a carton of cigarettes today. I will try and send cigarettes more often. I'll have to get some money out of the bank tomorrow, $1.00, and that will make it $63.52. I sent a check for a $1.39 to Spiegel's today as a down payment on the high chair. If you want me to send you $5 please let me know and I will send you some. You asked me if Larry was still getting fat. Yes he is, and his little arms and legs are sure cute. His hands are still short and chubby and I don't think they've grown very much. I sure hope you make good on your tests so you can get out of there when the eight weeks are up. If you don't pass, what do they do to you? Your supper you described sounded pretty good, but the way you talked it must have not been so.

June 30, 1943
Please forgive me for some of the letters I've written in the past. I was so blue I couldn't help writing them. I'm going to try not to write anymore letters like that. I know you're having a hard enough time without receiving letters like them. We're supposed to have a blackout tonight or tomorrow night so

I'm writing this letter about nine. I dread it, but if Larry is asleep it won't be so bad. I'm all ready for bed, but I've still got Larry's bottles to fill. Have you ever got paid yet in June? I went down to the dentist this morning. My tooth hurts worse now than it did before I went down there. He didn't pull it, but he cut the gum from over it and then cut the gum around it. He said it would get sore and it is. He charged me fifty cents. I left Larry with your mother this morning. When I came back, he had wet his pants and his bottom is sore. Your mother was changing him and he was mad. First he'd holler da-da and then mam-mam. He is really dark like his daddy. He laughs a whole lot now and sticks his tongue out. He wrinkles his nose when he laughs and twinkles his eyes. His eyelashes are getting long too. No, Larry isn't bull-legged when he stands up. One leg is straight but the other one is rather crooked. I hope we don't have to put a brace on his leg but we may have to. I'm going to take him to the Doctor when the check comes. When you get out of the Army, I'll probably have a good deal of money saved and after I get the debts paid I can save more. We won't have to worry so much about money. But I've found out money isn't everything and never will be. You and Larry and a home are what I want. How many words can you type a minute now? What are your other subjects about? PS. I am sending you a dollar. Be sure and let me know if you need money.

July 1, 1943
Just a few lines to let you know I love you. This college is very pretty. I took a test today, but I don't know what I made on it. I will be glad when this schooling is over so I'll see if I get shipped east or not. It would be good to see eastern soil again. Tell me how high the corn is and every detail like that. I saw in the headlines in the Los Angeles papers where the Yanks are doing alright for themselves. I sure hope it gets over sooner than the people say. I've got a feeling that within a year and a half we'll be able to see the end. Darling, it won't be long now till our boy will be crawling all over the place, will it? Madge wrote me and said his leg looked alright to her so be sure it's not right before you ever put a brace on it. Tomorrow night at 6:30 which will be 8:30 pm there, I'm going to take another shot. I sure dread it. It will make my 6th shot since I've been in the Army. This is my last tetanus shot, which is for lockjaw. The next ones are yellow fever. They say they're awful, but I won't mind them so bad if I set my head to it. That's the way I do things. If I don't like anything, I just set my head to like it and that's all there is to it. I've heard from everyone the weather is hot back home. I bet it is, but I bet there are a lot of boys who would like to see that kind of weather again. I

would sure like to be along Flatrock right now catching some bass. There's plenty of them there, but I never went in for fishing and hunting after Tom left. I will again when he gets back and all of us are together again. Tom was always classified the best fisherman, but I was the best hunter. If you don't believe Tom and I brought the fish in, ask Mom about it. We used to catch enough fish to supply Rushville and you know about our hunting. When this feuding is over, Larry will be big enough to learn to hunt, won't he? I'll have to teach him all the tricks to it. I'll also have to get him a gun when he's big enough. That's something every kid should have and know how to use properly. When I get home, I'll have lots of experiences to tell you. I'll beat Dad at telling tales and that will be hard to do. Darling, I'll have to close now. Be sure and be good. I'll see you all someday when this conflict is over.

July 2, 1943
Do you know it will soon be three years since you gave me my watch? I'll never forget the night you gave it to me. It has warmed up a lot and I sure am glad. We're beginning to need a rain. Larry is in bed sleeping. His little cheeks are getting so they're pink all the time. That is a sign he is healthy. He still hasn't got any teeth, but I guess he will have someday. My tooth is still awful sore. I'll be glad when it gets healed up. The dentist sure cut deep cut in my gum. I'm going to quit going to the show because it takes too much money. I want to send you things instead. Mom has got several little chickens so maybe we can have fried chicken when you come home on a furlough. Your dad's garden sure looks nice. I'll be glad when the tomatoes get ripe. I never got to even taste a strawberry this spring. I'm going to try and get some next spring. I'd give anything to see you again for a while, but I guess I'll have to wait for about three more months. You will soon be gone three months. It seems like you've been gone forever. I sure hope and pray this awful war ends soon.

July 4, 1943
I hope I do get to come and see you for a while. If you want me to bring Larry with me I will try to, but it would be awful tiresome on him. I know you want to see him as bad as you do me. Mom said she'd keep him for me, so whatever you want I'll try and do. It stormed after church, but it didn't rain much. Larry has been kind of cross, but I think the hot weather had something to do with that. He likes to play with paper, but he doesn't try to eat it. I cut my finger on a can tonight, but it isn't very bad. My tooth is still

awful sore. I'm afraid infection might set in. Mom told me Pepper (Madge and Dory's dog) *got run over Thursday, but it didn't kill him. It broke one of his legs and cut a big hole in the other. I guess they sure hated it, but they think he will get well. Tomorrow will be a holiday and I sure do dread it. I guess the International* (Karl's furniture factory employer) *is going to have a drunken party. That's the only kind they know how to give. We had fried chicken again today. It sure was good. I try and eat enough for you. I was going to give a pint of blood to the Red Cross but I can't unless you sign a paper or Mom and Dory do. I guess I'm not my own boss after all, but have to depend on you. I wish this awful war would end real soon. There are so many homes split up by it.*

July 5, 1943
In less than three weeks now I won't be here. I sure will be glad to get moved to some other place. After you're at a place so long, you want to go somewhere else. I'm hoping and praying I go east instead of staying out here. Still, I have a big chance of going overseas. They have been sending over about half of the units which already graduated but still I may not go, so don't ever worry about it. Does Larry do anymore talking yet besides da-da and mom-ma? I bet he puckers his mouth cute when he tries to talk. I never will forget when he was sick with a high fever. We didn't know what made him cry so. Remember? Honey, what did we do the last 4th of July? I've completely forgotten where we were then. Remember when I tried to teach you how to cast (throw a fishing line)**? Well, if you want, I'll really teach you someday. I'd also like to buy you a 4.10 gauge shotgun so you could go squirrel hunting with me. Of course, you couldn't do much good rabbit hunting as it'd probably wear you out walking and also it's too dangerous. That's something I don't think I'd trust a woman at. It's dangerous enough for a bunch of men hunting rabbits together let alone women going with them. Tell Mom not to worry about Tom. He'll get along all right. I also know it's a heavy burden on her as he never even got a chance to come home, but before she knows it, he'll be right back in his bed where he always was. I guess there are millions of mothers waiting for the same day and also thousands of wives aren't there? Well, to top that off, there are several million boys in the service who are praying night and day for the time to come when everything will be peaceful again. Remember darling, I promised you when I get back home, I'd start going to church with you again. That's a promise I'll keep.**

The Floyd gang was a brood of five brothers and Tom. The one they all admired and feared was their leader, Big Guy. He was their mentor and leader. He poked and prodded them to being proud of the family name. He was also a bit of a lightning rod for a fight. He didn't take, as only Big Guy could say, any "sonsabitchin' goddam shit" from anyone. He kept hearing everyone brag about Karl's achievements in California. This meaner than hell brother with a soft heart decided he needed to take his baby brother down a notch or two. He wrote a letter to remind Karl to keep his head from getting too big.

July 5, 1943
Dear Karl ass, I just found out your new address so will write. How is everything out there? I understand that you are nothing but a rookie. Well, I didn't expect much more out of you. I expect you sucked a little to get that PFC. Admit it. So you can shoot? If I was you I wouldn't talk about shooting if I'd gripe like you did about going out on the rifle range. Karl, there isn't much news. We were up home today. Larry sure is fat and cute. His mother was cute too. Ha. I sent Larry 4 bottles of Karo syrup addressed to him. He thanked me today for it. I wish you and that Tom was back so I could slap you both down. Karl, if you can, write to me and tell me how you had to suck and baby the sarge and officer to get such an easy job. If I get in, I want an easy job too but I am willing to work for mine. I would like for you to see the turtle I got the other day. He was a real big one. Well Karl, write and I promise to answer right back but write me a more interesting letter next time. I still remain your big brother.

Karl's mom was the backbone of Floyd family. Hers was not an easy life. She had married a stubborn, hardworking, razor edge tempered man who never backed down from a fight or argument. She bore fourteen children. She had buried six of them. She raised one grandson, Tom, from two years of age. She was raising four other grandchildren when Karl left for the army. She and Ott never had enough money. There was always some form of controversy among the kids. Someone in the family always needed her attention. Nonetheless, she and Otto always put food on the table. There was always room for others at her dinner table. She was a tired worn woman by the time Karl left for the war. She somehow found the time to write words of encouragement to Karl, wherever he was.

July 7, 1943
My Darling Boy, I will write you a few lines in answer to your ever welcome letter. I was sure glad to get it. I also got one from Tommy. He is Staff Sergeant now. He told me he has a pet tiger and said he expected it would be a good rug on the floor before long. Tommy said he got one letter from you but he was looking for another from you any time. I sure am proud of him, and you haven't done so bad yourself. Honey, I don't want you to worry about us back here as we are all very well. All I want you boys to worry about is getting back home. I gave Evie and Larry their kisses from you. He laughs when I kiss him. I am glad you got the cigarettes I sent and will try to send more as soon as I can. I haven't got any flowers to bloom yet this year. Dad has a nice garden and we have got some nice potatoes. He is working every day and makes pretty good money but it all goes away as everything is so expensive. He made $41.30 this week. He goes hunting groundhogs early in the morning, works all day, and then works in the garden till it gets dark. Big Guy and the kids were here yesterday. Big Guy brought Uncle Ed (Ott's missing thumb brother) *a goat but he wasn't home so Dad gave him $1.50 for it. The kids are crazy about that goat. It bawls all the time. Evie and I went downtown yesterday. I got Tommy another bond and the $5 stamp for his car. Honey, I hope they don't send you over as there are some boys that have been in the army over two years so let some of them go first. Well Dear, there is not much to write about. I have to write Tommy a few lines so will close. I will write again in a few days. Everyone here sends love and best wishes. Lots of love, Your Loving Mother*

Evie and Karl continued their conversation.

July 10, 1943
We sure did have a storm here this afternoon. The lights went off and we couldn't see much. I also got my book back from Rhodes-Burford and we only owe them $12.10. You asked me if Larry keeps me awake much of a night. No, he doesn't. He usually goes to bed about nine and wakes up about once for a bottle. Yes, I remember the night he was sick and cried and we didn't know he was sick. He is sure picking up some cute habits now. This afternoon he was lying in the crib and his bottle was down by his legs. He picked the bottle up and put it in his mouth and held it up so he could get the milk. Another habit is he'll hold his little arms out to you when he wants picked up. He laughs almost all the time anymore. He has got the sweetest little grin. I tell him his daddy is my big boyfriend and he is my little one. The other day he got to looking at my ears. He was standing up in my lap, and he'd hold his head to one side and just look. Then he'd look on the other side. I suppose he was seeing if they were clean. Yes, I think I'd like going squirrel hunting and learning how to cast. Remember the day we all went swimming? We sure had fun. Yes, I remember you promised to go to church with me when you get back. I'm going to hold you to that promise. When you come back are we going to buy another car? In two more weeks, your college work will be done. I'm sure hoping and praying you'll get sent back east. You know Larry and I will be waiting for you forever if it takes that long, but I sure hope and pray not. I hope you're not sent overseas.

July 11, 1943
This hot weather sure is hard on babies. I went to Sunday school and church this morning, but didn't go to church tonight on account of Larry. Larry is nine months old today. When he goes to bed, he lays real still until he goes to sleep. His bowels are loose and he has lost weight. He doesn't act a bit sick, but something is making him do that. It sure worries me. I don't know what I'm going to do with him. It won't be long now till he'll be crawling. He scoots backward now. That is what they do before they start crawling. The corn sure is looking good. Mom had a chicken hang itself this afternoon. It got caught in the fence by its neck. It was the first one she's lost out of 100. When you come back on a furlough we'll have fried chicken. Remember how we used to get ice cream of a night? In two more weeks you'll be out of college. I'll sure be glad when you do get a furlough. I'll be so happy you'll think I'm kind of goofy. I hope you get sent east.

July 15, 1943

If I could only see you for a while I'd feel lots better, but I guess I'll have to wait. Larry is in bed sleeping. He sure looks cute laying in his bed. He's had the laughs almost all afternoon and laughs at almost anything anybody said to him. I got my permanent this morning. My hair looks a lot better. I paid five dollars for it. I also got my new dress. It fits like it was made for me. I like it awfully well and I kind of think you would. Something in the neighborhood sure smells awful. It's about to make me sick, it stinks so bad. I caught a mouse in the trap this afternoon. Remember how you used to kill them with the broom? The Allies sure are cleaning up in Sicily. Also, the Russians are stopping the Germans. You sure have been doing good on your exams making 98. I'm sure you'll keep up the good work. When you get home you'll be like a walking encyclopedia. This war can't end too soon to please me. I wish it would end tomorrow. Be good and go to church once in a while.

July 15, 1943
Darling, I got assigned to my new post today. I'm coming to Ohio. It's going to be Camp Perry which is located up near Toledo. Boy, when I found out, my heart almost went up to my throat. I almost broke my neck to get up here and write you this letter. I was tickled to death to think I'm coming back east at last. Us easterners call it God's Country. I'll leave here a week from this Saturday night or around that time. It will take me about 3 days and 3 nights to make the trip. After I get there, maybe I can get a 3 day pass or something and I can get home for a little while. It sure will be good to see Good Old Indiana again. I'll come through Chicago, but at least I'll see the northern part of the state. I don't know how long I'll be there, but I'll at least have a better chance of seeing you all again. I had choices of Oklahoma City, New York, New Jersey, another place in Ohio near Lake Erie, Santa Anita, California, Los Angeles, and Tennessee. I also had a chance to go to Dallas, Texas, but give me the east any day. We had quite a variety to choose from. That's something a guy in the Army doesn't get very often. I'm going to be a stock record clerk. I imagine that don't mean much to you, but that's all they've pounded into our heads since we've been out here. I went back to school tonight to try review for the test we're going to have next week. It's going to be a killer. There are ten out of our bunch who are going across (overseas to Europe) **this time. I don't mind if I go across, but I'd sure like to see everyone once more. We have a mighty small chance of getting a delay in route, which means we can stop over for a few days but don't count on it. There were**

several different places we could go and Ohio was the closest place for us. Are Larry's teeth starting to come in yet? Let him take his time about cutting them. The longer they take the better they'll be. How is your wisdom tooth coming along? Have you had it pulled yet? I've gotten up to 36 words a minute in typing class so far. That isn't bad for a greenhorn, is it? I'm beginning to know this course up one side and down the other. It's pretty nice to actually know what you're doing. When we first came out here, we couldn't tell heads or tails about the whole thing, but now it's a whole lot better. Some different forms we have to make out are: Requisitions, Shipping Tickets, etc. There's about a hundred of them. Darling, be sure and let Mom and everyone knows right away where I'm going. It will ease all their minds. It sure did mine. Yes, I'll always remember my promise about going to church. If I ever try to avoid it, just remind me. I'm still fit as a fiddle. See you in Ohio. That is my next stop.

Evie's struggle raising Larry continued while Karl was in California. She sometimes got mad. Karl seemed to be enjoying himself, but she couldn't afford to have simple pleasures. Now he was heading toward home and he might get to see Larry. She was excited that she might get to see Karl, but she feared what he might think when he saw Larry.

July 16, 1943
I bet you know and have known for some time you are going to be sent overseas and just haven't told me. I sure hope you don't. I want to see you soon and can't if you go overseas. Larry is in bed, but far from asleep. His bowels are better today, but not well yet. I gave him a dose of castor oil. That seemed to help him some. He laughs like you do and spreads his mouth great big. I'm going to have to get him some new sleeping clothes as his little nightgowns are getting too little. He's got so many nice things such as sweaters and other things that he has outgrown, but I just can't give them away. It looks like he is going to have big feet like his daddy. It's so hot tonight the sweat is running down my face. I'm not exaggerating one bit. Do you ever dream about me anymore? I haven't had even a taste of watermelon and I don't suppose I will because they're too high priced. I didn't get any strawberries and I haven't had fresh tomatoes. I don't get very much candy either. I'm not aiming to go to the show tomorrow night, but I think I'll go next week. I don't have money for things like that since you've been gone. I have to squeeze pennies since I got my permanent. I kind of wish I hadn't

paid so much for it but you can't get a very good one under $5. PS. The news sure sounds good today. Maybe this war will end before long.

July 18, 1943

I want to come see you if you get closer to home. I want to see you so bad I don't know what to do. I suppose you know by now where you're going. If you do get sent closer to home, let me know and get a place for me to stay. Larry's bowels are a lot better today. He has been real good all day. He is in bed now talking himself to sleep. How many words a minute are you typing by now? Do you have very much to memorize? Somebody just shot a shotgun and scared me. Remember how we used to ride around on Sunday afternoon? I have to tell you something. I don't go out very much. When I do, I'm usually with either your folks or my folks. I'm trying to keep to myself so nobody will have a bit of room to gossip, but someone said a man was with me. If someone writes and tells you he was, it's a lie. I think a man who starts after woman so soon after his wife dies is no man at all. You know I'll always be true to you no matter what people ever say. I don't feel complete without you. I'm part of you and you're part of me. The day you come home for good will be the happiest day of my life.

July 18, 1943

I'm okay and feeling fine. Some of the boys and I took in a show which I enjoyed very much. Today I woke up at 11:00 by the Church bells. This is my last Sunday in California so I thought I'd take some of the sights in. This afternoon, I went out to a guy's house who is here with us and only lives about 13 miles away. He took his father's 1942 Buick-8 and we drove all over Southern California. We took in Hollywood and several different places there. We saw Will Rogers place. We also took in his ranch. I saw the great Brown Derby. Also, I had my picture taken along the seashore. When I get it developed, I'll send it to you. We also paid a visit to the camp in San Anita this afternoon. Boy, that place is pretty good. We went into a little palace out there, which had all kind of relics. It had several skeletons heads. One of them was a pony express rider who had been shot by the Indians with a bow and arrow. The arrow head was still in his skull. We saw human heads which were cut off and shrunk by the South American Indians. I saw a Mummy's arm which was better than 3000 years old. We saw all types of pianos and organs one to two hundred years old. They still played. They had all types of guns and even one of the first trains ever built. I'm telling you it sure was worth seeing. We're also having group pictures made this week of

our class at the college. I didn't get to do my washing this morning like I planned, so I'm going to try and do it between letters. I have to wash my own clothes this week. I'm not allowed to turn my washing in on account of leaving next Saturday night and I may not get them back. I think I may be able to talk Dad into selling us the house at a very reasonable price and we can fix it up the way it really should be. I've got great plans to change it when I get back. Being out here in California and seeing all the ways and different kinds of houses, I could be able to change the place into one of the prettiest homes in Rushville. I can hardly wait till the train starts for Ohio. I figured the miles out last night from Toledo to Indianapolis and it's just about 200 miles by crows' flight, so I imagine it's about the same to Rushville.

July 22, 1943

It's almost time for the lights to go out now. I sure have been busy tonight. I did some of my washing which was dirty and I've packed my barracks bags. That sure takes a lot of time. By this time next week, I should be in Ohio. I won't be sorry of it either. Have you ever figured out how far I will be from home in Toledo? I'll be about 200 miles away. That isn't so bad, is it? Darling, if I can, I'll try and write to you while I'm on the train, but I may not be able to. In the previous case when I was being shipped, I wasn't able to write, but if I can I will so you will keep on getting my mail. I was going to send the rest of my letters home, but I can't find any paper to wrap them up. Don't ever worry about me darling. I'll be alright anywhere I go. PS. Our class had our picture taken today at noon and another tonight. I don't think you can find me. I can't even see myself.

July 23, 1943

Darling, this is my last full day at Woodbury College. I'm not sorry about it, but I hate to leave my friends that I've made so far. I guess that will happen no matter where I'm at. Some of us are going together so that's better than nothing. Honey, I never got any letters from you today again. Our train will leave tomorrow night. If I don't get any tomorrow, it'll be too late till I arrive in Ohio. I hope to get a letter telling me that you received my letter about me coming back east. I would like to have seen you when you got my letter about coming back. I bet you were all smiles. Is Larry still in good shape? Be sure and keep him that way. I'm aiming to see you all someday and I'm looking forward to the romps with him. I'm also sending you my address where I'll be, but don't mail me any letters as I won't be able to get them. It seems to be a new rule in the Army. When I arrive at my new camp I'll write you all about it. I'm certainly looking forward for the train to pull out tomorrow night, and I know you're wishing for me to get closer to home. Have you ever looked on the map and seen how much closer I'll be to home than I am now? Evelyn, I'm going to get a furlough as soon as I can, but don't count too strong on it. If I can't, you can come up, but I'll let you know about it first. I'm all out of cigarettes again, but I'll buy my own tomorrow sometime. We get paid $15.00 before we leave here so we can have some money with us in case we need anything extra on the train, such as candy, gum, etc. I don't think we'll be riding a troop train this time, but will ride with civilians, only we'll have cars by ourselves. This is my new address, but don't write till you hear from me there. PFC KARL R. FLOYD 35140696, 983rd ORD. DEPOT CO. (ASF), CAMP PERRY, OHIO. (ASF=Army Service Forces.)

July 24, 1943
I'm still thinking of you all the time. I'm longing for the day when we can all be back together again. What would you like to do first when this war is over? Myself, I think the best thing is to rest awhile. Today is my last time I'll be in this typing class and then I'll be on my own. We're leaving Los Angeles about 5:30 this evening. No one is supposed to know about the time. That is why I couldn't tell you before. We will be coming on the Southern Pacific railroad. It will take us 11 meals to get there. That will be three days and nights and a little more. It will be a long train ride, but it will be worth it. I'm longing to see good old Indiana soil again. Tell Madge to have the chickens ready in case I do get a chance to come home, but don't count on it too much. I'm in the Army and you can't tell what they might do. Honey, is Larry still getting along alright? Well, I'd better close for now and get back in my room. We're supposed to be called down to the auditorium for our final instructions on our graduation. I wish you were here to see it take place, but that's something that can't be done. Remember, we can all expect this war is going to take a lot of lives before it is won. No matter where I'm at, I'll be doing my best in getting this thing over with in a hurry. I think it can be done in at least a year and a half. Tell everybody hello for me, sweetheart. Tell them I'll write them when I get situated in my new camp. PS. Be sure and take care of yourselves till I get back and then I'll help you out.

Woodbury graduation class.
Karl is in the middle, second row from the top.

The *Republican* carried an article begging for blood donors while Karl was travelling east. It started, "Are you sending your blood to the battlefront?" Another article reported that a British official predicted the invasion of Europe could start very soon. Roosevelt told the nation that Hitler's Europe was about to experience "the beginning of the end" to its aggression.

FURLOUGH

Private Floyd suspected he was headed for Europe when he found out he was going to the east coast. He didn't know what was ahead, and he didn't care. He just knew he was going to be closer to home. He might even get a furlough for a few days.

The four day train trip back East took an eternity. The trip was in an overcrowded, cigarette smoke filled car. All there was to do was watch the miles go by, eat, smoke, and sleep when he could. He continued his conversation with Evie. He wrote postcards along the way.

July 26, 1943
I'm on my way to Ohio. I'm at Phoenix, Arizona. It's hotter than Hell in this train. I sure would welcome a good shower right now. I will

get in Ohio sometime Wednesday instead of Tuesday. I sure will be glad to get there.

July 27, 1943
Just passed through El Paso, Texas. We're now heading east through Texas. Pretty soon we'll be going north. I'll try and mail this card at my next stop. Darling, this train trip is really hot. So far, we've been traveling two days and two nights. We've got that much further yet to go. We've come through California, Arizona, New Mexico, and Texas. It's a long hard ride back to Ohio, but it'll be worth it. I don't know whether I'll be able to get to come home right away or not, but I'm going to try to get there before I leave Ohio.

July 27, 1943
We're almost in Kansas City. This morning was the first time we've seen cornfields. They really look swell. We ought to be in Ohio by tomorrow morning. I'm still thinking of you both and will continually love you. Tell everyone hello. I hope to be seeing them all some of these days.

July 28, 1943
I'm in Davenport, Iowa. I haven't got time to mail this card, but I will when I can. Darling, I should arrive at my new camp sometime Wednesday morning. Remember, I'm continually loving you both.

July 28, 1943
I'm now in Chicago. It's 1:15 am. We'll be in Toledo about 10. I sure will be glad to get this trip over with. I've been on the road since Saturday night and I'm telling you, it's been a long ride. I've been writing cards whenever I can, but I can't always mail them. I will send them out as soon as I can.

July 28, 1943
Just a quick line to tell you I'm now in the depot at Toledo, Ohio. I'm getting ready to eat breakfast. I guess we're about 30 miles from our destination. That means we got about one more hour to go. We'll get off at La Carne, Ohio and to our camp by some other way. I'll write you all about it as soon as I can.

The reality of life for an army grunt hit Karl when he arrived at Camp Perry, Ohio. He was no longer living in a plush California hotel. The barracks were dirty and mouse infested. His bunk stunk to high heaven. Worse yet, he was not allowed to leave the base to make a phone call to Evie. His next letter couldn't hide his disappointment.

July 28, 1943
Just a few lines to let you know I'm okay but plenty tired. This is the first time I could write since I've been here. We spent 4 days and 4 nights on the train. I'm telling you it's not what it's cracked up to be. We arrived here at the camp at about 12 o'clock noon. This camp is right next to Lake Erie. It's not very big, but it sure disappointed me to see it. This is sure a change from the other places I've been. Then, I was hoping to surprise you and call tonight, but the first thing we were told was we would not get any passes or anything because we are confined to our company grounds. To top that off, they told us we're getting ready for overseas shipment. I'm sending my civilian things home since I don't need them. Honey, I may not be able to see you all again for some time. I was hoping I could get a furlough, but now it looks like I may not be able to. I'll have to wait to see if our confinement is lifted or not. If it is, I'll try and get to the nearest town and try and make some kind of arrangement for you and Larry. The captain kind of talked like I was due for a furlough before I went over, but you can never tell about the Army. To get ready for oversea duty, I'll have to drill from six in the morning till 9:30 at night. Its 10:10 now and I just got through. It's so disappointing to be so near home and we can't even get a chance to leave the company area, but maybe after Saturday we will be. Honey, in case we don't get to see one another till after the war, please remember I love nobody else but you and our boy. Honey, will you please send me five dollars when you answer this letter so in case I do get a chance to come home, I'll be prepared. I got a map this morning. It'll take five hours to go from Toledo to Indianapolis, and it'll cost me almost $5.00 for a round trip. If I don't get a chance to come out home and if I can get out of confinement, you can come out here pretty cheap. I don't know how soon I'll be shipped over, but darling, don't worry about me. I just hope and pray we can be together again soon. Tell Mom and everyone my address and tell them to write. I'm not in the mood to write everyone right now. I'm dead tired and sad. Be sure and kiss Larry for me. Tell him his dad will be home before long or someday to kiss him by myself. Darling, my address is: Pfc. Karl Floyd 35140696, 983rd Ord. Depot Co., E.P.G. La Carne, Ohio. E.P.G. means Erie Proving Grounds. Please give this to the rest of the family.

July 31, 1943
I just got in from camping yesterday afternoon, all night, and all day today. Darling, I'm going to call you up tonight sometime. It sure will be good to hear your voice again. I still don't know when I will get to see you. I'm going to try and come home next Saturday night and Sunday. I'll know more about what I'm going to do when I call you up. Honey, how's our boy getting along? I got your pictures today. They really are good. I sure wish I could see you both in actual life again and I'm going to try and make that wish come true. Darling, you ought to see what us guys stay in. It doesn't look like it's been taken care of by the Army. This camp was a concentration camp during the last war (World War One) **and they're aiming to condemn it again this September. When I came through Indiana the other night, I couldn't see a whole lot, but it sure was great to be on good old Hoosier soil again. The corn out here don't seem to be very good this year, does it? How is Dory's corn coming along? Is his up to standard? I sure hope so. I hope it makes a lot this year as everyone will need everything they can get. After this war is over, we'll have such wonderful times together. Just sitting at home together and knowing we belong to one another forever and ever will be a lot of thanks. I know I'll be the happiest man after this war, but I want to stay in the Army now and do what I can so it'll help out some toward winning the war. I'm going to close now and take a shower and shave, then go over and call you up. It sure will be like heaven to hear your voice again. Darling, this letter isn't very long, but remember, I'm aiming to call you up. That will be a lot better than a long letter.**

Karl did get a five day furlough. He had five days to get home and back. He took a bus to Indianapolis where Evie, Dory, and Madge met him. He and Evie couldn't take their eyes off each other on the way home. She sat so close to him that Dory whispered to Madge that there wasn't space for a pig's hair between them.

Just like that, he was back in Rushville. Everything looked the same as the day he left about four months earlier, but something wasn't right. Either he wasn't the same guy or the town's people had changed.

As luck would have it, the Rush County Fair was going on. Karl and Evie went one night. They had to leave shortly after they arrived because he got mad. He felt really uncomfortable. He was out of place. Seeing civilians having fun made him fume. He wanted to go back to his unit. Walking home, he told Evie, "Those goddam people are having fun. Don't they know there's a war going on?" His behavior scared Evie. The fun loving guy she married had become a soldier. He was focused on his responsibilities and fellow soldiers more than the folks at home.

Karl felt confused. Seeking some solitude, Karl went to Flatrock River on his last morning at home. It would have been a good day to fish for carp, but he didn't feel like fishing. He sat alone on the bank of the river. Memories came out of storage. He thought of the day he learned to swim. He was no more than five years old. Big Guy told him to swim across the river. Karl answered he was afraid he would drown. He immediately knew he had made a mistake. Big Guy and another brother picked him up by his hands and feet. They swung him. Big Guy yelled "One, Two." On "Three", they threw him in the river like he was a sack of grain. He was pretty sure they wouldn't let him drown, but he knew better than to yell for help. He had a conundrum. He could sink or swim. He ended up on the opposite side of the river. He had learned to swim.

That memory made him feel better. He walked home to Evie with a smile on his face. She had breakfast ready, fried eggs, sunny side up, just the way he liked them. Perfect.

Evie took the bus to Ohio with him so they could have a few more hours together. There was so much to say, but there were long stretches of uneasy silence. They were living separate nightmares. How could they talk about the future? They didn't know if they had a future. Evie could not hide her fear that she would lose Karl. She told him she wasn't sure she could live if she lost him. He responded that he accepted he might not make it back. He told her he would rather die than to stay home like some cowards he knew. He reminded her that he had survived his childhood. How could a war be any worse? He told her, over and over, that he would be careful.

Evie took the bus home alone. She cried until there were no more tears. Broken hearted, she wasn't sure she could go on, but knew she had to be strong for Larry's sake. All the way home, she prayed for strength. She begged God to keep Karl safe.

GOING OVERSEAS

USS General J. C. Pope

Karl had a foot locker in which he could store personal items during his stays in Wyoming and California. He saved the letters he received from home and gave them to Evie when he came home on furlough. Going overseas was different. He now had no such luxury as a foot locker. He had only a large duffel bag to carry his military clothing, toiletries, personal items, and any souvenirs he might find. There was no room for letters. For the rest of his time in the Army, he read letters, responded to them when he could find time, and then discarded them. He kept pictures that Evie sent in his bag, but nothing else from home.

A soldier's life meant long periods of waiting and grumbling about what was going to happen next. All hell would then break loose. Then more waiting and grumbling.

Karl's next stop was Newport News, Virginia. He didn't know where he was going from there. There was one thing he did know. Censors were now scouring his letters with a fine tooth comb. He couldn't tell Evie his whereabouts, what he was doing, or where he was going. The censors crossed out any words that might aid the enemy. He and his buddies played a game. They tried to outsmart the censors. Karl put hints in his letters. He hoped Evie would catch on to what he was trying to say.

August 9, 1943
A friend is mailing this for me. He's from a different Company. We're on alert. We don't know when we'll ship out and we can't mail any letters. I don't understand why we can't mail letters home. It makes it awful bad, but I guess the Army knows best. Boy, I sure did hate to leave you and Larry. I love you both so much I can't express it in words or writing. I think you know how much I do love you but I really can't tell you how much. Words aren't good enough for that purpose. I don't see why we had to be back at 12:00. All I've done is wash my dirty clothes. I've been thinking of you constantly all the time since I left you at the bus station and I will be constantly thinking of you forever and ever. Did you get your suitcases okay? Did you make all your connections okay on the way home? Darling, you won't get this letter for some time and I can't tell you why, but you can keep on writing me and I'll get your mail. PS. Be sure and take good care of yourself and Larry till I return and then I'll help you out in your duties.

August 12, 1943
Darling, here is what I know now. We're going to be shipped out real soon, but I don't know where we're going or when we're leaving. If I did know, I wouldn't be able to tell you a thing about it. Always remember I love you and Larry with all my heart and my love for you both continues more and more every day. I sure bet you were glad to get back home to Larry. How did he act while you were gone? Did your mother have very much trouble with him? Write and tell me all about it. I know he is one of the sweetest kids I've ever seen and no wonder since you and I are his parents. Does he still laugh as much as ever since I left? Darling, above all be sure and take good care of

yourself and our boy. I've been writing but I haven't been able to mail anything, but maybe they'll let me soon. I started this letter three days ago but I'm so busy I don't know what to say. I've been standing guard here at Camp Perry and I sure am sleepy so I'm going to close this letter for now. I'll write another one when I can.
My address: Pfc. Karl R. Floyd, 35140696, 983 Ord. Co. A.P.O. 473, C/o Postmaster New York City, N.Y.

August 27, 1943
Somewhere on the East Coast
Just a few lines to let you know I'm feeling fine and in the best of health. I've been thinking of you two all the time since I've been here. It sure was good when I was home, but I was always thinking about having to go back, so please understand how I felt sometimes. I had more enjoyment in those five days than since I've been in the Army. I get another shot this afternoon. That will end them for a while again, but I don't mind them very much now. I'm waiting on an answer from Tom's letter and see what he has to say about us two going into some kind of business. Personally, I think it would be a swell idea, don't you? I bet we could make a go of some kind of business. We both have the ambition. Are you both in fine health? I sure hope so as I'm looking forward to the days after the war. I want us all to have our health above all. I bet you wish Larry would start cutting his teeth, don't you? Be sure and let me know when you get your refrigerator and also about Larry's leg. I've been worrying quite a bit about it since I saw him. I'm anxious to know what you find out. Remember those days when we both went squirrel hunting together? Remember, you can't go rabbit hunting as that is too dangerous unless you and I go together so I can watch you. Of course, I don't think you'd like the idea of getting up before daylight but we could go in the evenings. I sure wish this war would soon end so we could all be together again. Darling, no matter where I'm at, remember I love you both more than anyone in the world. I'll continue to do so till I die and I'm aiming to live to be a ripe old age. PS. I'm almost out of writing paper and our payday isn't till next Tuesday. Remember our motto. Everything will be okay.

When Karl was home on furlough, he noticed that one of Larry's legs seemed to be bowed out at the knee. He also asked Evie why Larry wasn't sitting up by himself. She made excuses and promised to have Larry's leg checked out when she got her next check from the army. As Karl was about to be shipped overseas, she took Larry to a local doctor. He was the doctor who had removed Karl's appendix in 1942. The doctor sat down next to nineteen year old Evie after he examined Larry. He told her that there was something wrong, but he wasn't certain what. He arranged an evaluation for Larry at Riley Children's Hospital in Indianapolis.

August 30, 1943
I got two letters from you tonight when I got back from the detail work I was on. I was sure glad to get them. On the detail today, I ironed shirts. In fact, I ironed exactly 342 shirts in 7 hours. That isn't bad, is it? Of course, I had an electric presser to do it. It sure was hot too. I don't have to get up as early as I did in Wyoming, only when I'm on detail, and that's not very often. I've been getting up at 7:00 and eating breakfast at 7:30. It's not a bad life, but it isn't home. When I was home, we could sleep till noon if we wanted to, couldn't we? When this war is over for good, we'll take a camping trip for a few days. That ought to put us back in pretty good shape for a while, don't you think? If we can, I'd like for us to go to Lake Celina, Ohio for some fishing. I'll assure you we'd catch some fish. I've certainly seen enough water since I've been in the Army. It seems like every time they move me I go somewhere near an ocean or a lake, like now. I'd rather have it like that than to be out in the desert somewhere. Honey, I don't know whether Larry's leg could be double jointed or not, but I don't think it is. When the doctor returns, have it X-rayed and find out about it. I really think it's just a little crooked and it might straighten out later on when he begins to walk. I don't really know what I'd look like in my blue suit again, but it won't be so terribly long before us boys will be back in the running again. I don't know what kind of business Tom and I would go in, but I'll have to hear from him to see what he has to say about it, and then maybe we can make up our minds. A very good business for us would be an upholstering shop of our own. I actually think we could make good money at it on our own work. You know upholstering comes mighty high and furniture business is always pretty good when everything else is down. I know from experience the International factory (his employer) **kept going all the time during the depression. I was working there for a long time during it. If we could start off doing repair work on a big scale, maybe someday we'd be able to have our own factory and that would be good. Have you ever made up your mind yet what to get Larry for his birthday? You can get him**

anything you want to. I'll probably have to send money as I can't get anywhere to buy anything. That also goes for our Wedding anniversary. I wanted to send you both something nice, but it don't look like I'll be able to. I'll make it all up when I get back home. Honey, always kiss Larry for me every day and I'll make them all up with interest like I did when I was home on furlough. I never spent five better days in all my life. I hated to get back in camp, but if everyone stayed home this world would be in an awful shape by now.

September 3, 1943

Every day I continually think about you and wonder what you're doing. I sure wish I knew exactly what was going to happen to this outfit I'm in. I don't care, but we all would like to know. Honey, I'm going to tell you the works and hope for this letter to get through. We're all still in the dark, but I'll tell you all I know. If this letter gets through the censors, don't mention what I tell you to no one but Mom for at least three weeks. Thousands of boys' lives depend on it. First of all, I'm at a camp named Camp Patrick Henry. It's located about 15 miles from Newport News, Virginia. I've been into Newport News twice since I've been here on different details. We're going pretty soon to get our last physical before we leave for overseas duties. I don't know where we're going, but I have an idea it will be some cold climate by the way we're outfitted at the present time. I'm in an Ordnance Depot outfit as you already know. It's pretty safe so don't worry. We were supposed to leave two weeks ago, but our orders were changed. Darling, after this war is over and I don't think it will last so terribly long, you and I and Larry are going to take time off. We'll have a vacation of some kind and we'll have plenty of fun. I heard on the radio this morning where the invasion of Italy has started. From now on you'll see the Axis cracking little by little every day. In one year I think us boys will be home or so close to it. Personally, I don't believe it'll take very long to get the Japs off the map. They're beginning to get part of their punishment at the present time. Honey, how has Larry been acting lately? Has he been mischievous as ever? I don't want to have a sissy, do you? Have his teeth ever come through yet? Be sure and have his leg X-rayed. When you get it back, write and tell me all about it. Has Madge heard from Ronald or Dory's son recently? If she hasn't, tell her not to worry. They'll both be okay. Mom said she hasn't heard from Tommy for the past two weeks. Tell her that Tom writes home at least once a week, so whenever she receives any mail she'll get more than one

letter. Darling, till that final day comes when we can see the finish I'll be thinking about you both all the time and continually love you.

Karl shipped out from Newport News, Virginia on September 5, 1943. He and 6,000 other soldiers were packed like cattle into the hull of the USS General John Pope. He slept on a six foot long bunk which was nothing more than a piece of canvas stretched by ropes between two posts. Piled three high, each man had a vertical space of less than two feet. A fellow couldn't stretch his feet without touching someone's head. Karl was lucky. He got a top bunk. He looked at a bunch of pipes, not some guy's ass.

The trip was good preparation for what was ahead. There were no portholes to let in fresh air. The stench of sweat, stinky feet, stopped up toilets, and puke was overwhelming in the sleeping quarters. The only air movement came from guys crawling over the duffel bags and gear stacked on the floor. The ship's upper deck was full of military equipment and cargo. Seasick soldiers could barely find space to stand, eat, or puke. The eight day trip became a living hell when a three day long storm rocked the ship to and fro with such violence that the ship lost most of its lifeboats. Most soldiers became seasick. The smell worsened down below. Slew bags (also called puke bags) were used up quickly. To walk anywhere meant wading through the sticky mess of chunks of undigested food and green vomit covering the deck. Karl took the misery in stride. He decided the trip was good experience. It was no worse than what his brothers did to him when he was a kid. The horrible conditions re-enforced one fact. He was nothing more than a lowly, expendable GI.

Italy surrendered to the Allies while Karl bounced across the Atlantic. Allied Supreme Commander General Eisenhower, a four pack a day of Camel cigarettes smoker, stated, "Hostilities between the armed forces of the United Nations and those of Italy will terminate at once. All Italians who now act to help eject German aggressors from Italian soil will have the assistance and support of the United Nations." Germany was now all that remained of the European portion of the Axis Treaty.

The USS General John Pope docked at Greenwich, Scotland on September 13, 1943. It was one day shy of five months after Karl had left Rushville.

SOMEWHERE IN ENGLAND

> Somewhere In
> England
>
> Dear Evelyn & Larry:
> Just a few lines to let you know I'm feeling fine & in the best of health. I hope you all are the same. Darling I'll have plenty of things to tell you when I get back but I can't say much of the present time. I guess the War Department has notified you by now that I arrived safe & sound over hear.

Karl wrote no letters for fifteen days. He wrote nothing during the miserable, over-crowded trip across the Atlantic Ocean. Once he arrived in Scotland, he could not write until he arrived at his new base in England.

There was another problem. Soldiers and their families were mailing millions of letters and packages every month. Besides letters, families sent care packages containing candy, cigarettes, pictures, and other goodies. Soldiers sent the usual letters plus gifts and souvenirs to the folks back home. Mail transported on ships took up to two weeks, often longer. The government tried to keep the mail flowing using airmail. Airmail still took about a week for a letter to reach its destination. The volume of letters and packages became so enormous the system reached a breaking point.

The government's answer was Victory Mail (V-mail). A soldier or civilian had only one piece of paper to write a letter on. The letter writer gave the letter to a postal worker. The postal worker photographed the letter onto photographic film. Rolls of film traveled overseas by air. The receiving post office developed each letter on the film into a picture. The picture letter was then put in an envelope and forwarded to its destination. The military encouraged soldiers to write two of every three letters by V-mail. Karl did not like V-mail. It limited his letters to one small page. He preferred standard delivery because he could write longer letters.

The result was Evie did not get any mail from Karl for almost a month. She had become accustomed to hearing from him on a regular basis. She was beside herself with worry. She had no idea where he was. Why were there no letters? Would she receive the dreaded Western Union telegram? Was an Army chaplain going to knock on the door? All she could do was be patient, worry, pray, and let her mind run rampant.

Finally, there was a letter in the mailbox. It was the first letter in a month.

September 18, 1943
I'm well and safe. I'm somewhere in England. I guess the War Department has notified you by now I arrived safe and sound over here. I should be getting your mail now in a couple of weeks or at least I hope so. That's the only way we have of finding out things from home and that's what we all want to know. Those V-mail letters aren't long enough so I don't think I'll write many of them. I would rather write a long letter instead. Don't worry too much as I'll be okay. I'm thinking of you both all the time. Darling, I'll have plenty of things to tell you when I get back, but I can't say much at

the present time. I can say people over here sure talk a funny English brawl. I guess the slang we use sounds funny to them, but I'd rather hear good Yankee talk any day. Honey, I'm getting anxious to know what the doctor said about Larry's leg. I worry a lot about you two's health. I sure am waiting to hear how you're getting along. Since I've left home, a lot of people sure have died around the town, haven't they? Our Army seems to be having quite a hard time in Italy, but don't worry about them not getting in there and doing their best. The country over here is very beautiful, but it's nothing compared to our own country. When I get back, I'll have plenty to tell you which is not supposed to be said. The things which I've seen are actually amazing. If I ever seen it in our country, I'd be fighting continually. I'll tell you all about it later on. My hope right now is to get this war over with as soon as we can, then we'll all be free to come home and settle down for a nice quiet life again. Tell everyone hello and to write. I'll do my best in answering the letters.

PS. My address is: Pfc. Karl Floyd, 983 Ord. Dept. Co., General Dept. G-18, A.P.O. 51, New York City, N.Y. Also, we got our English money today.

September 19, 1943
I haven't received any mail yet, but I expect I will before long. All I can do is wait patiently till I do. It sure will be welcomed when it does arrive. I'd like to tell you where I'm at, but there'll be plenty of time after the war for that. I've got so much to tell you it'll take me a month to get it all out. Has your mother heard from Ronald or Dory's son lately? Is Dory's son still transporting prisoners? I can't figure him carrying a gun and guarding prisoners. I bet he'd a lot rather be home instead. Of course, I don't know of anyone who wouldn't but we all are seeing lots of sights and having lots of experience. I'll always keep my promise to you about going to church again every Sunday and I'll do my best in keeping it up to standard. I never did believe in quarreling in church like they did up there and I still don't, but if enough people think like that there won't be any churches. Darling, remember the night when we met each other? You were sure shy. Of course, I wasn't very far behind you myself. Also the times when Tom and I would go hunting? You always blushed when I kissed you goodbye. The night when Winkler and I went catfishing together, we had lots of fun together. I wish I knew if Winkler is in England or just where he is. If he is here, I'd try and get in touch with him. Honey, as I

sit here many miles away, these memories come back to me and I know there will be many more of the same. I'm going to write a letter of thanks for the cigarettes the International sent me and a letter telling them to send me a letter stating I'll have a job waiting for me after the war. I don't know, but I think if I have a letter stating that, I will get a discharge sooner so I may as well get one. I bet Larry is still saying Da-Da and Mom-Ma all the time isn't he? If I have my way, he's going to be all boy and no sissy about him. He wouldn't be a Floyd if he wasn't all boy, would he? Is your wisdom tooth still bothering you? If it is, why don't you go to the dentist again and let him cut the gum then maybe it'll come on through like the other. Honey, our second wedding anniversary isn't far off and our boy's first birthday too. I'm mighty sorry I won't be home for that day, but you can rest assured I will be thinking about you both all that day and hoping and praying we'll all be able to be there this time next year. I sure do hate to have to be away from you both in a time like this and I know you're having a hard time raising Larry by yourself, but it's better to be gone now while he's still very young than to have to wait till he gets older when he really needs a father's guidance. When he gets to be 3 or 4 years old is when he'll start looking forward to a father's care, and then I'll be there to give it to him. Since he's a boy, I'll have to teach him a lot of things which would be impossible for you to do. It don't seem possible for us all to be separated so far apart, but we all are living for the day when peace comes again. We all want to do our best in bringing this war to a close sooner. In the past few days, my address has kept changing around. Well, the one on the envelope is the correct one for a while, so always use it till I notify you again. If you write to any of my previous addresses, I'll receive the letters someday.

September 20, 1943
I've been waiting for the mailman to bring in some letters. We should be hearing from you all in a few days now, or at least I hope so. All of us would sure welcome some mail. I expect you are too but I've been writing to you since I've been here so you should be getting some soon. Some of the boys and I went to town yesterday to see what it is made of. It's not bad, but I'd just as soon stay in camp as go there. The censor says I can't say why. I'll tell you later, when I get home. You know how people back home think the English people don't have much to eat? Well, we ate dinner yesterday in town at a little restaurant and it served a

pretty good meal. We have 100% better chow at this camp where I'm at now than we did in the states. Just before we came over, the chow was terrible. I think they tried to starve us boys but that's almost impossible. I was never surprised so much in all my life to see the English people's ways. **The Limey's** (British soldiers) **are okay but some of the civilians I wouldn't wipe my feet on if they were a throw rug. I wondered how you came out on the x-ray on Larry's leg. I sure hope I'll hear from you about it before long. I'm anxious to find out. Has Mom heard from Tom lately? It sure will be great when all of the boys get back in civilization again. It'll take a long time to get used to civilian life again, but I'll learn. We been working pretty hard lately and I'm glad of it. I never was used to loafing around and sometimes we do a lot of loafing. The way I figure it, the harder we all work the sooner the war will be over. I've found out one thing since I've been here and that is, the weather gets colder over here in September than it does in the states. I expect frost is about due at home if you haven't already had one. I always like a good morning frost. I remember how us kids, when we were small, would wait for the frost to come so we could gather walnuts. Sometimes, we couldn't wait and gathered them too early. Remember when I took my sister's kids out and got some walnuts last year after I was operated on?** (His appendix was removed.) **That was some vacation I had. The best part of it was I never lost any pay. My side never has caused me much trouble, only when I lift a lot, and then its pains a little, but it always was like that even before I was operated on. Today is the day when all the kids started to school back home. I never will forget the first day I started to school, will you? My teacher was Miss Ham. She sure was cute, but I was too small to realize things such as that. I'd never dreamed I'd be in England 17 years after that, but that shows a person never knows. Darling, in 21 days will be our second wedding anniversary and Larry's first birthday. Of course, it will be impossible for me to be home with you, but you can rest assured I'll be thinking of you all day and loving you both. I sure hope and pray I'll be back to spend that day with you next year. I'm pretty sure the war will be over in Europe by then. I don't know about the other side of the world, but we can all hope for the best. Things are sure beginning to pop in Italy, aren't they?** (He was referring to the Allies' invasion of Italy.) **We're beginning to take the German's like Grant took Richmond in the Civil War. Today's paper stated some high ranking German Generals put**

Hitler out of command as far as running the Army. That makes the news sound better. When such things happen, you can be rest assured things are really going against them. By the way, I'll try and send some money home every 2 months. I'll have more than I need and there's no use of keeping it with me. I'll try and write to you when I can, but if something comes up and it's impossible, don't worry about me. I'll be alright, but will be busy and not have time to write. So darling, till the day comes when we'll all be together again.

Karl and some buddies playing baseball in England. Karl is middle of top row with his hands on his hips.

September, 25, 1943
I haven't got any mail except for one day, but we should get some more before long. I sure hope so. That's what we all wait for every day. That's the only way we have to hear from home, so you can see how much it means to us. I got more letters than anyone in our barracks the other day, so you all back home are doing alright. Tomorrow, the British are celebrating Harvest Festival. The 983rd will be there marching, so I'll be there. I always like to march, especially with a band. We got our first ribbon today for European Theater of War. Before long, we should get 1 or 2 more. I'll be dressed like a General when I do get home, only I won't have the stars on my shoulders. They keep us boys pretty well amused over here. We've got a theatre in camp so we get along pretty

well. Remember the Saturday night before we were married? We were parked and the cops came up and made us move on? They really thought they were doing some great deed, didn't they? Remember the same night, we both fell asleep and never woke up till almost daylight and how scared we both were. We were lucky Dory and Madge never woke up when you came in. Darling, regarding the picture you're going to have taken of Larry on his first birthday. I certainly would like to have one if you could get a small one and send it. I sure wish we all will be together this time next year so we can celebrate both anniversaries together instead of thousands of miles apart. Remember when I told you I was going to get you a 4.10 shotgun and you could go hunting with me? Well, that promise still holds good. Also the camping I promised you. It's really fun to camp, but the way the Army does it is altogether different. One ambition I've always had is to go to the Northern Lakes for some good fishing. After this war is over, I'm aiming to pack our car up and take off. It may seem funny to you about everything I'm planning, but remember we'll have a long time afterwards to do all of these things. As I sit here on my bunk, I can think of a million things to do and afterwards when we're reading the letters over at home, we can see what we aimed to do. Then we can eventually get it done. On the 11th day of October I'll be thinking of you both every minute as that's about as near as I can get to you. All I hope is on our next wedding anniversary we'll all three be together. Honey, I'm going to send you a little present for your wedding anniversary and Larry's birthday. It may reach you a little late but, nevertheless, it will come from the bottom of my heart. You can do whatever you want with it as I know you always put things to good use. I saw in last night's paper where Russia isn't very far from the Polish border so that looks pretty good also. Darling, no matter where I maybe during the next few months, always remember I love you and Larry more than anyone in the world. I'm continually thinking of you.

Evie wrote Karl about Larry's upcoming appointment at Riley Hospital. She knew he would worry himself silly if she told him everything. She said the evaluation was only for Larry's bowed leg. She prayed to God to forgive her for not being completely honest with her husband.

The farm was fifty miles from Indianapolis. The 35 mph Victory Speed Limit stretched the trip to Indianapolis to two hours each way.

Dory got up extra early on the day of the appointment. He emptied the chamber pot. He milked the cows. He fed the horses and pigs. Like he did every morning, he checked to make sure The Bull hadn't broken through the fence. Madge gathered eggs, fed the chickens, and made breakfast while Dory completed his chores. Dory siphoned enough gas out of his Ford tractor to get to Indianapolis and back after breakfast. He put the gas in his auto. Off they went.

A team of doctors evaluated Larry. X-rays taken of his leg revealed his bones to be fine. The doctors then gave Evie a startling diagnosis that she was not prepared for. Somehow, Larry had suffered an injury to his brain. Larry had Cerebral Palsy. That was why he wasn't sitting up or crawling. They told Evie his leg appeared bowed because his leg muscles were having spasms. The damage to his brain was irreversible if their initial evaluation was correct. Larry would never be normal.

They instructed Evie on stretching exercises to help Larry's legs to stop having muscle spasms. They advised her to consider placing Larry in a home for handicapped children. A return appointment was set up for more evaluation and discussion.

September 29, 1943
Our mail got in today. We all are sure a happy bunch of boys when we get mail. I got 12 letters from you. Last week I got more than that, but every letter counts a lot. I'm sorry I had to go so long without writing you, but I suppose you heard from me by now. I bet it sort of surprised you to know I was in England. I'm glad to hear you and Larry are feeling fine. I'd give anything in the world to be there with you and Larry, especially when you take him to the Riley's hospital for the X-ray on his leg. I know you'll take good care of him, but I'm hoping and praying there is nothing wrong with it. Have you heard from Ronald lately? Don't worry about him. He's tough and he'll be okay plus the Army looks after their men better than a person would think. How is Dory's son? Is he still in Massachusetts? Madge said he was learning to like Army life a little better. He may as well like it. It would do him more harm to dislike it. The way to take this Army is to take everything on the chin and say nothing about it. I went down a while ago to the PX (the Base Exchange was like a grocery and department store) **and got my rations for the week. I got 7 packs of cigarettes, a bar of candy, 1 package of mints, 2 small boxes of**

matches, and a small package of cookies. Most everything else we can get without rations. I forgot to mention a package of chewing gum. I also bought a box Brownie from a boy in my barracks that needed some money. We aren't supposed to have them, but with it I can take some pictures, I'll try to send them to you if the censors let me. Mom said she received a letter from Tom and he is getting along fine. I'm sure glad of that. The place he's at takes a lot of grit to keep your morale up. India has only two seasons and they're hot and rainy, so I feel sorry for him. I think he's doing swell in keeping his morale up. Darling, in a few more days our son will be 1 year old and we will be married two years. My present will get there a little late but I'm going to get it there as soon as possible. It certainly takes time to do everything you're supposed to do. Just remember I'm doing my best and I love you both so much. If anything ever happened to either of you, I don't know what I'd do. I wish I could be there this winter to keep you both warm at night. Of course, that's impossible, but we're doing everything we can do so we can be home as soon as possible. When the war ends and I get my discharge, I'll be willing to walk home after I get on U.S. soil, but till this war is over, my place is in the Army. I have no desire to get out of the service like some guys I know. If I did anything like that, I couldn't look anyone in the face again.

A Box Brownie camera

Stars And Stripes was the newspaper for the Armed Forces in the European Theater of Operations (E.T.O.). The newspaper was popular with the soldiers. Karl read it every day. It contained news of the war, tidbits from home, sports stories, and of course, comics. A quote from the U.S. Army Chief of Staff General George Marshall in the September 22, 1943 edition perked Karl's ears up. It pertained to the upcoming invasion of Europe. Marshall said, "Now at last we are ready to carry the war to the enemy overseas, thank God, with the power and the force which we hope will bring the conflict to a speedy conclusion."

The military announced it needed 445,000 more men by the end of 1943. Most able bodied, draft age, non-fathers were already in uniform. The Selective Service announced men who were fathers before the Pearl Harbor attack were no longer deferred from military service. This turn of events made Karl somewhat happy. He and Evie had gotten the short straw. The Rush County draft board had made him eligible while other men whose babies were Larry's age received deferments.

Evie wrote about taking Larry to doctors at an Indianapolis hospital to have his leg checked. She then wrote things that didn't make sense to Karl. Larry was almost a year old, but he still wasn't sitting up by himself? Larry was almost crawling? Karl sensed something was amuck at home. How could it be that he was almost this and almost that? Don't babies usually sit up around six months of age? Don't they crawl shortly after that? He wrote his mom and sisters and asked questions. They gave strange answers. What the hell was going on? It was like the feeling he used to get when his brothers were too nice to him. He couldn't get the idea out of his head that they weren't telling him everything about Larry.

October brought some good news for America. The noose was tightening on Germany. Recently liberated Italy declared war on Germany.

There was more bad news for Rush County. The October 1 *Republican* reported the death of the eleventh Rush County soldier. By the end of the month, the number of soldier deaths increased to thirteen. The twelfth man from Rush County to die had left on the bus for Fort Ben with Karl.

October 4, 1943
I'm still feeling good and in the best of health. I'd like to tell you what I'm doing, but it's against the rules so I'll wait till I get back and then we'll have lots of time to talk. I'm expecting some mail to come in tomorrow as it comes in about every six days. It sure is a happy day when the mail comes. It's better than payday. I see where the Allies are still going strong. If we all work hard, this war will be over before we think. There's still a long bloody road ahead of us, but we have to grin and bear it. Have you read about the new Jap plane? Don't think it's better than the P-38's of the Americans, because it's not. The Americans and British are holding land, sea, and air superiority now, so the Axis can't hold out forever. (The Axis was now down to Germany and Japan since the third member, Italy, had recently surrendered to the Allies.) Have you heard anything from Ronald? If he was in that paratrooper attack, I'm sure he'll be taken care of by God. We all have to take lots of chances. Some are just luckier than others. Has Mom heard from Tommy? He's in a worse place than I am, but I'd give a thousand dollars to see U.S. soil again and I know he'd give the same. Still, we have a war to win and we can't win it at home so the place for us boys is here so we can get it over with. Darling, how is Larry getting along? Is he still as mischievous as ever? Honey, I'm having a hard time to decide what to send you for Christmas. I can't get anything like we can at home, but I'll assure you I'll do my best. Is Larry's tooth completely through yet? Has he ever bit on your finger yet? What did the doctors say when he had the x-ray taken? Did you have to leave him at the hospital? If there is something wrong with his leg, do they have to put a brace on it? That's a lot of questions, but I want to find out all about it. Honey, one week from today is our second wedding anniversary and Larry's first birthday. I hope the little present I sent you will reach you in time, but if it doesn't, remember that I'll be thinking about you both all day long. I'm sorry it's impossible for me to be home on that day. I guess over here is where I fit in this war. All we can wish for is to be together next year. PS. This poem is from me to you.

Censoritis:
The censor says I can't say much,
Can't talk of so and so and such,
Can't even say we're having weather,
Or you'd put two and two together.

> Can't say just where I am, or what,
> Can't tell you why, or if, or but,
> Can't tell you what we do or don't,
> Or if we might, or will, or won't.
> But - I can send my love to you
> Without restriction - so I do.

October 5, 1943

I never got any mail today but I'm looking forward for some tomorrow or the day after. I'd like to see Larry's new tooth. I bet he really clamps down on your finger if you put it in his mouth, doesn't he? I'm getting anxious to find out how the X-ray came out on Larry's leg. I don't really think there is anything wrong with his leg, but I'll have to wait for your letters to find out. Isn't he even sitting up yet? What seems to be holding him back? I'd sure like to know. He should be almost crawling or walking by now. Maybe it's just because he's slow catching on to things. Madge often told me you were 18 months old before you started walking. If his leg needs medical care then give it to him. Be sure and do everything you can for him and no matter the costs. Money is nothing compared to his health. This paper I'm using was given us boys by the Red Cross on the ship when we were coming over. They also gave us a little bag with toilet articles and a cartoon of cigarettes. When we left the states, they gave us ice tea. When we landed they gave us tea again, but the tea over here is nothing like we have at home. By my estimation, England is about 25 or 30 years behind us in our standard of living in every way. It's so different it will be hard to get use to our living standards again when I return. Honey, the 11th Day of October will soon be here. Although I'm thousands of miles from you, remember I'll be thinking of you both continually all day long. I and you both know my part in winning the war is being over here, so I may as well make the best of it. I feel pretty confident the European war will be over by this time next year. Maybe I can spend the 11th of October with you two then. We're all working toward that goal.

October 11, 1943

Just a few lines to let you know that today is the day of all days to you, Larry, and me. When I wake up in the morning, the first thing I think of is you two and that thought lasts all day and night. All day I've been thinking of the last 3 1/2 years which we've spent together and all of the good times we've had. Remember how we use to take rides through the country about every night? Boy, those days I really enjoyed a lot. This morning when I woke up, it was really foggy but it sorta cleared up somewhat to turn out to be a pretty fair day. I imagine back home you all are enjoying fine Indian summer like it was 2 years ago. Is Larry's leg okay? Did you have to leave him at the hospital over night or not? Let me know if the $25.00 I sent you and Larry got there in time or not. You can use it any way you wish. That's the only present I could send you and I want you to make the best of it. Honey, there isn't any news over here I can tell you, but it looks pretty much that we'll have the war won over here by this time next year. I'm not saying we will, but if we don't we'll be pretty well near it.

Evie and Larry

October 19, 1943
Honey, your letters I received today mentioned about you all going down to the funeral home to see Omer Levi. I never received any word when or how he died. I'll assure you it was a great shock to me about him. I thought John or Court (members of the Courthouse Curbside Court) **would die before him. You asked me**

how I like England. Well, it's okay, but it's nothing like the states and it never will be. It's impossible for me to tell you how close I'm located to a town, but if I could I would. I can tell you the town I went to is pretty good size, but I can't say how large it is. The English camps are nothing like our camps back home on account of we're so close to the front, they have to build the barracks pretty far apart on account of certain reasons but I can't say what. The civilians over here are alright, but they're a lot different from us. I'll tell you what I mean when I get back in the states. I can't say how the English people cook because all our cooking is done in the Mess Hall by American soldiers. One thing that is pitiful is to see the kids over here. They hardly know what toys are. A lot of the American boys are making toys to give out to them this Christmas. It sorta makes me feel sad when I see such things. I work as hard as I did in civilian life and you know I worked pretty hard then. I always did like to work hard. I always will. I get up about 6:00 am and go to bed from 10:00 to 11:00 pm. On our wedding anniversary and Larry's birthday I was thinking of you both all day and night. That was the day I mashed my toe, but its okay now. It really hurt for 3 or 4 days. Honey, if you would, I wish you would do me a favor. Give Chuck (one of Karl's brothers) money and have him get me the best and biggest hunting knife he can find. Tell him to get one that has a good edge and which will sharpen easily. A person over here can never tell when he might need it, can he? I guess it won't be long before I get a letter telling about what the doctors said about Larry's leg. I sure hope and pray there is nothing wrong with it. He's sure had a hard time. I'm willing to do everything that lies in my power to make it all up for him when I get back.

P.S. I sure am glad to know you and Larry are back in the states where it's safe and plenty of things to get. People over here, honey, know what war really is. I hope you all never do. If we could, I'd be willing to call this whole thing off. There's a lot of Yanks that feel the same way.

October 24, 1943
Just a few lines to let you know I received five letters today and two Christmas cards. Some of the boys and I was aiming to go to Church this morning, but we had to work. I guess work has to be done before anything else right at the present. The way I look at it, every hour I spend working brings the end of the war that much closer. It won't be but a few days now that I should get the letter

from you telling me what the Doctors said about Larry's leg. I'm praying nothing is wrong with it. You said in one of your letters I got today that Larry is spoiled. That's the way I want it to be while he's young. If he ever wants anything, get it for him because I know it's hard on a child not to get things he wants. Don't get me wrong. He may want something he shouldn't have and, of course, he won't get it. A bunch of us boys went down to the recreation hall and played snooker, threw darts, and Ping-Pong most of the evening. When I came back, it was time for the lights to go out. After all these months in the Army, I met a guy last night that used to live near Rushville. There were a half dozen of them which came from another part of England to get some equipment and they stayed in our barracks all night. It sure seemed good to see someone who knew the same places I did. Darling, it won't be long till Christmas and I wish to take this time to wish you all the happiest and merriest Christmas you can have. Maybe next year I'll be home to celebrate it with you. Our motto will always hold true.

The GIs understood the need for secrecy. The Nazis were looking for any hint that might tell them where and when the European invasion would occur. Even so, the soldiers were frustrated to not be able to tell where they were. The *Republican* published a little snippet written by Aviation Machinist Mate Dale Hawley. It summed up the secrecy situation fittingly, "After leaving where we were before, not knowing we were coming here from there, we couldn't tell whether we had arrived here or not. Nevertheless, we now are here and not there. The weather here is just as it always is at this season. The people here are just as they look. I had better close now before I give too much valuable military information." Such was the life of the American soldier.

October 31, 1943
Honey, it's pretty hard to write a letter when you can't say a thing about your surroundings, but I can always say the most important things, such as our love for one another. The news which I can write about is very little, but I will say the news is going to look much better very shortly. You can count on that. I went to church this morning for the first time since I've been in the E.T.O. (European Theatre of Operations) **except for the time we attended the parade. I certainly enjoyed it a lot. I'm aiming to go with the**

other boys every Sunday from now on. Tomorrow night there's going to be a U.S.O. show at the theater. We're going down to see it if we don't have to work. That's about all we've got to do so we may as well make the best of it. The funniest thing happened to me a while ago. I got sort of ambitious and decided to wash some socks out. I got a bucket of water and put three pairs of socks in it and put it on the stove to boil. In the meantime, us boys went to chow. When I returned, the water had boiled dry and the socks practically burned up. There sure was a smell in the barracks. It sure was funny. Honey, I had to take time out from writing and go help the boys play some Halloween pranks. We fixed about everyone's bed in our barrack and also went over to some of the other barracks to do some dirty work. They'd do the same thing to us if they had a chance. I'd sure like to get the letter tomorrow telling me what the doctors said about Larry at the hospital. I'm praying there's nothing wrong with him. Tell everyone I said hello. I wish them all a Merry Christmas.

Sightseeing in England

November 8, 1943
In a couple of days, hunting season will begin back home. I sure wish Tom and I were there to start it off like we always did. A good hind leg of a rabbit or a pheasant would sure taste good right now. I saw in the paper today where all us boys overseas will have 1 pound of turkey for our Thanksgiving dinner. That won't be hard to take. We have it pretty good over here, although we all are working hard. It's worth it, I guess. When I shaved last night, I left my moustache on but I think I'll shave it off tonight. I don't like it. Honey, the boys told me to tell you cigarettes aren't very good to eat. They'd rather have candy instead. It was all in a joking manner. Everything you sent to me are things I need every day. You know this war won't last forever. Think of the days when we were going together and how much fun we had. I never will forget the night when I was coming back from taking you home. I turned there at the railroad and saw a horse in the road. For a while, I never knew what to do next. Remember when I'd pick you up every day at noon and ride you and your girlfriends all over town? I just thought up a swell idea for us boys for our Christmas Eve night, and that is for each of us in our barracks to draw names and exchange presents like we used to do in school. It will be about the closest thing we could do next to being home. Everyone has agreed to it, so I guess that's what we'll do.

Evie continued to tell Karl good things about Larry. He was cutting teeth. He was eating good and gaining weight. His leg didn't need a brace. He talked all the time. She didn't mention the bad news. She never mentioned Cerebral Palsy. She had convinced herself that the doctors were wrong.

November 10, 1943
I got several letters from you today. Honey, thanks a lot for everything. I think I've got everything now that I need. Ott Jr. (another of Karl's brothers) **sent me several bars of good American candy and a bag of popcorn. We all like popcorn and we'll have plenty if we can scrape enough butter together. We'll have it some of these nights. Maybe on Christmas Eve. I've got enough cigarettes now to last me a long time. I have cut out a little of my smoking, but I still smoke plenty. After I get my ration of cigarettes each week I don't have to draw many from my reserve. So Larry is eating good now, is he? I'm sure glad to hear that.**

Maybe he'll get along a lot better now. You said he has three teeth and more ready to come through. I'd sure love to see you and him this Christmas, but honey, we have to realize it's impossible, so we have to make the best of it. I saw in the *Stars and Stripes* today that Churchill said the war would undoubtedly be over sometime in 1944. I hope it's in the early part of the year. There's a rumor out that a Lt. and Corporal are betting the war will end tomorrow. Personally, I think they're both nuts, but still the feud could end at any time now. Germany is in poor shape and each day the Allies get stronger so one of these days something is bound to pop. What kind of weather are you having today? I'd like to know so I can know how the boys came out hunting rabbits today. I'd have given a lot for all us boys to be there to start the season off, but we're determined to be there next year. Darling, we've all been working pretty hard but I went on sick call today to get my wrist and back taped up. There is nothing the matter with me, but my wrist was always weak from when I fell when I was a kid and I didn't want to weaken it any more. My back is a little sore next to my spinal cord, but it'll be alright, so don't worry about me. A lot of boys over here have the flu. Maybe I'll be lucky and not take it. Us boys in this war are pretty lucky to have good doctors. The ones in the last war never knew too much about different diseases. I already knew the Japs are stinking and have almost every kind of disease. That's one of the first things they teach us in training so we'll be more careful if we come in contact with them. When Ronald was in battle he probably did lose several of his buddies. That always happens. He's mighty lucky to come out safe and sound. Sometimes I wish I was fighting Japs instead of the Germans. Maybe we'll get home a little quicker by me being over here, but one never knows. The Army sure teaches a man how to do a woman's work. So far I've been lucky on K.P. and as far as mopping the floors and making beds, I'm tops. I'd sure miss those duties a lot.

PS. England is really blowing their top. They're saying the U.S. is giving them a raw deal in the way we're telling them off. In fact, we're making up for some of the things we lost out on in the last war.

November 12, 1943
I didn't receive any mail today from anyone, but I haven't been doing so bad this week at all. I've received 35 letters and 4 boxes. The handkerchiefs you and Larry sent me sure come in handy over

here. Everything you've sent me has been awfully nice and I can use it all. I would like to have some milk chocolate bars a little bit after Christmas. I still like them a lot and we can't get them over here at all. I'll be glad when this feud is over so we three can be together again. Sometimes I think it will be over right away and sometimes I don't. I can hardly believe it will be over before spring though. I guess the best way is to wait and learn. If the Russians keep on, they will be in to the Polish border before long. One of the boys in the Company next to us has got a guitar. I'm going to try and borrow it and maybe I can keep my practice up. I sure do miss mine a lot. Do you still have it in our front room? In fact, I miss everything back home, but I've got enough morale in me not to be homesick. Some of the boys are pretty well homesick sometimes, but they get over it after a while. We certainly had a nice trip over on the boat except one big storm, and it was terrible. I saw some big sea monsters, but I can't tell you what kind, because if the enemy got a hold of this letter they could figure out the route we take coming across. We left the states on Sunday, September XX (The date was blacked out by the censor.), 1943. It was a day before Labor Day. In the next letter, I'll tell you the day we landed so both dates won't be in the same letter. Honey, how is Larry feeling? Is he still mischievous as ever? So he is getting several teeth, is he? I realize it's a hard job and may God help you in any circumstances which you may get stumped on. Darling, you said you have to take Larry back to the hospital on January 12? I don't know, but I think he'll be walking before they said. I knew all along he was nervous. If you remember when you met me up at Indianapolis (for his furlough) how he tightened his mouth up. That was the first time I noticed it. I want Larry to be alright. I think if we hope and pray enough, he will be. May God see him and you through safely till I get back. PS. Wait till the invasion starts, honey, and you'll be able to see Germany falter. It'll be a hard fight, but we'll win.

November 14, 1943
Just a few lines to let you know this is Sunday morning and I'm aiming to go to church pretty soon. The other evening I told you the time we left the states so now I'll tell you when we arrived here. The boat dropped anchor early on September 13, 1943. We never left it, though, until September 14. Now if you put both letters together, you can determine our time. It's almost 10:30 am

here so it should be about 4:30 there at home. I can almost tell what you're doing about every hour of the day according to the time. Did you go to town last night? I haven't seen a town for a long time, but I may go in this afternoon. It sort of helps a guy out a little. We had different arrangements made in how we work, 13 days straight and off 1. Not bad, is it? We've got lots of work and we're the boys to get it done. Maybe someday sooner than we think, I'll be back to help you out. Honey, we had mail call and I just received two letters and a V-mail from you so I'll continue this letter. I remember quite well the nights we would listen to the radio and I'd act scared afterwards. You really thought I was, didn't you? Really, I wasn't. If you can't think of the woods I wrote about, think "Robin Hood" (He was trying to tell her he was near Sherwood Forest). That may freshen up your memory a little and let you know where I am. It sure surprised me to hear that Eurine (one of Evie's friends) has, at last, found her true love. Maybe she'll settle down a little from what she used to be. I think she'd like any boy with pants on, don't you? How come, if her future husband is 24 years old, he isn't in the Army yet? Honey, you must be getting along pretty good if you weigh about 120 lbs. I'm glad to hear Larry is beginning to talk. I'd sure like to be there with you both during his young days so I could help you out. Mom wrote and said he sits alone now for 10 or 15 minutes at a time. I'm awfully glad to hear it, but still I can't believe it yet as you haven't written me about it yet. She also said that he pulls himself up in bed. I remember quite well the night when you and I both got mad at him. We never knew he was sick. I always did hate that we didn't know, but we'll make it up to him. I want him to be happy, don't you? The wind is sure blowing hard here today. I sorta look for some snow before long. I always did like snow and I guess I always will. Bing Crosby's program is on the radio. He's singing "Among My Son". Boy, its sure pretty. You may be listening to the same program as its coming short wave and it's for the boys overseas. Honey, trying to get out of the Army is the last thing I'd do. I know too many boys that have done tricks like that and I think very little of them, don't you? I may be gone for a long time yet, but when I do get back I can say I've seen it through and that's something some of them can't say. Personally, I still think the Army is okay, but civilian life is better. It gets dark about 5:30 here and daylight doesn't come till 8:30 or 9:00 in the morning. We have to be in bed by 11:00 and get up at 6:00 in the morning. It sure is dark when we get up in the mornings. The reason it's so dark is on account of the fog we have here. Our barracks aren't nothing like the ones we have in the states, but we can't have them like that. We're so close to the Germans they have to be far apart on account of bombing. You've heard tell of the German bombers no doubt. Tricky little rascals aren't they? But they're not tricky enough. Lieutenant Fitzgerald who censors my letters is in my company. He is the youngest Officer is our outfit. He turned 21 years old just before we left the states. I think you'll find where Lt. Hale does a lot of the censoring and also Lt. Susan. They're all pretty good boys. As far as that goes, our whole outfit is okay. I imagine they get pretty tired of reading letters but that is part of their job. I'm aiming to send you a little souvenir from England, but so far I haven't had time to send it. Yes, I think it would be a good idea to get all the kids some kind of little present for Christmas as I never did miss getting them something. If you could carry on this year, maybe I'll be there next year to do like I always did. I think I'll write Firestone a letter about when they tried to but didn't fix the brakes on the old car I sold. Send me the last bill they sent and let me take care of it from here. They may pull that stuff on some people, but not on me.

November 25, 1943

I got 16 letters from home today. I sure was glad to get them as today is Thanksgiving. I decided I have lots to be thankful for. I promised you I'd send you our menu for today, so here it is: turkey, pork chops, mashed potatoes, peas, gravy, cranberry sauce, bread, butter, and coffee. What did you have at home? We borrowed a guitar from Headquarters and I've been playing it a lot tonight. When was Bill Hartzler killed in Italy? There will be a lot more Rush County boys go down in action before this is over. War is awful, but some people just can't realize it yet. Wait till the final great invasion comes from the British Isles. Remember when the invasion started in Italy and you would see lots of boys getting killed? It will be worse when we invade from here, but it will draw the war nearer an end. You'll see more and more killed than ever before. What is the matter with Chuck? (Karl's brother) He usually kills more rabbits than the limit every year on the first day of hunting season. I bet I could have got more, or at least I always did. Tell him I said maybe he's saving the rabbits for seed next year so all of us can enjoy hunting. Well darling, this is about all I know for tonight except for the news about all the bombing of

Berlin. I guess it's practically in ruins. They laughed when England was getting the same thing. The table has turned. It's awful for so many people to have to die for no reason, but war is war. P.S. I'll keep my promise in going to church with you.

November 28, 1943
I'd just as soon forget about this dump. It's been raining a cold rain all day and I'm glad I don't have to work in it. This is my Sunday off. I never went to church this morning. I was tired so I laid in my bunk almost all morning. We very seldom get a day off, and when we do we try to rest up a little. I've still got a slight cold yet and I've had a little sinus trouble, but don't worry about me. I'll be okay. I saw in yesterday's paper where the Allied Nations leaders expect a collapse of Germany before Christmas, but I really don't. It could be, and I hope it does even though I have got several bets that it doesn't. I'd be glad to pay those bets off. I suppose you and Larry are getting ready for Sunday School and church right now. It should be about 8:00 am at home as it's around 2:00 pm here now. The camp has been under some kind of quarantine, so they never have any shows for us. I very seldom go to town but some of the boys and I went to see a show last night. There's nothing you can do there but go to shows and I've seen the majority of them. They have practically all American shows here. In fact, about everything they have here is American. It was the first one I've seen in a long time. Have you ever got the three glass Swans I sent you through the mail? If you have, were any of them broken? I tried to pack them the best I could. They will be something to remember dear Old England by later on. How did Dory's son enjoy his furlough home? I hope he doesn't have to go overseas for his and Norma Jean's sake. (Norma Jean was the wife of Dory's son.) I can't express how much I love you and Larry in words because of the censors, but in action I can. That's the biggest trouble with the Army. You have to get permission to do almost everything.

December 9, 1943
I got four letters and a V-mail from you today. The V-mail I got today was written Sunday night, November 28, 1943 so it takes almost two weeks now to get a letter. If I'm back by next fall, I'll be right in what I said when I left. Remember, I told you I'd be gone for a year and a half? Well, next fall the year and a half will

be up. It may be sooner than that if the war keeps going the way it is now. Boy, I'm sure glad to hear Larry is getting along so well and he may be walking before he's three years old. When Larry says caw maybe he means cow? Does he talk a lot anymore? Try and teach him a lot. When I get back, I'll teach him to be a real boy. He certainly is starting in young if he is loving the girls so soon. I guess he is a chip off of the old block. I'm glad to know Larry is like me. That makes me feel proud. You don't have to worry about me cussing in front of him if I can help it. You know it's a pretty bad habit I've got, and maybe I can control it. Honey, I know you love to do things for me and I do for you too, but I won't ask too often for things. We need every bit of shipping space we've got on our vessels. I'll probably ask about once a month for candy, and of course, I prefer milk chocolate. I don't want you to spend too much on me. You have to get along at home and I get everything I really need. The boys and I went to the show tonight and seen "Rose Marie" with Nelson Eddy and Janette MacDonald. I've seen it before but it was still good.

December 15, 1943
Darling, I'm one of the happiest men in the world tonight. I got your letter today containing Larry's picture. Boy, he sure is sweet and cute. I can see a 100% change in him since I left. I never did notice about Larry's eye drooping a little, but I don't think it amounts to much. Let me know about what they say at the hospital on January 12. I remember the nights we had the water fights and also how you liked to tickle my feet when I was laying down. I cherish them days among some of my best memories. Those days will soon be back again and we'll have lots more fun. Last but not least, I received my hunting knife. It's perfect, honey, and I'm glad you never sent any other. It'll come in handy. I suppose I'll receive my candy pretty soon. I sure like my American candy as anyone else would after tangling their teeth in this Limey stuff. I went to the show tonight and watched the movie *Ariel Gunner*. It was pretty good. So my sister got her divorce at Brookville? She'll be smart if she leaves that no good rat alone, but I still kinda miss my Saturday night fights with him. Boy that was sure fun whipping his ass. Honey, sometimes the Airmail letters come by plane and sometime by boat. The ones that come by plane take about 8 or 9 days and the others usually 14 or 15 days. I'll be thinking of you both all day and my prayers are with

you always. This war can't last forever and when it is over, I'll be back.

December 21, 1943
I got a V-mail from you today. It was written on December 6. You were out to the farm then. It's been raining here all day, but it does that all the time so that isn't news. It wouldn't be so bad, but it's always a cold rain. Maybe I will be back next winter with you and Larry. If everything keeps going the way it is now, I'm almost sure I will be. Maybe it won't be long before us boys can move over to finish this war and get back home. In four more days it will be Christmas. I hope and pray you and Larry will enjoy it the best you can. Don't worry about me on that day. I'll have a good meal then, although it's just another working day for us.

December 23, 1943
It's always good to get a letter from home. Since tomorrow is Christmas Eve, it would be lots better if I get one. A couple of the boys and I went to a couple of different school houses this afternoon and tried to bring the kids a little enjoyment. We played them several songs such as "Jingle Bells," "Johnny Got a Zero," and "Silent Night", then we gave them lots of candy, gum, and cookies. It was sure a treat to them. They get very little sweet things over here, so you can imagine how they felt toward getting the different things. The Chaplain arranged the programs and they came off pretty good. It's does a guy's heart good to see so many children so happy. At the last school house, we were invited for tea so we stayed. We had tea with milk and very little sugar, unflavored cake, and some little meat puffs. That's what they were going to have for a Christmas party so we joined them. It was plenty of fun. My only hope is to see the war end so the kids over here can get some decent food to eat. I don't see how the people live on such stuff. Darling, it won't be much longer till you'll have to take Larry back to the hospital. I hope and pray the Doctors will find him a lot better. He should be able to crawl by now shouldn't he? I'd love to see him as he scoots across the floor. Maybe he's slow with cutting teeth like I was with the girls. If all the reports in the papers are right I don't see how this conflict can last much longer.

December 24, 1943
I never got any mail today. If I get some tomorrow, that would be a nice Christmas present to me from you. I hope you heard from me today. I sure hope you're enjoying yourselves this Christmas Eve. I wish you both have a very, very happy one. They just got through playing and singing "Goodnight Sweetheart" on the radio. I'm telling you honey, that hit the homesick spot in my heart. I bet you're at Dad and Mom's tonight, aren't you? How I recall those Christmas Eve nights when old Santa would come. Are you going to be at your folk's house tomorrow for dinner? If you are, be sure and eat enough for me. I'll try to eat enough turkey for all three of us. We got a swell dinner planned for tomorrow. Of course, a G. I. meal isn't anything compared to a good home cooked meal like we have at home. Well darling, those good old days will be back someday and when they come we can at least say I wasn't a shirker like some guys I know. Myself, I'm proud to be a soldier of the U.S. Army although it brings us all lots of hardships. Darling, remember last year at Christmas Eve night when you gave me my ring, house slippers, etc? Then we went over to Mom and Dad's to give out the other presents. If it wasn't for you and Larry loving me the way you do, I wouldn't care how long this war would last, but since I love you both so much and you love me, the sooner we get his feud over with, the better things are going to be. A while ago, we heard part of Roosevelt's speech and it was very interesting. Also they've put some good programs on the radio for us boys. For instance, there was Edgar Bergin, Charlie McCarthy, Roy Rogers, Sons of Pioneers and lots of others. There's another program on now which is combined between British and Americans. Earlier in the evening, we got some butter and salt and took our mess kits and popped the corn which Ottie sent me a long time ago. They were about a dozen of us boys which ate it and there was enough for everyone. My only wish for tonight is that you, Larry, and all the family are in good health and enjoy this Christmas very much. Maybe next year Ronald, Tom, and I will be there with you all again to celebrate and help bring Peace and Goodwill Toward Men once again. Remember our motto darling. It will always be true as long as either of us live.

December 25, 1943
I spent a happy Christmas over here. We had a very good dinner and I got two letters from you, including a V-mail. Last but not least, I got the candy you sent. Boy, that candy couldn't arrive at

any better time. Another boy and I almost made ourselves sick by eating so much dinner and then eating lots of candy. I guess today is when a boy is supposed to eat lots though. Darling, did you have a happy Christmas? I hope you got something nice for yourselves with the money I sent you. It wasn't much but about all I could think of. Honey, what did you get Larry? Did his eyes get big when he saw his presents? Next year, he'll be old enough to expect and look for Christmas to come. I'm glad Chuck (Karl's brother) got a deferment and of course he isn't any better than anyone else, but I hate to see anyone go to the Army who has children. It's pretty tough to leave your wife and child behind. Believe me. I know. Do you really think Larry will be pulling himself up to things before long? That's the best news I've heard in a long time. If he does, he'll surely be walking before he's three or three and a half years old. I bet he's cute sitting in his high chair, isn't he? Honey, don't you really know why they're sending so many men to England? Remember the next invasion? Well, that may be the reason. I hate to estimate when the war will end, but I really don't see how Germany can last much longer. After that, I think it will be just a matter of time before Japan will surrender. Of course I could be wrong, so don't quote me on it. I wish you both had a very merry Christmas.

December 31, 1943
Your 20th Birthday and end of the year. Honey, I sure hope you enjoyed your birthday. I wish you many, many more of them. Maybe next year I'll be there to help you celebrate it. Did my little present get there in time? If I'm home next year, I'm going to get you whatever you want. We got paid today. I got $29.70. I'm aiming to send you some. We're having turkey again tomorrow. It's getting so we're having meals like that pretty regular. Darling, has Larry got any more teeth yet? This is one year I don't mind seeing go by. I sure will be glad when this war is over so we all can be together again. Won't that be a wonderful day? I really think 1944 will end the war with the Jerries. The sooner victory comes the better everyone will be, including the German people themselves. I bet it'll be a long time before they want to start another war. Are you staying up and seeing the New Year in tonight? Some of the boys have gone to town. The rest of us are staying up and we're going to play some music on the guitar. When I get back I think I'll take a month or so off from work so all

three of us can lay in bed in the morning and talk and have a good time with Larry. Remember when I was home on furlough how he enjoyed getting in bed with us every morning? Also the romps we had every night. You mentioned in a letter I got the other day that the burn Larry got was getting along good. I never even knew he'd received a burn. How bad was it? How did it happen? Did he cry much when he did it? I guess all children have to go through the same thing, or at least it seems that way. If it wasn't for the censors, I'd write a letter to your doctor and tell him what we thought of him, but I doubt if that would go through. When I get back I will, and don't think I won't. He's really did us a dirty trick and I'll never forget it. Honey, I'd better close for now. There's no news to write about. Happy Birthday.

At the end of 1943, the *Republican* reported that twelve Rush County soldiers had died in the war.

FINAL PREPARATIONS FOR THE INVASION

The Germans weren't going to surrender without a fight. The Allies were about ready to grant them their wish. The anticipation was so great you could almost taste it.

Eisenhower stated the ground work for the European invasion was almost complete. Churchill said the upcoming invasion would involve an equal number of American and British soldiers. The transporting of equipment and materials to England was well underway. Stockpiles of tanks, weapons, ammunition, supplies, trucks, and jeeps occupied every nook and cranny in England. The Allies were bombing the French coast to neutralize German gun placements and plane runways.

The pace of activity increased for the boys who were going to have to do the hard work and the dying. They knew their jobs. They had practiced very detail over and over until they could do it in their sleep. The boys had matured into men who understood the invasion was the only ticket home. They also knew many of them would not come home.

The soldiers were busy and pre-occupied. There was little free time. This meant fewer letters from Karl. When he did get to write, he continued to tell Evie everything the censors allowed him to tell. He still worried about Larry, but mentally he was indoctrinated in the Army way. He was ready. He tried to prepare Evie. One thing though, for some reason he changed how he dated his letters.

1/1/44
Darling, I got a v-mail letter today from you dated December 16. Honey, today is the first day of the year so I've made several resolutions which I'll probably break within a week's time. I usually do, but I'm going to try not to. Remember last year I tried to quit cussing? Well, I'm trying it again this year. Darling, is Larry sitting up alone yet? Is he crawling yet? In 11 more days you'll

be taking him back to the hospital. I hope and pray the doctors find him 100% better. I'll be thinking of you both all that day. It's really been windy here this afternoon and is getting colder all the time. I'd like to see a snow on the ground in the morning. It hasn't snowed over here but for a few flakes one day. I went to the show last night and saw *Hoppalong Cassidy*. Boy, was it a thriller. Ha! I'm going to the show tomorrow night and see a Gene Autry movie. It's just one thriller after another. I used to enjoy them a lot, didn't you? Maybe it won't be long till we can go to the shows again together. We got off about 3:00 this afternoon from work on account of it being New Year's Day. We put in a good day's work though before we quit. Tomorrow is Sunday and it's my day off. I think I'll stay in and answer all the letters I owe to different ones at home. I guess you know the war is supposed to be over in Europe this year sometime. If we all pull together, I hope we can get it over with sooner.

1/6/44

I got a V-mail you wrote on December 20 today. Yesterday, I got mail that was written December 28. Pretty good delivery, isn't it? I'll try and describe a full day in the Army to you as far as I'm concerned. I get up at 6:00 am, eat breakfast about 6:30, then I come back to the barracks and make my bed and clean up around my bunk. Then I listen to the 7:00 news on the radio. After that, I lay down for a while and listen to the program the War Department puts on for the boys overseas. It's still pitch dark outside at 7:50, but nevertheless we fall out and start for work. We do different jobs inside till it gets light enough on the outside. That's usually about 9:00 am. I quit work at 11:45 and come to the barracks, eat dinner, and read the mail whenever I have any. That's been pretty regular lately. I usually read the paper then too if it's here. We fall out for work again at 12:40 pm and work till 5:00. We eat supper as soon as we get back to the barracks. After super, I sometimes take a nap or go to the show. About 8:30 I start writing you a letter. A couple of the boys and I usually find a few minutes to play the guitar a little also. I listen to the 9:00 news and after that, continue writing. I go to bed about 11:00 pm and that finishes a complete day for me in England. It doesn't seem like much, but a person can get really tired at the end of the day. Darling, in your V-mail today you said Larry could stand up in his walker some. He should be walking sooner then we think.

He included a poem that he thought was funny. He didn't realize how it would play to a young woman who had been left behind in the States. Evie didn't think the poem was funny. After she read it, she put it back in the envelope it came in and stored it away.

An English Girl Comment
Dear old England's not the same
We dreaded invasion, well it came.
But though it's not the beastly Him
That gosh darned Yankee army came.

You'll see them in a tram or bus.
There isn't room for both of us.
We walk to let them have our seats
Then get run over by their jeeps.

They moan about our lukewarm beer;
Say "Beer's like water over here."
Yet after having two or more
You'll find them lying on the floor.

You should see them try to dance.
They grab a partner, start to prance.
When you're half dead they stop and smile
Say "How ya doing Honey Child?"

The officers give us cause to smile
With their superior habits and lack of guile.
We wonder if they are wolves or mice or men
Decide they're wolves and avoid their den.

With admiration we would stare
At all the ribbons these Yankee wear.
We think of deeds so brave and daring
That won the ribbons they are wearing.

Alas they haven't fought the Hun,
No glorious battles have they won.
That pretty ribbon just denotes
They crossed the open seas in boats.

If we should speak, they all look hazy.
They think we're nuts, we know they're crazy.
But to our Allies, we must be nice.
They love us, yes, like cats love mice.

They laugh at us for drinking tea.
Yet a funnier sight you'll never see
Than a gum chewing Yank with a dumb looking face.
He'll raise a laugh most any place.

They tell us they can shoot and fight.
Its love they fight, when they are tight.
I must admit their shootings fine
When they're shooting us a line.

You are their life, their love, their all,
And for no other they would fall.
They'll love you dear till death do part
And if you leave, you'll break their heart.

And then they leave, you broken hearted.
The camp has moved, your love departed.
You wait for mail, it doesn't come.
Then you know, you're awful dumb.

In a different town, in a different place,
To a different girl, with a different face,
I love you honey, please be mine,
It's the same old Yank with the same old line.

Though the war consumed Karl, Larry's well-being was tearing him apart. He wasn't a religious man, but he was talking to God daily when it came to his son's health.

1/11/44
I got two letters and a Christmas card today which were mailed in November. I don't know what took them so long to get here, but better late than never. Maybe the ship got lost. Darling, tomorrow is the day you take Larry back to the hospital. I'm hoping and praying with all my heart and soul the doctors find him okay. Of course, it will probably take some time yet before he actually gets

to where he should be, but maybe he'll pick things up faster now. Honey, can he stand up in his bed yet? I hope his bones get to be stronger. I don't want him to be injured in any way. I'll be thinking of you both from daylight on tomorrow. I always have you both in my mind constantly but tomorrow will be more than ever. You said in the letter I got today that you thought I was issuing clothing. Well, I'm sorry to disappoint you but you're wrong. In the first place, that's the Quartermasters job. I'm in the Ordnance, so you see that couldn't be right. I can't tell you what I'm doing, but wait till I get back. I'll tell you all about it. It's about 9:15 now and I just finished listening to the news. It sounds pretty good all over the world. Us boys have been making guesses when the war with Germany will end. I guessed September 3, 1944. Most of the boys guessed from March to July. I'd rather see them guess right, but I'm afraid they're a little too hasty. I may be guessing a little too soon myself. Well honey, it won't be long till I'll be overseas for six months. Time sure does fly over here, but after I give it a little thought, it has been a long time since I saw the old U.S.A. coastline fade away in the distance. That's one ride I'll never forget if I live to be a thousand years old. I didn't get seasick on the way over, but most of the boys did. I don't care if I get so sick I can't stand up on the way back.

For Larry's next appointment at Riley Hospital, Dory and Madge again did their chores earlier than usual in the dark. The weather was cold and windy. This time they made sure the animals had water to drink and enough straw to keep them warm. The Bull was in the barn with the cows. He was in a peaceful mood since none of the girls was in season. Dory had siphoned some gas the night before. He had also put a blanket over the engine because of the cold weather. The auto's engine was grateful. It fired right up when he cranked it. It purred like a kitten. Off they went.

Evie did get not the answers that she prayed for. The opinion of the doctors hadn't changed. Larry was not progressing like a fourteen month old. His legs weren't as stiff as they were on the last visit, but they still weren't straight. They told Evie she would have to work with Larry every day just to teach him to stand. They said Larry would need to use a walker if he was ever going to learn to walk.

Madge went with Evie to hear what the doctors would say. She wanted to make sure Evie asked the right questions. One of the young doctors started to talk about placing Larry in a home for handicapped children. The doc said it would not be fair to future children to have Larry at home. Madge stopped him midway through his spiel with one word. She just said, "NO." She then told him that God had a plan for Larry. That simple response from her mom made Evie realize she wasn't alone. With family and lots of prayers, she felt a calmness that she would somehow get through the burden that had been laid upon her.

1/12/44
I woke up this morning real early. I guess I was thinking of you two so much. You and Larry are the first ones on my mind every day and the last at night. This is the day you took Larry back to the hospital. I've been hoping the doctors find him one hundred percent better than they did the first time you took him. Darling, ever since I've been gone from you and Larry it seems like I've left half of myself there. At least my heart is with you and I know I've got yours with me wherever I go. I'm sure proud of you both. I'm going to make you the best husband and father that I know how when I get home. It's been rainy, foggy, and sloppy here the last couple of days, but the work goes on just the same. I bet its cold back home now. Over here, no matter how the weather may be, we have to carry on since the war won't be won if we lay down and do nothing. I'd like to be home to keep you warm, but since that's impossible, all we can do is hope that everything will be all right next year. Let me know right away what the doctors say about Larry.

Evie knew Karl was anxiously waiting for news. She wrote Karl about the latest appointment. She emphasized the progress Larry had made. He could sit up without assistance. He was trying to stand up. She told him the doctors wanted Larry to use a walker to help with his crooked leg.

Karl seemed relieved with what Evie wrote about the last doctor visit. He asked fewer questions about Larry's wellbeing.

1/30/44
The mail has been coming through pretty regular lately. I saw in our paper where it's been pretty warm back home and the temperature went up to 62 degrees. Over here, today is a little

cloudy out and no rain so far, but probably will by night. I just got back from chow and we had fried chicken again. It was pretty good, but nothing like a home cooked meal. When I get home I'm going to help you fry chicken about three times a week so we can catch up on it. You said in your letter that Larry sits up alone. Does he sit up by himself much more? I wonder how long he sits by himself. Let me know how much he weighs also, will you, darling? In a couple of days, it will be Tommie's birthday. He'll be 26 years old and in 12 days, I'll be 24. It seems like only yesterday when I was 20 and we met. I've never regretted once about meeting you. I only wish it was sooner so we could have had more time together.

2/1/44

Today is Tommy's birthday. I hope he's back in the states before he's 27 but I sorta doubt it because where he is, it isn't very easy to reinforce troops. My candy hasn't come yet but maybe it will get here for my birthday. I didn't get any letters today. I hope I get some tomorrow as I'll be gone after tomorrow for a couple of days. I'll write you when I get back, and if the censors let me when I get back, I'll tell you how I spent my next 48 hours. Does Larry pull himself up yet? Let me know as soon as he does. Honey, have they heard any more about Bus yet? (Bus was a friend of Karl's from Rushville.) For some reason I think he's okay, but I may be wrong. I guess we'll know some day. I bet his folks are almost crazy. They always were so close to him. He was the one of us all who was always unlucky. It seems like the Allies are having a little tougher opposition now but don't worry. Everything will turn out alright in the end. Whenever the invasion comes off, you'll be able to see Germany crumble a little at a time or at least that's the way I think it will be. I had a dream last night about you. I dreamt you, Larry, and I were together. We were all three sitting in our big lounge chair with one of you on each of my knees. It sure seemed real. I was really disappointed to wake up and find myself in the same old bunk. Maybe it won't be long till dreams like that will come true.

2/5/44

I've got about 23 letters in the last two days. I can picture what Larry looked like when he got all the lipstick on him. You never spanked him for it, did you? Myself, I think it would be cute of him.

I hope you have your **specks** (eyeglasses) by now and be sure the doctor gives you a good fit. Honey, when you take your driver's test, don't be scared or nervous. There isn't any use in it and it may prevent you from getting your license. I expect the war will be over whenever I get back to the states. At least Germany will be licked. I may get a discharge as soon as I get back or I may not. I will probably just get a furlough. If I don't, I'll probably take one anyway. Darling, remember what I always said about you coming to stay with me? I don't think it's a woman's place to stay with their husbands in the service. Well, I still feel the same way, but we'll see about it whenever the time comes. It's according to where I'll be stationed. Honey, in some of your letters you act like you're getting lonely and blue. I know you are, but darling, try and keep your chin up the best you can. Maybe someday before long we'll all be together again and we'll all be happy. We all are doing our share in winning this war. You're doing as much as anyone else and I want you to understand that. It's simply crazy to have girls in the **WAC's** (Women's Army Corps) and so forth since they've got the idea they're doing everything that we do. I think their main object is to keep up the soldiers' morale. I can tell you a few stories when I get back about WAC's, but not in this letter. Tomorrow is Sunday and my day to work. It'll be just another day for me.

2/10/44

It's My Birthday. I didn't get any letters from you or anyone today. I can't say much bad about the mail because it's been coming through pretty regular. I saw **Dick Cohee** (A friend from Rushville) again today. He's stationed about 8 miles from me. We had a darn nice visit and he's working this week in the building next to me. I must have talked to him two or three hours and we're aiming to spend Sunday together. Honey, there's something else I want you to do for me and that is, have my blue and gray suits cleaned. You don't have to have my black one cleaned. It's out of style or worn out. Is Larry still saying, "how do" and "bye"? He should be talking a lot by summer. Mom said you were teaching Larry to know me. Darling, that's what I want you to do. I imagine he'll almost have forgotten me by the time I get back. I wish I could be there when you take Larry back up to the hospital. Maybe I will someday. You'll probably have to take him up several times yet before they release him. May God Bless him. I hope and pray everything turns out for the best.

2/13/44
I got three letters and a card from you today. I sure was glad to get them. I didn't get to go in town today. I may later on, but I guess the Army comes first. Honey, if you haven't gotten your drivers' license yet, I'll try and give you a pointer. Remember, you can't cross a yellow line unless you're making a turn onto some other road. I hope you pass okay and also wish you get your glasses and they fit your eyes. Honey, are you sure your eyes tested 20-40? They're supposed to test 20-20 so you see if yours is 20-40, it couldn't be so very bad off. Maybe it would be worse if you never got it corrected with glasses. I'm supposed to get G-I glasses but so far they haven't got here. I guess they will some of these days after the war is over. I had them examined before I left for overseas and maybe that is why they haven't got here yet. I've still got my civilian glasses so I wear them whenever my eyes start hurting and that isn't very often. Remember when your grandfather was buried and when we came back from the cemetery? (Evie's Grandpa Lewis was buried the week after Pearl Harbor.) I think your step-brother thought he could drive away and leave us in the dust with his Chevrolet. If he did, he got fooled by my car. I sure do hope Larry doesn't have the croup. The little fellow has had enough. Let's both hope and pray he gets along okay from now on. I do believe in children taking their little knocks now and then. That helps teach them to look after themselves. It was like getting a Christmas present when I got the candy on Christmas day. I never have got the candy yet that you mailed on January 6 or around that time so counting the package you mailed on the 18th of January, I've got two on the way. Yes honey, I'd like to have our own home before we have any more children. I think that can easily be arranged after I get back and we can talk it over with Dad and Mom. We can really make it a cute place. Every Saturday, we get a magazine called *Yank* and its good reading, only a lot of it is propaganda. It costs me $2.20 a month, or two shilling and two pence. I imagine Larry will lead me a merry chase when I get back. Those days will come again sometime. We'll have to wait patiently till this grudge is over.

2/14/44

I got a letter from you today. It's dated January 15th, so it must have come by ship instead of air. It'll be good not to have to write letters back and forth every day, but instead we can sit together and talk. I see in *Stars and Stripes* where it's really cold back home now. I guess February still holds its name for being the worse month of the year. I hope for your sake the winter breaks pretty soon and spring steps in. We been having pretty good weather here in the last week but a person can't tell much about it. Larry must be getting along swell since you said he can stand up by the bed now and also get around good in his walker. I bet he's cute when he paddles his little feet across the floor as he goes across the floor in his walker. I don't see how the German people can take the terrific pounding they're getting from every direction they turn. Last month alone the U.S.A. Air Force dropped 22,000 tons of bombs on Germany and German occupied countries besides what the other Allies did. Remember, I'll love you all the time wherever I may be, now or later.
PS. Please send me some candy. Put a little of homemade fudge in it if possible, but don't use the cocoa if it's rationed.

2/29/44

Honey, I'm worried about you. I never received any letters from you today, but the V-mail I got yesterday said you weren't feeling good and were awful weak. I'll be glad when I do get some mail from you so I'll know what the trouble with you is. I hope you're feeling better. I got paid today. I drew 7 pounds, 8 shillings, and six pence British. That's $29.70 American. I'm going to try and send $20.00 or $25.00 home because I don't need much money over here. All I need is enough to get my rations for the month. I'm going to send a pin home to you after I buy something else so I can make a bigger package. Is Larry still feeling good? Try and keep him mischievous. That's the way I like to see boys, don't you? I don't think there's much use to worry about him ever having tantrums as we can take that out of him as soon as he's old enough to realize it. There's a little snow on, but it's melting pretty fast every day.
PS. Right now there's a big crap game going on here in the barracks. It's the same old story. One guy usually walks off with all the other boys' money. Aren't you glad I don't drink or gamble?

Larry with his walker
The little girl is the daughter of Evie's paratrooper brother.

3/2/44
I got two letters today. I'm glad you're feeling better. I guess most of your letters are coming by boat right now so that's the reason for the hold up. Has Larry ever learned to crawl on his hands and knees yet? (Larry was now almost 17 months old.) He may start walking before he crawls. Let me know whenever he picks up any new things. I bet it sounds cute when he jabbers. When I get home he should really be rambling the words off. It really snowed hard today for a while, but most of it is all gone now. Reminded me of the April showers we have in the states. I see in the paper where Finland is seeking peace with Russia, and Bulgaria is talking about the same thing. If they do reach an Armistice, I think it won't be long till the rest of the smaller countries do the same. If they do, it will drain Germany of most of her raw materials and then they can't last much longer. In a short time I may be moved to the same place Dick Cohee is. That would

be alright as he and I could get together once in a while and talk over some old times. Remember when the car caught on fire when we were driving around town? I jumped on another car to go get the firemen to put it out, and the car I was riding on got side swiped? Remember how my shoe was cut? I've often thought how easily that accident could have proved fatal to me. Boy, I really hung to the side of that car. I was lucky I did because if I hadn't, the other car would probably have massacred me.

3/7/44
I just got back from a U.S.O. show. It was pretty good. It's a darn good treat to see one of those shows. We get to see them about every two months. Your step-brother's wife wrote and told me about Gene Posey being home some time ago. I can't see how some guys can get home while others can't. I'm not speaking for myself, but Ronald and Tommie both have been across much longer than he. So at last the miracle has happened? You're actually learning to make pie crust? Maybe if this war lasts a few more years, you'll know how to make it. Don't take that to heart. I was just kidding. Since my outfit moved the other day, we've had **chocolate pie.** (He was giving a hint that he had been re-located. The comment made it by the censor) **Honey, I do think it's a swell idea to get Larry a bedroom suite of his own, but about him getting a little sister is something we have to wait to talk about when I get back. It may be a good idea. I believe very strongly in sharing all kinds of burdens, and when I do get back we'll do just that. We can sit down every week and budget our money. I always tried to give you and Larry anything you wanted, but maybe I slipped up somewhere.**

3/26/44
I hope my mail is coming to you pretty fast. Two of the boys and I went riding on bicycles today. It sure was fun. We rode several miles all total. We sure were tired when we got back to camp. The sun was really bright and it was real warm out. It reminded me of spring back home, but still there's 100% difference. I'm sending you a pamphlet of an old castle I had the opportunity to visit recently. It's a pretty place and it's somewhat like the castles you read about in history books. I never thought when I was studying about them I'd ever have the chance to visit one. I also visited an old church that was made back in the 12th century.

They still use it and also use the graveyard for burials. I've seen graves which dated back farther than the 12th century. It's sure something to talk about when I get home. I cut two fingers pretty good the other day. The cut on the forefinger wouldn't grow back together so they cut all the skin off. Maybe it'll be alright some of these days. Well, darling I'd better close for now. I'm pretty busy and have to rush.

Sightseeing in England

The pre-invasion news back home was staggering. The March 8 *Republican* reported 1,000 American bombers, in a daylight attack, had dropped 1,700 tons of explosives on Berlin. America lost 38 bombers and 15 fighters in that one raid.

The government reported 37,853 military personnel had died so far in the war. 20,592 of the dead were in the army.

The *Republican* also reported the death of Rush County's 19th serviceman. A War Department Western Union message was received on Saturday evening, March 18. It reported the death to the family of Pvt. Wilder. He was the parent of a 23 month old son. Pvt. Wilder was Rush County's first soldier father to die in the war. The last word from him was a letter to his sister received on March 12. He wrote it on February 23. That was the day the War Department reported in the telegram that he died. Evie sat in stunned silence after she read the article. It had been almost a month before the family received notification of his death.

He left a widow behind. Worse yet, he had a child.

Pvt. Wilder's tombstone in Rushville's East Hill Cemetery

4/9/44

I worked all day today and I sure hated to as it is Easter Sunday. Now I'm on C.Q. again tonight and I have to stay awake all night long. (C.Q. was army slang for Charge of Quarters. The soldier on "C.Q." handled his unit's administrative matters after hours.) **I've**

been wondering all day if the sun was shining back home like it was here. It's really been pretty today and I would have liked to take a long walk. Honey, did you and Larry get your new Easter clothes? I want you both to be the best dressed of anyone in town. If you did, write and tell me what the outfits looked like. Maybe next year I'll be able to doll up too. We sure will have lots of fun when we get back together and when a holiday comes, we'll enjoy it instead of having to work. After work today, some of us boys went out on the town and had a little wrestling match, or maybe you could call it a fight, with some **Limeys** (British soldiers) just to keep us in shape. Boy, it was fun. Honey, remember me telling you about hurting my fingers pretty badly? Well, both fingers are pretty good now, but now the nail on one is coming off. I think I'll cut it off with a knife so I won't tear it off later by accident. I'll always take the best of care of myself for you and I will be back home as soon as we put the finishing touches to the Jerries. Keep your chin up, honey. Don't worry. Everything will be alright in the end.

Larry was seen a third time at Riley Hospital. The doctors told Evie that nothing had changed. They urged her to keep working on his leg flexibility. She told them he was trying to use his walker, but he often lost his balance and fell.

Evie wrote Karl after the visit. She told another little white lie. She said everything was going well. She didn't mention there was no change in Larry's condition. Karl was satisfied with what he read. His mind was totally focused on what laid ahead for him and his buddies.

4/12/44
It sure has been pretty here today. It's the best weather we've had since I've been in England. We all have a touch of spring fever but we still plug on. Today is the day when you took Larry back to the hospital. You're probably coming home about now. I sure wish I knew what the doctors said about him. If I could only be there to go with you and him, it would be so much better. Honey, I've got a little present for you. I'll send it when I get time to wrap it up. That is, if someone doesn't take it before I get to mail it. I've got it deep in my foot locker and it's pretty safe there. Honey, I'm afraid you're wrong about the oversea stripes. They don't issue them anymore. Maybe we can put them on when we get back to the states, but I

don't know. In another month it will be Mother's Day. Since the mail is so slow, I want to take this time to wish you a very happy Mother's Day. I wonder if you'll win the flower at Church for being the youngest mother there. Maybe next year I'll be home to get you something nice. I hope so. Your mine, I'm yours, and Larry's ours. That's the way it will always be.

P.S.   My address now is: Cpl. Karl Floyd 35140696, 983rd Ord. Depot Co., A.P.O. 507, c/o Postmaster, New York City, N.Y.

Karl wrote on the back of this picture:
One of our units lined up in New Brighton, England

4/28/44
I got several letters from you today. I sure was glad to get them. You said one time you got eight letters from me in one day. Boy, you had plenty of reading for a while didn't you? Sometimes I've gotten 20 letters at once. It takes me a long time to read them all and it takes a long, long time to get them answered. We've been having some pretty weather over here, but still it's pretty chilly. I guess it gets pretty warm in July and August. If we all pull together, I'm sure we can have the Germans whipped by the end of this year. The biggest thing we all have to learn is to keep our mouths closed. It's a hard thing to do since we know some things, but you know I'm keeping pretty quiet. Darling, I also got yours and Larry's pictures today that you had made downtown. Boy, Larry is

really getting fat, isn't he? In one of the pictures he looked a little scared, but I guess he was hugging you so tight. I wish I could hug you both real tight right now, but that has to wait along with the many other things.

General Eisenhower predicted on April 11, 1944 that the European Invasion would start soon. He had made similar comments in the past to keep the Nazis guessing. He wasn't bluffing this time. The Allied intensity went into overdrive. Bombing raids occurring daily in Germany, Nazi occupied France, and Belgium. Every raid seemed bigger than the last. Berlin radio reported the Allied bombing offensive was likely the immediate prelude to invasion.

Back home, the *Republican* reported overwhelming evidence the invasion was imminent.

- April 21: Allied bombers on one day dropped 5,000 tons on German occupied territory and German cities.
- April 26: Allied bombers carried out attacks for a twelfth straight day. Using a smidgen of comedic cockiness, the article reported no bombers were lost while they "laid their eggs".
- April 28: Germany announced that Allies were amassing ships on the southern British coastline. German bombers had destroyed some ships.
- May 6: Allied bombing was in its 22nd straight day. No enemy fighters opposed the bombers when they "planted their bombs".
- May 11: The bombing in France was so powerful that houses in England shook.
- May 29: 8,000 Allied planes participated in a raid that dropped bombs in Germany and Western Europe.
- Photos in the *Republican* showed concrete obstacles the Germans had built along the entire French coast.
- Photos were published of Yanks in full battle pack practicing maneuvers.
- The military announced the English Channel had near perfect conditions for a crossing.
- British civilian train traffic was halted to clear the way for the military.
- London radio told French citizens to stay home and keep off the roads. Allied troops would have the right-of-way.

- The American Secretary of War announced on June 1, 1944 the "great aerial offensive in Europe" was moving steadily toward its goal and the United States now had 3,657,000 troops on foreign bases. He speculated that June may be the time to act. He asked the American people to "remain cool and patient".

Things were getting real. Theories and rumors circulated on both sides about when and where the invasion would start. The Courthouse Curbside Court convened on Saturday, June 3. It made predictions when the Invasion would happen. A few bets were made. The Germans also played the game. They mocked that the Allies dared not attempt an invasion when each date they predicted passed. One Nazi astrologer tried his luck. He predicted the invasion would begin on Monday, May 15th. In return, Secretary of War Stimson said, "The day will come, but it will not be the one which the Nazis have selected. When the moment for telling of the news arrives, we shall try to tell it speedily and adequately."

Families braced themselves. Churches were full on Sunday mornings. Prayer circles popped up everywhere. Little kids couldn't sleep. Neither could their mommies. Evie's apprehension paralyzed her. She met the mailman at the box every day. At best, the mail took two weeks to get delivered. Letters from Karl seldom came. She knew he was safe on the day he wrote a letter, but he could have been injured or killed after he wrote it.

While the buildup intensified, Karl wired a Western Union message to Evie on Mother's Day. Evie didn't want to open it when she received it. She knew how the military used Western Union messages. She finally got the courage to open it. Karl's message was intended to give her comfort. It said: **My love and greetings on Mother's Day. My thoughts and prayers are ever with you. God Bless you.** She cried herself to sleep that night.

Ott usually spent his springtime evenings working in his garden until sunset. During the spring of 1944, he preferred to spend his evenings listening to the radio with Clara. He was worried. There wasn't a goddamned thing he could do to help his son. As May turned to June, even he, the Old Man, let his guard down. One evening, he looked at Clara. He saw the worried look on her face. His mind raced through the tragedies they had gone through over the years. He felt so helpless. He didn't know what to say to comfort her. In typical Ott Floyd tough guy fashion, he put on his game face. He reached over and put his hand on her knee. His raspy voice said "Hon, the shit's about to hit the fan."

Ott and Larry working in Ott's garden in 1944

GIs were acutely aware of the intensification. They also knew they would be the last to know when the invasion would start. Corporal Floyd's 983rd Ordnance Depot Company was busier than a one armed paper hanger. They and other units who were going to participate in the invasion were prohibited from mingling with civilians. His letters became reflective when he did find time to write. The family back home was on his mind.

5/14/44
Just a few lines to let you know I love you with all my heart and I always will no matter where I may be, now or later. I know you're

okay, but still there's always a worry in my mind. I always liked to take care of you both. When I get home, I'll sure do that. Darling, today is Mother's Day. I hope you spent a very happy one. It sure will be a grand day when you, Larry, and I can go out like we used to do. I don't think Larry will be too much trouble. I want to teach him all the things I know about nature. It will always come in handy for him. I remember when Dad would take us kids fishing. Boy that was really fun. It seems like only yesterday when all of us kids would get together and go fishing and swimming. What a time we had. I'll never forget any of it. I want Larry to enjoy those times like I did. I guess every kid has experiences like that, but I can't see how anyone could have enjoyed their childhood any better than me. I worked hard when I was small but I didn't mind that much. Honey, although we're apart now because of this war, there is no reason why we can't be happy. It makes me feel good to think of what good times are ahead for us. We really have our life ahead of us yet, and we've got everything a young couple could ask for. We have our home, furniture, a little money in the bank, and best of all, we have a big boy. Every time I feel blue, I think of all those nice things and it makes me feel a lot better. I'm on guard duty again starting tomorrow night. If I don't write, remember I'm thinking and loving you just the same. I'd better close for now and write Mom a letter as it's Mother's day. I don't want to miss out writing her on that day.

5/23/44

I sure hope you're getting letters from me okay. You're the only one I'll ever love, honey. Sometimes I wonder what would have happened to us if Donald hadn't introduced us to each other. (Donald was a friend. He told Karl in March, 1940 that Evie would like to meet him.) I think we would have met some other way, don't you? Honey, what kind of flowers did you get from me? I can't get anything over here for Dad or Dory for Father's Day, so if you will, try and get them something pretty nice. Boy, the Allies are really going to town again in Italy, aren't they? Maybe this old war will be over with one of these days and then we'll all be happy. I was going to sign up tonight for a swimming contest with the Limey's, but I couldn't find anyone else in the outfit that wanted to so I didn't either. It's too cold anyway. You understand please, no matter how hard a person tries to watch out for himself, something may happen, but don't worry. I can take care of myself.

Corporal Floyd was physically and mentally ready. He had pictures of Evie and Larry in his battle shirt's left pocket. There was nothing left to do but wait for the order to come. He wrote his last letter before D-Day to Evie.

5/30/44
Well darling, today is Memorial Day. I wonder if you all went out to the cemetery to put flowers on the graves. I used to go with Dad every year to do that. I bet the roses are really in full bloom back home right now as they always were around Declaration Day (Memorial Day). The old cemetery there by home sure is full of them too. I got the box of candy today. Thanks a million. You seem to know the right kind of candy to send me. That fudge you made was swell. I've almost got it all eaten already. I'm saving the bars though. I lost my ration card and I've gone without rations for the past two weeks. It was really a good thing I had plenty of spare cigarettes on hand. Honey, you said in a letter I got the other day you bought a qt. of strawberries, but they cost 49 cents a qt. Don't pay any attention to the price of things. Honey, I had an awful dream the other night. It was about the Perkins Street railway crossing. I dreamt the car you were driving stopped on the tracks right in front of a train. I've been worrying ever since. I decided to tell you to be sure and be careful whenever you cross a railroad track. I don't know what ever made me dream of such a thing, but I was really scared stiff for a while. I've been anxious to get a letter from you since then, but so far I haven't. As the days go by, they find me falling deeper and deeper in love with you. I thought it was impossible to love you any more than I did the day you and I were married but, darling, I do.

A story in the June 1st *Republican* said, "The possibly fateful month of June opened in Europe with the English Channel shrouded in mist...The period of decisive action is at hand in the war...The Allies are ready to strike victory winning blows by land, from the sea, and in the air."

America had all of its ducks in order. Everyone was ready. The whole world was watching and waiting.

Karl wrote on the back of this picture:
Jim Curran and Bob Weidoff in one of our pup tents.
These pup tents are our home most of the time.

Staging area in England just before the invasion

Karl wrote on the back of this photo:
Our mess in southern England. We had some
of our best meals in the Army served off of that table.

Karl in England before the invasion

Pre-invasion two ton truck in England

INVASION

D-DAY June 6, 1944

Any soldier who said he wasn't scared was lying through his teeth or was a fool. Indiana born war correspondent Ernie Pyle explained it as well anybody could, "There are no atheists in a foxhole."

Ernie's quote also applied to the folks back home. It was impossible to go anywhere without meeting someone with a loved one in harm's way. Moms carried bibles and comforted each other. Dads talked tough, but they couldn't sleep well. Dread and fear consumed the soldiers' wives. Churches kept their doors open day and night for praying.

Ott tried to make Evie and Clara feel better. He kept telling them that Karl was a Floyd who knew how to take care of himself. He even said he felt a little sorry for any goddamn Jerry who got in Karl's way. Despite Ott's macho assurances, Evie was terrified. She wasn't getting letters from Karl. She didn't know where he was. She didn't know what his responsibilities were during the invasion. She didn't even know if he was alive.

Tuesday, June 6, 1944, started like any other long summer day at Dory and Madge's farm. The roosters crowed at the crack of dawn. The wind-up alarm clock rang at 5 am. The cows made their way to the barn for milking. The Bull surveyed his pastureland kingdom for victims to harass. Dory took the chamber pot to the outhouse. Madge boiled water for coffee. She made the usual breakfast of fried eggs, bacon, and fried potatoes. They had much to do that day. Besides the usual chores, Dory needed to be out in the fields disking between the corn rows to keep the weeds down. Madge planned to weed the garden. She hoped to pick some early beans for supper.

Like he always did, Dory turned the radio on when he came in for breakfast. He adjusted the dial to the station he listened to every morning for the farm news and weather forecast. An unfamiliar voice was talking. Both he and Madge stopped dead in their tracks. They sat down at the table and listened to what was being said, "Bulletins have been coming in to our newsroom in New York. During the course of the last hour or so on these broadcasts we have been hearing from London. You have heard a statement by General Dwight Eisenhower, the supreme commander of this great operation which has begun in the early hours of the morning. He said a landing was made this morning on the coast of France by troops of the Allied Expeditionary force. German radio statements admit that our troops are now ten miles inside Europe. That apparently means we have broken the first German defense line. We've pierced a hole in it! We are ten miles inside the fortress of Europe. That wall of steel and concrete which Hitler boasted could never be broken apparently already has been broken...."

Dory and Madge listened in silence for several minutes while they ate breakfast. The significance of what they were hearing finally sank in. They held hands while Dory said a prayer. After the prayer, Madge went upstairs to wake Evie. Dory went to the barn to milk the cows that were bellowing in misery. Dory did no field work that day. Madge didn't pull one weed in the garden.

The *Republican*'s headline that day said in large, bold print: MIGHTIEST MILITARY INVASION OPENS. The story followed with, "It's here. D-day has arrived. Allied invasion troops hardened by months of training are storming the German west wall along the French coast. Allied soldiers leaped onto shores which the Germans have been fortifying for four years. Our invasion troops have penetrated several miles inland into France. So far as we know, no bells or whistles heralded the invasion nor were churches opened for public prayer. How many breakfasts went undigested as folks attentively listened to invasion bulletins will not be learned."

President Roosevelt addressed the nation that evening. He ended his speech by reading a prayer he had personally written. His prayer ended with, "Some will never return. Embrace these, Father, and receive them, Thy heroic servants, into Thy Kingdom."

Evie didn't know Karl remained in England on D-Day. Nineteen month old Larry was accustomed to his twenty year old mom crying when she read Karl's letters. That night, there were no letters to read when they went to bed. She held Larry as tight as she could. She sobbed until she fell asleep.

The June 7 *Republican* reported that everyone expected the invasion to be a blood bath, but initial reports said the invasion had gone well. One correspondent, who was on Utah beach, not Omaha, wrote that it was like seeing a play in which some of the leading actors failed to show up. He wrote of watching thousands of men tumble safely across the beaches with no enemy to be seen. The Associated Press reported the Allies had penetrated twelve miles into France on D-Day. The disaster on Omaha beach was not mentioned.

Sadly, in the same edition of the paper the War Department announced that sixty-nine additional national cemeteries might be needed for the American soldiers who could die before the war ended.

Karl wrote his first letter in three weeks on the evening of D-Day. Evie had not received a letter from him in five weeks when it arrived two weeks later.

6/6/44
This is the day of the Invasion of Europe. I finally got back from where I've been for a while and have some time to write. I will try and do the best I can. Please excuse me for not writing while I've been away. It was impossible. I hope you understand. We're mighty busy right now. We can't do as we please. We've been going through some pretty tough things here lately but don't worry about

anything. What did you think when you heard the news of the invasion? It sure did come at an unexpected time, didn't it? Maybe it won't be long now till all of us are back home again. When I got back from the trip I was on, I had several letters from you. I sure was glad to get them. I got my receipt from where I sent you $25.00 and I've still got a little money left. I always like to keep a little just in case I need it. I'm going to make out an allotment as soon as possible so you'll get $100.00 a month, and then I'll probably send you some every month. Larry must be getting pretty strong now, isn't he? You said he could run in his walker. That's pretty good. Tell him to be a good boy for daddy. If I don't write as often as I did, remember I can't help it. I'll write when I can. Our motto will always be true. I'll never forget it. I love you and Larry.

Tom was in India, but news sped fast in the military. He wrote a letter to Evie when he heard that the invasion happened. He tried to encourage her, but he couldn't hide his anxieties for Karl's safety.

Tom (wearing the helmet) in India

June 12, 1944
No doubt the news of the past week has caused you much worry and anxiety. It's the news we have all wanted to hear

for a long time, yet it struck a lot of fear inside of me. No use to tell you I worry about Karl, knowing the position he is in and the job facing him. Let's not give way to this fear or to worry, but face the facts with hopes for the future when once again he will be home. I bet old Karl is excited, don't you? He realizes what the outcome over there means to all the generations to come. I sincerely wish I were right beside him so I could keep an eye on him. I have all the confidence in the world that he will be back home sometime in the future. I will end by saying again, don't worry about Karl. He expects all of you back there to keep a stiff upper lip. Don't ever write him that you're worried for him, as this is sure one factor on his morale.

The military attempted to make it sound like the invasion had been a piece of cake. Like always, reports of what really happened leaked out. One reporter wrote that gains were made, despite furious Nazi counterattacks all along the 100 mile invasion front.

In responding to the invasion, the Nazis began launching one of its secret weapons of the war, buzz bombs. One reporter described the horror of the buzz bombs, "The enemy is sending flame spitting pilotless planes to southern England. The planes look like they are about twenty-five feet long with a wingspan of twenty feet. They fly at terrific speed in a straight line. They have bright lights to make themselves visible to Allied soldiers on the ground. Flames shoot from their exhausts which suggests they might be jet or rocket propelled. They drop super heavy explosives which explode on or near the ground. The explosions have caused many deaths and considerable damage. The Germans report this new invasion weapon works most effectively." This report scared the bejeebers out of Evie. From Karl's hints, she was certain he was somewhere in southern England.

The War Department confirmed the terrible news. There were 15,883 American casualties, including 3,283 dead, in the first eleven days of the invasion. A reporter described the first Allied cemetery in Normandy, "Stretched out on their backs with their pitiful personal belongings lying beside them on this bomb blasted, shell scorched bit of the Normandy beach lie the American dead. They lie there mutely waiting while troops dig long trenches for temporary mass burial.

When the Americans swarmed onto the beaches through murderous surf, angry German guns mowed them down. The cold greedy water of the wrathful channel, lashed by a three day wind, clutched at some, sucking them down. This battle was so fierce that our grave registration officers, the men who bury the dead and tell the folks home about them, had to spend most of their time in foxholes."

Rumors spread in Rushville that two or three Rush County boys were casualties in the invasion. No families had been notified…yet.

Karl was not able to write again until one week after D-Day.

June 13, 1944
Just a few lines to let you know I love you both. I haven't written you for a while, but it was impossible. Don't worry about me. I'm still okay. I'm getting along swell. I guess it is okay to tell you now that I've moved since I wrote you last, but I can't tell you where I'm at or anything. I haven't got any letters from you for quite a few days, but I'm looking for some most any day. Boy, from what I hear, I guess the invasion is going along pretty good, but we don't get much news here. I guess we're the ones making the news. Really, honey, I can't see how the Jerries are holding out, but they hang on somehow. Maybe they'll crack some of these days. I've been so busy lately I haven't had a chance to do anything. If I'm not able to write, remember I'm always thinking of you and loving you both with all my heart. I always carry yours and Larry's picture in my pocket when I'm on the move. Whenever I'm in a pup tent, I put it so I can see it all the time. I haven't got the box of candy yet with the films (photos)**, but I probably will before long. My address is still the same. If it changes I'll let you know. I'll try to write you, but if I don't from now on, please don't worry. Everything will be okay over here.**

Karl boarded a troop transport ship two days later. Fourteen months after he left Rushville to join the army, he crossed the English Channel for Normandy, France.

SOMEWHERE IN FRANCE

Omaha Beach, Normandy, France
Karl is first on the left, second row

Karl's unit made the twenty mile trip across the English Channel on June 15, 1944. This wasn't anything like the first day of hunting season back home. His palms were sweaty. He could feel his heart pounding in his chest. As he boarded the transport ship, he couldn't get out of his head that he might not live. Worse yet, would he be a coward and run? He squeezed the barrel of his weapon. That, somehow, made him feel better. So far, it was like any other training run he had gone through. There was one big difference this time. At the dock, ships full of injured men were returning from France.

It took most of the morning to get across the English Channel. He had prepared himself for noise. He thought it couldn't be much worse than the noise his shotgun made on the first day of rabbit season. Was he ever wrong! A few miles into the trip, it started with a rumbling sound coming from the east. It reminded him of the distant thunder of an approaching Indiana thunderstorm. Then there were frequent what sounded like explosions which became louder as the transport moved toward Normandy. Those booms reminded him of when a storm was overhead at home. He and his brothers called them thunder boomers.

He discovered the source of the explosions a mile or so from the Normandy coast. Two huge U.S. Battleships were firing 2,000 pound bombs at speeds of 2,600ft/second. Their targets were German bunkers ten miles beyond the beach. The sound became deafening as his transporter passed close to the battleships. His ears started ringing. It was so overpowering that he couldn't hear the guy next to him.

Finally, Omaha beach was in sight. Karl's transporter stopped to wait for its turn to dock. He made his way to the rail to see what he could see. He got his first glimpse of the horrors of war when the ship resumed its quest for the beach. Something unimaginable caught his eye. It was nine days after D-Day. Floating, bloated bodies still bounced up and down like fishing bobbers. Some were face up. The expressions on the swollen, bluish colored faces told Karl they had experienced horrible deaths. He couldn't help but think that each of those bodies had family back home that would soon be grieving. He came back to reality when he heard some guys around him puking. Others shit their pants. He thought of Evie, Larry, and his mom. Tears welled up in his eyes.

Welcome to World War Two.

Looking to the mainland, Karl saw what used to be a beach. It was now a junkyard of blown up landing craft, disabled machinery, and destroyed tanks. Unbelievable amounts of debris were everywhere. The dump back home where he and his brothers shot rats popped into his head. Rushville's dump was neater than Omaha beach.

Finally, the transporter docked at one of the temporary piers. The beachhead was secure, but the place was a chaotic zoo. Fierce German resistance had stalled Allied progress a few miles inland. There were soldiers who seemed to be trying to direct traffic, but their efforts were to no avail. There was not enough space on the beach for everything and everybody. Arriving troops were everywhere. Tanks, jeeps, trucks, artillery, and other supplies were being unloaded. Wounded soldiers were being loaded for transport to medical ships.

Karl looked around when he finally got off the transporter. At the water's edge were helmets, weapons, and personal items. Body parts washed to and fro with the waves. The beach was in utter chaos.

Karl saw an indescribable sight when his unit made it beyond the pandemonium at the shore. A few hundred feet inland, stacked like firewood were piles of soldiers' bodies. These were the poor souls who on D-Day had run into the ambush on the beach. Many were missing arms, legs, or heads. Some had their guts hanging out. Dog tags with those twenty-eight inch chains were on most of the bodies, but not all. Karl thought, "It's nine goddam days after D-Day. Why haven't they buried those boys?"

He felt like he was going to pass out because he was hyperventilating. It wasn't just the sights and smells that got to him, but it was the realization he was in the middle of a war zone. He covered his nose in an attempt to reduce the smell of rotting human remains with a handkerchief Evie had sent him.

He reminded himself how lucky he was to not be in the infantry. His unit then did what the army had trained them to do. They started by clearing debris on the beach. They then loaded their trucks with supplies and ammo and moved forward, toward the fighting.

Like he always did, Karl adapted to his surroundings. His life depended on keeping his wits about him. The next day, he found time to write. He needed to be careful. He didn't want Evie to know he had landed in Hell. From his words, it appeared nothing was amiss.

6/16/44
I got 16 letters and two cards a few days ago. Thanks a lot for the Father's Day card. I forgot all about Father's Day. I never even knew when it was. The last letter I got from you was written on the 8th of June. It came pretty fast, didn't it? What did you think when you heard the news of the invasion? Were you surprised much? Did the churches in Rushville open up? I know they were going to try and have every church in the states open all day. Someone should have prayed for the boys. They needed it. I just heard the American casualty list. There were 3,000 and some killed and a little more than 12,000 injured. That's a lot of men for a few days of fighting. I'd like to tell you where I'm at now, but I can't. I will someday. I'll tell you everywhere I've been since I've been overseas. I've been a lot of places and expect to go farther.

I'm sorry to hear Ronald is in the hospital again. (Ronald was in the Pacific theater of war. He had malaria). **Maybe he'll be okay now. He's sure had a time of it since he's been in the Pacific, hasn't he? I forgot to tell you that I also got a letter from Madge today. She said Dory's son was transferred to the Infantry. I bet he hates that. Those boys have a rugged life. I don't think he'll go overseas anytime soon unless he's had quite a bit of infantry training. So far I'm doing fine and in the best of spirits. Sometimes my morale gets pretty low, but I get yours and Larry's picture out of my pocket and look at it. That makes me feel a lot better. Try not to worry about anything. Everything will be okay in the end.**

Karl took a picture of a disabled tank near Carentan, France

6/17/44
I think of you and Larry every moment I'm away. I didn't get any mail from you today, but I'll get a bunch of it again some of these days. They're doing their best to get the mail across to us, but we can't expect too much right now. Maybe things will change as we move along. Myself, I'm fine and my morale is as high as ever. It has really been warm here today, but the wind blows just the same. If I stay in this part of the world a lifetime, I'd never get used to the climate. Darling, when we get together again we'll have lots of fun. I'm anxious to see you shoot the 4.10 gauge shotgun I'm going to get you. I'm doing my best to save money so

we'll have a good start when this war is over. Have you been listening to the invasion news? The way things are going, I don't see how the Jerries can hold out much longer. We hold supremacy on about everything in warfare and we seem to have better equipment which counts a lot. I guess by now you have heard of the "Doodle Bug" the Germans are using. By the way, Doodle Bug is what we call the flying bomb. So far it hasn't put much of a scare into the Allies. About all its fit for is to build up some propaganda for the German people. Also, you better start getting some coal in the basement for the stove too as it may be plenty scarce this winter. I don't want you and Larry to get cold. Larry should be getting to be a big boy by now, isn't he? How much does he weigh? Our motto will always be true and I'll never forget it. I'm continually thinking of you both, honey.

Families back home were encouraged to send goodwill packages to their soldier. The military emphasized not to send useless articles that cluttered up the mail. It even published advice on what the soldiers needed and wanted. A soldier's ration of cigarettes was only seven packs a week, so families were encouraged to send cigarettes if their soldier smoked more than a pack a day. Good books, magazines, snapshots, and a subscription to the local newspaper were much encouraged. Of course, soldiers never turned down candy, gum, cookies, or chocolates. Using a bit of military humor, moms, girlfriends, and wives were reminded that soldiers would be "very embarrassed" to receive "foxhole pillows, pajamas, or other sissified equipment."

The *Republican* reported Rush County lost its twenty-first soldier on D-Day. His family was not notified of his death until June 30th, twenty-four days later. The government announced more grim statistics. 24,162 Americans were killed, wounded, or missing in the first two weeks of the invasion.

Karl's letters became infrequent. When she did receive a letter, Evie feared she might be reading the words of her dead husband. She did not receive his next letter until mid-July. The letter told her where he was. Karl was in France.

7/4/44
France. I think of you continually. I'm hoping for the day when we can all be together again. Today is July 4th, but it's not any

different from any other day over here. The way the guns are sounding off, it must be 4th of July every day. I wish you all back home could hear them for about an hour. How is Larry getting along? Does he like his playpen? How does he like his new walker now? Honey, don't send me anymore candy or anything unless it's for Christmas. I don't need a thing and I've got no place to keep it anyway. I'd better close for tonight. I have to clean my rifle. It needs it. I'll try and write again but if I don't, try not to worry. Everything will be okay.**

Karl told Evie that he was a clerk in an Ordnance Depot Company when he was on furlough in 1943. She had convinced herself that a clerk would be far from the front. He would be out of harm's way. The July 4 letter scared her. What was he referring to about guns sounding off? Why did he have to clean his rifle? Why wasn't he receiving any mail? Why was he talking about killing? Karl's next letter didn't reduce her anxieties.

7/9/44
Somewhere in France
On this Sunday evening, I'm feeling fine and in the best of health. I'm hoping and praying this letter finds you and Larry the same. I still haven't got any mail since I've been in France, but I know it's on its way somewhere and will get here someday. I hope it's soon. It's been a long time since I've heard from you and the other folks at home. I can picture you and Larry now in Church as it's about that time back home. It would be lots better if we both could be with Larry while he's still young, but that can't be helped. Maybe it won't be many more months till I'm back home, then we can do anything and everything we've planned in these long months we've been apart. I thought I saw Cuttie (a friend from Rushville) **yesterday, but I was mistaken. It was the same kind of outfit he's with. From a distance it looked just like him. I'd like to know if he's over here or not. If he is, I've a swell chance of running into him. I suppose it's so hot back home a person can hardly breathe. It's pretty darned hot over here too, but it's not caused by the weather.** (He was giving Evie a hint as to what he was doing.) **I guess the Yanks are still moving according to plan as we're going right along, but I think the Limeys** (the British army) **will still be at Caen** (a town in France) **when the war ends. At least they will be at the rate their going now. Honey, whenever I get back to the**

Karl looked around when he finally got off the transporter. At the water's edge were helmets, weapons, and personal items. Body parts washed to and fro with the waves. The beach was in utter chaos.

Karl saw an indescribable sight when his unit made it beyond the pandemonium at the shore. A few hundred feet inland, stacked like firewood were piles of soldiers' bodies. These were the poor souls who on D-Day had run into the ambush on the beach. Many were missing arms, legs, or heads. Some had their guts hanging out. Dog tags with those twenty-eight inch chains were on most of the bodies, but not all. Karl thought, "It's nine goddam days after D-Day. Why haven't they buried those boys?"

He felt like he was going to pass out because he was hyperventilating. It wasn't just the sights and smells that got to him, but it was the realization he was in the middle of a war zone. He covered his nose in an attempt to reduce the smell of rotting human remains with a handkerchief Evie had sent him.

He reminded himself how lucky he was to not be in the infantry. His unit then did what the army had trained them to do. They started by clearing debris on the beach. They then loaded their trucks with supplies and ammo and moved forward, toward the fighting.

Like he always did, Karl adapted to his surroundings. His life depended on keeping his wits about him. The next day, he found time to write. He needed to be careful. He didn't want Evie to know he had landed in Hell. From his words, it appeared nothing was amiss.

6/16/44
I got 16 letters and two cards a few days ago. Thanks a lot for the Father's Day card. I forgot all about Father's Day. I never even knew when it was. The last letter I got from you was written on the 8th of June. It came pretty fast, didn't it? What did you think when you heard the news of the invasion? Were you surprised much? Did the churches in Rushville open up? I know they were going to try and have every church in the states open all day. Someone should have prayed for the boys. They needed it. I just heard the American casualty list. There were 3,000 and some killed and a little more than 12,000 injured. That's a lot of men for a few days of fighting. I'd like to tell you where I'm at now, but I can't. I will someday. I'll tell you everywhere I've been since I've been overseas. I've been a lot of places and expect to go farther.

I'm sorry to hear Ronald is in the hospital again. (Ronald was in the Pacific theater of war. He had malaria). **Maybe he'll be okay now. He's sure had a time of it since he's been in the Pacific, hasn't he? I forgot to tell you that I also got a letter from Madge today. She said Dory's son was transferred to the Infantry. I bet he hates that. Those boys have a rugged life. I don't think he'll go overseas anytime soon unless he's had quite a bit of infantry training. So far I'm doing fine and in the best of spirits. Sometimes my morale gets pretty low, but I get yours and Larry's picture out of my pocket and look at it. That makes me feel a lot better. Try not to worry about anything. Everything will be okay in the end.**

Karl took a picture of a disabled tank near Carentan, France

6/17/44

I think of you and Larry every moment I'm away. I didn't get any mail from you today, but I'll get a bunch of it again some of these days. They're doing their best to get the mail across to us, but we can't expect too much right now. Maybe things will change as we move along. Myself, I'm fine and my morale is as high as ever. It has really been warm here today, but the wind blows just the same. If I stay in this part of the world a lifetime, I'd never get used to the climate. Darling, when we get together again we'll have lots of fun. I'm anxious to see you shoot the 4.10 gauge shotgun I'm going to get you. I'm doing my best to save money so

states, if I don't get a furlough or discharge right away, I think I'll go **AWOL** (absent without leave) **for a while and come home. Personally, I think they're aiming to give us discharges right away. Would you want me to go "over the hill"** (AWOL) **for a few days? Really, I'm a better soldier than to do a trick like that, but I'll be glad when this is all over and everybody can go home and live like they should instead of killing each other by the thousands just for the profit of someone else. Try not to worry about anything, honey. Everything will be okay in the end.**

Caption on the back of this photo: "Dwyer took this picture of me just fooling around. Notice my foxhole in the background? We use them quite often.

Tom wrote another letter to Evie in an attempt to lift her spirits.

July 16, 1944
I received your letter recently and immediately went into mourning. The news of the death of my pet duck "Flash Gordon" was hard indeed. In my hour of grief, I wore a stiff upper lip and found consolation in the fact that "Flash" was at one time the king of the farmyard. I only hope his life was successful and he leaves behind many more just like him bearing his name who will in future years live up to his fine reputation. Oh, if only it were possible that I be there to sprinkle a few grains of corn on his grave as a token of my esteem. Tell me, how come he died a natural death? Seems to me he would look better swimming around in his own gravy banked by a mound of baked potatoes. I think I know what is wrong with the kid (Larry). He probably is girl crazy and even at his age, he takes after his old man. I hope the doctor says he is fully recovered and no further treatments are necessary. I have a feeling Karl is safe and will continue to be so and will one day return home a little older, a little wiser too perhaps. I have no fear for myself; never have as far as that goes. I have no immediate reason to come back, but with him it's different. So, don't worry. Let the war run itself out. It won't take too long, I'm sure. Tom

Karl sent a flurry of V-mails when his unit got to rest after fighting at Cherbourg, France ended. His mail finally had caught up with him.

7/23/44
Darling, I won't be able to write airmail for a while. There aren't any airmail envelopes here. I'll write V-mail in the meantime. I got 12 letters today. I sure was surprised in reading about Wayne dying from an airplane crash, but things are just planned by God that way. I'm sure the doctors found Larry much better this time, although I haven't got your letter yet telling me what they said. Honey, I expect to be home by Christmas, but don't be surprised if I'm not. We're doing our best to get this war over.

7/25/44
I'm still fine and in the best of health. I sure hope these few lines find you all the same. Honey, go ahead and get a new radio with a big cabinet. Be sure and get one so we can put a record player on it. Is Larry still as mischievous as ever? It seems like the war is about over as far as Germany is concerned, but they may spring up with something that will prolong it for a while. If they don't, I aim to be home by Christmas or shortly afterwards.

7/26/44
Honey, I'm still okay and in the best of health. I think I've got some mail today, but we haven't had mail call yet. I hope I have a letter from you saying what the doctors said about Larry. I'm sure they found him a lot better, but I'll feel better about it when I get your letter. Yes, honey, it's perfectly alright for you to get lots of new dresses. I want you and Larry both to have everything you want or need. Honey, they say the war with Germany is going to be over shortly. I hope they're right.

7/27/44
I can wait hardly till this war is over and we can all be together again. Darling, give Larry a big kiss for me. Tell him to be a good boy. I can't tell you much about things over here. The censors will cut it out so I'll wait till I get home. Keep your chin up and take care of yourselves. I'll do the same.

The government announced 53,101 American soldiers "on all fronts" had died in the war by the end of July.

Karl had other things on his mind to tell Evie.

8/1/44
Do you recognize this stationary? It's what you sent me last Christmas. I've been saving it till I ran out in some place where I couldn't get any more paper and this is the place. The envelopes are stuck together, but the Army has issued some to us. They look like they're made of toilet paper, but they'll do. The reason I worry so much is because I haven't seen either of you for so long and I try not to worry about Larry's legs. I know he'll walk pretty soon. I guess I weigh about 165 pounds now. That isn't bad considering everything I've been through. You'll be able to fatten me up again when I get home. I'm really longing for some of those home

cooked meals. I'll probably eat us out of house and home when I do get back. I've been getting mail pretty regular lately and it sure helps. You sure should see the snails over here. They're 4 or 5 inches long and the darn things crawl right in the blankets with a person. We sleep on the ground now or in foxholes, or I should say mud, and that's the logical place for them. The French people eat them. I got a letter from Don Young tonight. He didn't have much to say only about Wayne getting killed. I also got an awful nice letter from Tom telling me to be very careful. I sure hope he does get home. I'll feel much better and I know Mom will.

Private Ronald Yoder

Sunday, August 6, 1944 was a beautiful partly sunny day in Rush County. The annual Rush County Fair had completed its festivities two days earlier. The crops were growing well. The garden was yielding more green beans and peas than Madge knew what to do with. To help with the canning, Evie and Larry were staying with Madge and Dory. As they did every Sunday, Dory drove to church in Rushville. Madge was the Sunday School Superintendent, so they arrived early and stayed late. It was a bit after twelve noon when Dory finally pulled into the barnyard. Pepper greeted them with the usual tail wagging and doggie bows. Nothing seemed amiss until they approached the back door. Stuck between the door and doorframe was an envelope. Clearly visible were the words Western Union. Evie's heart sank. Madge fought back tears. Dory felt faint. There were three young men in their family who were in the military. They knew of the dreadful stories about the Western Union telegrams. Madge finally mustered the courage to open the envelope.

The *Republican* in its war news section reported the contents of the telegram two days later, "Mrs. Dora Brown received word Sunday from the War Department that her son, Pfc. Ronald C. Yoder, 24, was slightly wounded in action on July 3 in New Guinea. No details were given but the message stated Mrs. Brown would be kept informed of her son's condition. Pfc. Yoder is a paratrooper. He has been overseas 21 months and has taken part in several battle engagements." There was a lag of over one month from the time Evie's brother was injured until the family was notified. More prayers than usual went up that Sunday.

By now, Karl's letters to Evie were few and far between. When she got one, she was aware he could already be injured or dead. Karl seemed to know this. He assured her that he was fine in the next letter he wrote.

8/21/44
I'm sorry I haven't been able to write. If I'm not able to write, remember that I'm always thinking of you both all the time. It's been raining here all day. I hope it clears up tonight though. I don't like sleeping in the rain very much, but if a soldier has to, that's all there is to it. I can tell you of a few towns I've been in now. They are XXXXXXXXX (The first town's name was crossed out by the censor who read this letter), **Pontanbault, Fourgeres, Rennes, and several others, but I can't tell all of them to you now. It shouldn't be long till Paris falls and then we'll go hell bent for Germany. I can't see how Germany is holding out. We'll find the weak link some of these days and they'll give up all at once. All the American soldiers' morale is pretty high, but if we don't get some better food over here, it won't be high for long. They say we're the best fed Army in the world. If we are, I'd hate to see the worst. I'm getting so sick of K-rations I can't see straight, but we're always hoping for better rations the next day.** (K-rations were high caloric but almost tasteless, pre-canned meals for soldiers in battle. The soldiers called them K-Rats.) **Darling, I sure hope and pray Larry starts eating better than he is now. Maybe he will if his teeth would come through. I don't know whether I'll be home for Christmas or not, but it sure would be nice. Surely everything will**

be over by the following year so we can be home. **PS. This ink I'm using is German. It seemed to be better than ours.** (He was giving a hint to Evie that he had been up close and personal with the enemy.)

The Allies liberated Paris from the Germans on August 25, 1944. The anticipation for an end to the war in Europe intensified. The *Republican* quoted a British general who told his troops the Germans faced "definite, complete, and decisive defeat. The war's end is in sight." Even the Selective Service seemed to think victory was near. It talked of a planned "gradual demobilization" when the war ended. It did acknowledge a gradual demobilization would be unpopular "because when the war is over, people will want their boys to immediately come home."

The War Department released new casualty numbers. 64,468 army soldiers had been killed as of August 29, 1944.

8/30/44
It's still raining and it looks like it will continue. I would rather see the sunshine. Are you having pretty weather back there? Mom said it was still plenty hot. We're getting a break tonight so we're going into a town and see a U.S.O. show. I don't know who it will be. Darling, are you and Larry feeling okay? Maybe it won't be so much longer till we three can be together again. I hope so. Take good care of yourselves for me.

8/31/44
I got seven letters late last night. Five were from you. I also got two from you today. I hope mail is getting to you okay. At last, it's quit raining and the sun is shining again. I don't know how long it'll last, but it's welcome as long as it stays. Has the hot weather broke back there yet? Darling, I have often looked up at the moon and stars in the sky and watched them and I knew the same moon and stars were shining down on you. Some of these days we'll be side by side watching them instead of being so far apart. I hope that day isn't far off. I sure wish Tom and I could have opened squirrel season together this year, but maybe we can next year. I don't know whether I would rather hunt squirrels or rabbits because I like both. Yes, I remember when I used to hold Larry in the palms of my hands when he was born. Have the Doctors ever

given you any reason why he doesn't eat? Yes, we can wait till after the war is over before we get a new radio, unless ours goes bad again. If it does, get a new one. Tom and I have thought it over. We've decided the first thing to be done is get our jobs back and then take off on a vacation The first three or four weeks after I get home will probably be harder on me than my whole Army career as I've got lots to catch up on. We'll have plenty of time to decide about our next baby, but beyond a doubt, we'll have one. I'd like for Larry to get a little older before we do. Yes, I remember popping corn the night before I went to the Army. We played some music during the evening. I still play a guitar quite often as a boy in the outfit has one that he got in England. I turned mine back into the special service. Personally, I don't think it will take long to whip the Japs after the Jerries are cleaned up. My worry right now is when are those damn Germans going to give up? The papers say they're getting ready to use gas on us. If they do, it will be the last time they will as we'll kill every damn one of them. Let me know when you get the last $100 and the German equipment I sent. What I'd like to say about West Virginia in this letter would never pass the censor, but I will say most of our outfit is from there. You can draw your own conclusions from that. This is the longest letter I've written in a long time. I can hardly wait till this war is over and we get back home. It'll be a lot better when we can discard all the writing and talk to each other instead. Try not to worry. Everything will be okay.

Karl took a picture of soldiers somewhere in France.

The war created another economic problem. The American civilian labor force was largely made up of women since most of the young men were gone to war. Even with women working, the labor shortage reached critical levels.

The government found a partial solution to the labor shortage. The march across Europe had harvested thousands of German prisoners. The sheer numbers of prisoners overwhelmed the military's capacity to imprison them in Europe so German prisoners were brought to America to help with the labor shortage. The August 31, 1944 *Republican* reported German prisoners were in a POW camp fifteen miles from Rushville. The prisoners were available, accompanied by a guard, for labor. Residents were warned to not fraternize with the prisoners.

September started with hope the war in Europe was about over. The U.S. Army thought it was going to enter Germany soon. Talk started to circulate about being in Berlin by Christmas. The enemy wall of resistance the Allies met was an obsolete collection of easily-cracked concrete pillboxes. The pillboxes were manned by old men and teenage boys.

There was one problem the American brass had not anticipated. After Paris fell, the news reported the Nazis were desperate. Somehow, the Germans continued to put up a vicious fight as they retreated toward the German border. The *Republican* reported the reason to the folks back home. Those old men and boys, plus some war hardened Germans soldiers, were incented to fight. They had been told that one in ten soldiers who ran from the fighting would immediately be executed by firing squad.

The Americans were forty miles from arriving at the western German border by the end of September. The American enthusiasm had been premature. The Nazis still had some fight left in them.

9/8/44
I saw in the paper where my demobilization center will be at Camp Atterbury (Camp Atterbury was in southern Indiana). **If I ever get that close to home, they had better watch me or I'll be long gone. You said you couldn't get the joke in the clipping I sent you.** (He had sent her a picture from the *Stars and Stripes* kneeling by a pile of dirt.) **The caption said, "The kindly group of French people**

solemnly placed fresh cut flowers on the little mound of dirt. They paused for a moment then walked away. They couldn't read the lettering on the pasteboard and wooden cross which said in English, Old Latrine July 8, 1944." Well, a latrine is army language for a toilet. When in the field, we dig a place similar to a trench or grave. When we move on, we cover it with dirt. In this case, there was an old latrine which had been covered up on July 8, 1944. It looked like a grave where someone was buried. That's what the French thought. Catch on? Fried chicken would be awful tempting right now, but I'd probably make myself sick by eating so much. By the way, we had a pretty good supper tonight, mashed potatoes and canned chicken. I won't be so choosy about my eating when I get home like I was before I left. I forgot to tell you, but I got a small box of candy from the factory yesterday. They sent me a deck of cards, but I gave them away as I don't need them. I can picture you sitting in front of the stove in the kitchen writing letters and trying to keep warm. You must be having some early fall weather, but don't worry. Indian summer will come and it'll warm up. The weather here in France reminds me of home a lot. It's chilly over here. At the present, it's raining like hell. Maybe it'll quit soon. I couldn't say how soon I'll be home after the war is over, but there have been some rumors about shifting us boys to the Pacific theatre. As far as I'm concerned, they can keep that war. I've had enough of it all.

9/10/44
I'm sure glad to hear Larry is starting to pull himself up to things. Maybe it won't be long now before he'll be able to stand up alone. Larry will soon be two years old and we'll soon be married three years. I was going to try and send you both something from over here, but haven't had a chance to do it yet. You and your mother must have worked pretty hard if you canned 38 quarts of peaches in one day. About another baby when Larry gets a little older, well, it's a pretty hard question to answer. Of course, I want one, but the tough part is if we'll be able to wait that long or not. A mistake may happen. My heart will always be with you no matter where I may be. I know yours is with me.

Karl was now de-sensitized to the horrors of war.
He started taking pictures of dead German soldiers.

9/24/44
The letter I got from you today was written September 7th. By now I bet you have the heating stove up as it's probably chilly back there at night and in the morning. I got a letter from the factory saying I have a job waiting for me but if I decided to go into some other work besides furniture, they would help me out in any way and help me get accustomed to the work. He also said that promise would always be remembered. Pretty nice of him, don't you think? I got to see a show last night. It was good to see one again after not seeing any for so long. We used to see a lot of them, didn't we? I'm sure glad to know Larry is doing so much better. Maybe before long he'll be taking a few steps. By all means, don't let anyone use the German canteen I sent home. I want to boil it first. I washed it, but I couldn't do a thorough job.

It still looks as though the Jerries may give up before long, but no one knows. Take the very best of care of yourselves for me. I'll do the same for you.

Churchill issued a warning in late September. It was almost like he had read Karl's letter that the enemy was near defeat. Despite the fact the Allies had already lost nearly one million men in Western Europe, Churchill said, "No one, certainly not I, can guarantee that several months of 1945 may not be required to finish off Germany."

The war continued to haunt the folks back home. A picture of a para-trooper landing on his head appeared on the front page of the *Republican*. Two more Rush County boys died. It was three weeks after their deaths before their families were notified. One family received a letter written by their soldier two days before they got notice of his death. He had written letter the day before he was killed.

From Karl's Box Brownie camera. He wrote on the back: Some of our boys trying out a 50 caliber just to see how it is lined up. Isigny, France. June 14th.

Photo from Karl's Box Brownie camera of another 50 caliber gun.

American cemetery, Omaha Beach, Normandy, France
This picture was taken in 2011.

SOMEWHERE IN EUROPE

Dead German soldiers

Chain smoking 1940 presidential candidate, fifty-two year old Wendell Willkie died from a heart attack on October 8, 1944. Rushville was again in the national spotlight. His body was transported to his adopted hometown for burial. His final trip through downtown was nearly the same route he followed when he victoriously arrived in 1940. The funeral procession traveled down Main Street then circled the Courthouse square. His car turned west toward his mother-in-law's house in 1940, but his hearse turned east on Second Street in 1944. It traveled under the quarter mile long canopy of sycamore trees that had saluted Rushville's dead for almost one hundred years. The procession turned into East Hill Cemetery which overlooked Flatrock River. He was laid to rest.

Karl knew censors read every word in his letters. He was careful about what he wrote, but sometimes the censors were caught napping. He had been in France for months. He always started his letters "Somewhere in France." Now he wrote "Somewhere in

Belgium." He even was able to throw in a tantalizing hint to Evie that he had made a few trips into Germany.

10/11/44
Somewhere in Belgium
This is our anniversary and Larry's second birthday. Honey, today is the day when we three should be celebrating together but since it's impossible, I guess a letter will have to do for this time. I've been thinking about you both all day. I've also thought of the many things we did together since we've known each other. Darling, we've had a good time and we'll have a lot more of them when this war is over and everyone gets back home again. The card you sent sure was pretty. I can't tell you how much it means to me. I'll do my best to keep it if possible. I'm sure glad Larry wants to pull up to something all the time. That's the first thing they do when they start to stand up. I'm sure if things keep going the way they are now, he'll be walking before much longer. Yes, a lot of the boys (from Rush County) **are in France now, but I think I was one of the first from home to get here. In the Miscellaneous section of the *Republican*** (This was a military column in the local paper.) **that you sent, I haven't seen but one person that landed before I did. That was Myers and he was killed. He was a glider pilot who landed twenty minutes or so before H-hour.** (H-hour was the hour when the troops started landing on the beaches on D-Day) **I didn't care about getting here that soon. I doubt if I'll drink coffee when I get home. I much more prefer cocoa, but lately we haven't been getting any of that. A good cup of cocoa with marshmallows melted in would sure taste good right now. Boy, it's raining to beat hell right now, and it has been for the past four or five days. I guess winter is finally starting over here for sure. It slows down the drives I take with supplies, but nevertheless, we're still doing our best to whip the Jerries by the end of the year. Germany is whipped right now but they haven't got enough sense to realize it. If I do come back to the states after Germany is whipped, I'll probably get a discharge. I've got some more to add to my points now since I've been awarded the Bronze Star for the invasion. I don't know how much it counts for, but it's that many more steps toward home. I sure hope you enjoyed the anniversary today. Honey, here's hoping I get there by next year.**

The military brass made its next blunder. They hinted that a small number of soldiers might get discharged when they announced they were developing a point system to determine a soldier's discharge eligibility. Length of service, overseas time, combat credit, and number of dependents were likely part of the formula. Nobody knew what else would be a factor. This announcement created more excitement than the brass anticipated so they felt the need to remind everyone of a big variable. Germany had to surrender first before such a point system would even be considered.

That didn't work. Rumors spread faster than an August brush fire in Indiana. The possible point system discussion grew to epic proportions both in Europe and at home. People sought any information they could find. The Courthouse Curbside Court even weighed in on the topic.

To extinguish the rumor mill, the military poured water on the blaze it had created. It reminded Americans that the bulk of America's manpower would go to the Pacific after Germany fell, but that didn't put out the fire. It continued to smolder for the rest of the war. Soldiers kept a tally of their imaginary points. If nothing more, the point system issue made for good foxhole conversations.

10/16/44
I'm still okay and in the best of health. I have a slight cold, but not anything to worry about. Let me know when you get two small boxes from me. I hope you like what's in them. It's the best I could do over here. The pack and canteen I sent were taken off a dead German at Cherbourg. The gun case never has been used. I sent those things because I'll be able to use them on fishing and hunting trips when I get home. I can tell you I was in Paris a few months ago. I'll tell you all about it when I get home. Tell the ones that tease you about French girls that we're in a war over here and have no time for lovemaking. Girls are the least of our worries. People back home don't realize it, but the so called good looking girls over here are the ones who stab the boys in the back when it's turned. I guess it is okay to tell you I've been awarded the Bronze Star medal for military action in the invasion of France. I hope that answers the question you asked a long time ago. At present I've been awarded the E.T.O. (European Theater of Operations) **ribbon, one year good conduct ribbon, a good conduct medal and the Bronze Star medal. Yes, I think a wedding ring**

would get here okay in a letter if you make sure it couldn't tear out.

Karl sent home more pictures of dead German soldiers

10/27/44
I'm back in France. The mail seems to be coming through pretty good again now. I hope mine is getting to you just the same. I'll sure be glad to get one of Larry's pictures so I can see how much he's changed since last year. I imagine Larry could walk if he'd try, but he will in time. I've still got yours and his picture in the leather frame you sent. I carry it next to my heart all the time. It's gone through some pretty tough places with me, but we all got through okay. I'll sure be glad to get the fountain pen you got me. This Limey pen I've got isn't worth a damn. It loses ink all the

time. **Maybe I'll be able to write better when I get the new one. Honey, it would be a lot better if you would go out to the farm. I'm pretty sure I won't be home this winter as I expect the war with Germany to last through the winter now. PS. I'm sending you the copy from General Eisenhower I got the day before the invasion.** (A letter from General Eisenhower was given on June 5 to every soldier who participated in the invasion. Eisenhower praised their efforts and wished them the best.) **The other paper is one of the leaflets the Air Corp dropped on Cherbourg so the Germans could surrender without being shot or anything. The Germans were scared to come out and surrender on account they were afraid we'd shoot them, so we had these copies printed. It proved very successful.**

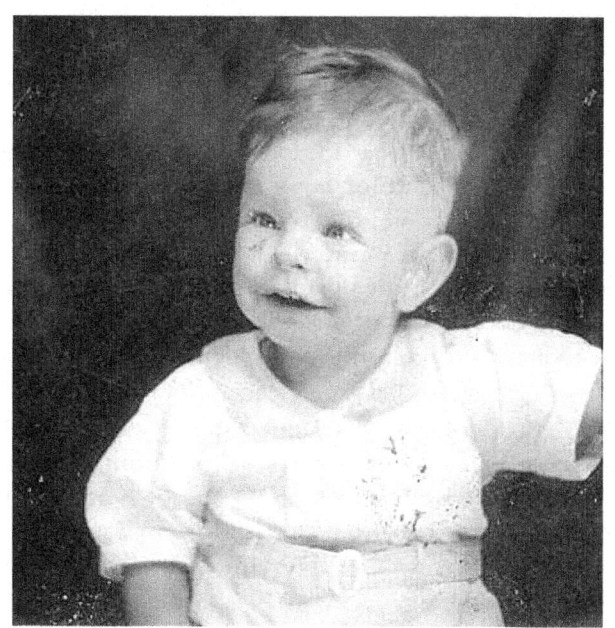

Evie kept sending happy pictures of Larry

The military's appetite for supplies, equipment, and troop transportation was ravenous. Over 560,000 motor vehicles and 23,000 planes went to European and Pacific war fronts in 1944. 93,072 injured soldiers returned from Europe to ports in the eastern United States that year. Thousands of "green as hell" replacement troops arrived in Europe to fill in the gaps. Families also contributed. The folks back home sent 2.6 million Christmas cards and packages to the troops in Europe.

The guys doing the dirty work were always last in line. Shipment of mail from the troops to their loved ones was not a priority. (Remember, War rule number one.) Karl was a crusty and experienced veteran by now. He knew the mail service was slow and unpredictable, so he sent his Christmas cards to Evie and Larry on Halloween.

10/31/44
I'm still anxious to see you go hunting with me and shoot at squirrels. I wouldn't doubt if you don't kill as many as I do, if not more. Today is Halloween. Boy, what times us kids used to have on that night. Remember when I took you and all the other kids riding on Halloween night? It doesn't seem like it's been four years ago. Time sure does fly, but over here a person hardly notices it much. Honey, tomorrow is when you take Larry back to the hospital. I sure hope the doctors find him much better. I also hope it's a lot better weather back there than what we're having over here. It's rainy and cold out. The dampness goes right through all the clothes a person can put on. I'm sending a box which contains a lot of stuff that isn't worth much, but I've kept it with me a long time. It contains my civilian eyeglasses with one of the lens broken and also my old address book. (The eyeglasses, address book, and several jagged pieces of shrapnel were in the bread box with the letters.) **I bought a small notebook in England and I keep addresses in that now. Has Mom heard from Tom recently? I'd sure like him and Ronald to get home for Christmas, but it's very doubtful. It looks like this war is going to last on through the winter, but it can't be helped. I sure hope that it ends some of these days.**

He wrote in his Christmas cards.

Dear Larry, Although your dad is far away, be sure and keep in mind his heart is with you and he's always looking out for the best for you. Tomorrow is November 1, 1944 and your mother is taking you back to the hospital. The best Christmas present your father could get would be for the doctors to say you're well. Here's wishing Santa Claus don't forget you and I don't think he will. Dad

My Dearest Darling, Another Christmas time is upon us and it still finds us far apart, but remember my heart is right there with you. It sure would be nice if we could be together for this Christmas, but someone has to do the suffering. We're just one family out of millions that has been chosen. Let's hope and pray that next year we'll all be together again. Karl

Smoking two packs of cigarettes a day, President Franklin D. Roosevelt appeared much older than his age. That didn't stop him or the voters. He won a fourth presidential term on November 7, 1944. Rushville's voters were still angry about Willkie's spanking four years earlier. They voted for Roosevelt's opponent. The *Republican* wasted little ink on Roosevelt's landmark victory. Its front page headline only said, "Voters Here Give Support to Dewey, Losing Candidate."

The strain and fatigue of battle was wearing Karl down. Neither dates nor the day of the week mattered much to him anymore. His next letter startled Evie. He didn't even know the date.

I think its November 7, 1944.
I'm still okay and in the best of health. I'm Corporal of the guard right now and it's raining pitchforks and handles. It's rugged but I can take it. Honey, it's best you start your Christmas shopping early. Most of the things will probably sell out early this year as most everyone is making good money. My heart bleeds for the old drake of mine for his life coming to such a sad end. (The drake was Karl's duck that he won at the Rush County Fair in 1940. Its name was Buck Rogers) **I feel sorry for the sows that ate him. He must have been plenty tough. Anyway, I'll raise another one when I get home. I suppose I should tell you I lost a bet on the Notre Dame and Navy football game. I bet 1,000 Francs, or $20.00, that Notre Dame would beat Navy and they didn't come anyways near it.**
I won't do that again. Honey, if you're counting on me being home before the winter is over, I think you had better change your mind. It looks like the war will last up into the spring anyway. No one really knows but the way things are going now, it will be a long drawn out affair.

11/23/44

Well, darling, it is Thanksgiving Day again and it finds us far apart. Remember, I'm thinking of you continually. We certainly had a good dinner today, turkey, mashed potatoes, dressing, gravy, cranberry sauce, and several other things I can't recall. It was good, but nothing compared to those good dinners we have at home. I and some of the boys attended Church today and it was a very good sermon. I'll keep my promise to you about going to Church again when I get home. I wish the pen you sent would get here. Cigarettes are really scarce over here. If you can buy some, I wish you'd send me some. If they're hard for you to get, don't send them. I've just got a carton left and don't know when we'll get any more. I've got a couple cans of tobacco left so I'll manage to get by somehow, even if I have to roll my own cigarettes. Good things are pretty hard to find over here, only perfume and I've sent you some of that. I didn't vote in the election. We really don't know what's going on back home. All the news we get from home through magazines and papers are heavily censored so I don't even know who was running for any office, only the President and Vice President. I'm glad Roosevelt was elected. I don't believe in changing horses in the middle of a stream. I'm sending another small package for Larry today. It contains a pair of little wooden shoes like the people wear over here where I'm at. Those shoes are about the only thing I could think of to get him. Here's wishing you had a very happy Thanksgiving. Maybe next year we can all celebrate it together once again. Here's hoping Tom was home to celebrate Thanksgiving with you and the folks.

11/28/44

Somewhere in Europe

I'm still okay and in the best of health. I'm a happy boy tonight. I got twenty letters today and that really is a lot of reading material. I still haven't gotten any packages from you, but there will probably be more mail tomorrow. I got the picture you sent of Larry and I'm rather disappointed in it. It seems like his eyes are crossed. It may be the way he was watching the camera. I wouldn't take anything for him. Of course, it will be okay if you buy Larry a new walker so you can take him places with you. I can picture how pretty it is back there when the leaves are changing colors. Maybe if everything goes okay, by next year I'll be there to see it. Of course, honey, I'll go to basketball games when I get home again. I always go in for any kind of sports. I'll also be glad to get those packages you sent me. I don't know what the special thing could be unless it's a ring? I can't imagine why Dory's son called up his wife and told her not to come see him, unless he was moving out. Hope he doesn't have to come over here right now. It's pretty rugged. If he comes over here, it would be best for him to be in the Army of Occupation. (After a war is over, the winning side maintains troops in the conquered country called the Army of Occupation.) **Today ended the clear weather we have had for the past three days. It's been raining pitchforks and handles again all day long. I'm sure glad I'm inside for now, but I don't know for how long. I hope for the duration. It would be nice if we could be together for Christmas, but I think it's impossible. It's really hard to say when we'll all be home again. Let's all hope and pray it isn't far off. Don't worry about me as I'll be alright.**

December started badly for Rushville. Two more local soldiers were reported to have been injured. Pictures of dead Belgian civilians (where Evie thought Karl was located) were printed on the front page of the *Republican*.

12/2/44
Somewhere in Europe
I'm still okay. It makes no difference where I may be, remember my heart is always there at home with you and Larry. I know I have yours with me. I sure hope you're hearing from me oftener than you were as I know how you worry. It won't be much longer till Santa Claus will be visiting you all back home. I know this Christmas won't be very happy for you, but darling, try and forget that I'm so far away. How I wish I could be there with you and Larry so I could make you happier. I want you and Larry to have the best Christmas you can. Don't mind the cost. Try and think I'm there with you. Although my body isn't, my heart and soul will be. It won't be much longer either till you'll be 21 years old. You'll be a big girl then, won't you? I'll soon be 25, but right now I feel like I'm 50. If this war doesn't end soon Larry won't know what a father is, will he? It seems so awful to be so far from you and him, but someone has to take the brunt of it all and be over here. Surely we'll be together by next year, but no one knows. All I really care about now is getting this war over with.

12/12/44

I got five letters from you and one from Mom today written on the 12th of November, so you see the mail is moving at a snail's pace. About the German pistol Dad asked about. I would also like to have one, but it's strictly against Army Regulations to send one home. Let me tell you, I could get several but would take a big chance in keeping them. Maybe I can when the war ends. If so, I'll send one home. They're really not much good though because they use a different size bullet than we have. I sure would have liked to have been there for rabbit season, but no luck. I saw in tonight's paper where the brass is predicting that it could take us until 1949 to beat the Japs. If they would just turn us GI's loose, it wouldn't take that long. It seems like they don't want this war to end very soon. Surely next Christmas the war will be over, but it's beginning to look like this is a 100 year war.

12/14/44

I'm still in the best of health. I hope and pray these few lines find you the same. Honey, I'm so happy tonight. I got the package which you sent the ring and pen in. The ring is really beautiful. It fits me perfectly. I almost cried when I put it on. I'm writing this letter with the pen and it writes swell. It's the best one I ever owned. I wouldn't take anything for either of them. Darling, your Christmas card in the package sure was nice and very pretty. Thanks a million for everything. I had my picture taken again. I've got five small ones and one large one being made. I should get them December 28th and I'll send them to you as soon as possible. This time I left my cap off so they may look awful. Does Larry still say "daddy" or does he say "pappy"? I'll be glad when he starts walking. Bless his little heart. I hope and pray he's on the road to recovery now. If you can, darling, how about sending me a dozen handkerchiefs. I'm getting pretty short on them. I'll be glad to get home so I can repay everyone for the things they're doing for me. I'd sure like to know if Tom is home yet. I hope he's there for Christmas. The talk is still pretty strong about a lot of the boys from Europe being switched over to China or the Pacific. I wouldn't mind it so much if I could just get home for a furlough. Maybe my chance will come some of these days. Let's hope and pray we'll be together next year.

The news was encouraging. The Allies in Europe were at the German border. Some American soldiers had penetrated into Germany and met minimal resistance. News from the Pacific was also good. American forces had reoccupied the Philippines. The United States Navy was sinking Japanese ships "almost at will."

Allied Supreme Command felt the Nazis were as good as done. Even Eisenhower let his guard down. In a bit of enthusiasm he later regretted, he made a bet with British General Montgomery in early December. Eisenhower wagered five pounds the European war would be over by Christmas.

Allied Supreme Command had let the cart get before the horse. The officers at the front with more level heads worried that Hitler wasn't close to being defeated.

The grunts on the ground were about to pay a terrible price for the Allied military leaders' premature and reckless over confidence.

Another photo from Karl's camera

THE BULGE

A cocky attitude breeds careless mistakes. So does an inadequate and poorly managed supply line. Allied Supreme Headquarters was sleeping at the wheel. They were happy and festive. Eisenhower and his staff scheduled a holiday party for the evening of December 16, 1944. They ignored field officers at the Belgian front who told them there were not enough soldiers manning the front line in the Ardennes forest. The sad, stupid part was Eisenhower had replacement soldiers at his disposal that could have bolstered the troops on the front. He chose to hold the replacements in reserve for use in an "Army of Occupation" once the war was over.

Eisenhower was also getting inaccurate reconnaissance reports which downplayed reports of possible German movement. American POW guards told of German prisoners of war talking of a big build up in the Ardennes. Eisenhower chose not to believe them.

Sloppy management had bogged down all American supply routes throughout Belgium. Not enough was done to control the traffic on the main supply route. Troop movement and supply convoys traveled the same pot holed, snow covered roads. The troops needed food, ammunition, and winter clothing, but supply trucks could not get to them. To make things worse, the weather provided the icing on the cake. Weather forecasters predicted a very cold winter.

Hitler had other plans for the Allies on that cold winter day. He was not about to surrender without a fight. He had planned a top secret attack to isolate the Allied armies from each other. His ultimate goal was to recapture the seaport city of Antwerp, Belgium.

His plan almost worked. The Nazis attacked the sparsely protected Belgian Ardennes forest. The massive offensive started at 5:30 am on December 16 when 1,600 Nazi artillery pieces commenced a ninety minute bombing barrage of the American front line. A savage tank and infantry attack followed. The under supplied, outnumbered American troops were up the creek without a paddle. German armor and soldiers encountered widespread confusion and feeble American resistance. The American front line crumbled in short order. Panic stricken American soldiers hastily retreated and ran for their lives.

Hitler's plan caught the Allied leaders with their pants down. The surprise attack succeeded. It opened a bulge for the Nazis to rush through. The Nazis were on the move toward Antwerp. Field officers scrambled to stop the Nazi thrust. It was too late. The cat was out of the bag.

American military leaders were not only warriors. They were acutely aware of the politics and psychology of the war. Several had post-war political aspirations. Caught with egg on their faces, they tried to hide their mistakes from the folks back home. Allied Supreme Headquarters attempted to impose a strict blackout regarding information of the extent of the Nazis advance.

Their effort to hide the facts didn't work. The self-serving policy ultimately increased anxieties back home. News soon trickled out that something bad was happening in Belgium. The *Republican* announced the battle on December 18.

- The Nazis had launched a counterattack and had penetrated twenty miles into Belgium.
- Unconfirmed reports said the Germans were using a Vengeance weapon. (more buzz bombs)
- Belgium citizens were alarmed by the German advance.
- Reporters described American soldiers riding toward the battle with grim and serious faces.

- There were large numbers of American casualties.

German forces penetrated thirty-five miles into Belgium by December 21. Allied Supreme Headquarters tried to settle the folks back home with a bit of good news. It announced the American First Army had stopped the Germans "cold." That was a barefaced lie! The truth was the Germans had broken through American lines. American soldiers were being massacred.

More bad reports from Belgium were in the *Republican*.
- Some soldiers snatched kisses from Belgium girlfriends before their unit pulls out.
- Tanks and truck roared toward the front with their red lights flashing.
- Destroyed vehicles cluttered the roads.
- There was deafening noise everywhere leading up to the fighting zone.
- Soldiers coming back from the front had blank, dazed looks on their faces.
- Reporters wrote that to mention being home by Christmas now brought only tired smiles to solder's faces.

Belgium was once again a major battle front. The reckless talk about the war ending in the near future ceased.

Evie was a few weeks from turning twenty-one when the Bulge started. Scared and panic stricken, she re-read Karl's letters. WHERE WAS HE? He hinted months ago he was no longer in France. A pair of wooden shoes he had sent home suggested he was in Holland, not Belgium. Why wasn't he writing? She prayed, "Please God, don't let him be in Belgium."

A few weeks into January, 1945, she finally received a letter that Karl wrote on Christmas day. His hints suggested he had participated in the Battle of the Bulge.

12/25/44
Just a few lines to let you know I love you both. I haven't had time to write you for the last several days, so I'll try and make up for it in this one. I just had to write to you today. I'm thinking of you every minute and will continue to do so forever and ever. I'm feeling fine and I sure hope and pray these lines find you and Larry

feeling fine. I hope you all had a very happy Christmas. Ours wasn't so happy over here. Have you been reading in the papers what is taking place? It may be Germany's last stand and everything seems to me to be pretty well in hand now. I sure hope so. It had been snowing a lot over here, but now it's clear and really cold. Remember the gloves you got me one Christmas and how I raised hell about them? I'm so cold I think I'd even wear them now if I could. I'm sorta worried about Cuttie. I think he was in the place where the Germans broke through. I hope not. I think Joe Goodson was in there too and I haven't heard from Red Spoon for a long time. Maybe he got lost over here somewhere. In one more week, you'll be 21 years old. I'd sure love to be there to give you 21 big smacks on the place where it stings. Maybe I'll be able to give you 22 next year. I'm sorry to hear Dory's son is going overseas. My heart bleeds for him. He'll be alright if he's careful. I sure hope Tom made it home for today. He was really looking forward to it. (Tom did make it home for Christmas. He enjoyed a three week furlough in Rushville. On January 9, 1945 he left for an Army base in Miami, Florida.) **I'd better close, darling. I'm writing this in a few spare moments. Remember, I love you both with all my heart. My heart has been with you and Larry more than ever today. Merry Christmas and Happy New Year to both of you.**

The *Republican* printed a picture from a captured German camera on December 26. It showed large numbers of American soldiers in German prison camps. Reports had leaked from Belgium of large number of American casualties. The military admitted that the Nazis penetrated fifty miles into Belgium. The *Republican* finally reported good news on December 30. The Germans had made no gains for three days.

American reinforcements finally arrived at the front to bolster the American front lines. The Americans stopped the German progress. Now the goal was to move them back to Germany.

January of 1945 arrived in Belgium with a burst of record setting cold weather. It was so cold that rifles and artillery froze. Oil in military vehicles turned to jelly. Many GIs' fingers, toes, and ears suffered frostbite. The ground was frozen. Digging a foxhole was next to impossible. After the war, Karl liked to say that he learned one lesson during the Bulge. A soldier discovered he could dig through frozen ground if bullets were flying and bombs were exploding.

Karl found time to write letters when he had a few minutes to himself. After the battle had ended, Evie started receiving the first letters Karl wrote in early January. His letters confirmed her fears. Karl had participated in the Battle of the Bulge.

1/1/45
Belgium
Darling, it's been so long since I've heard from you that it worries me. I haven't been able to write you since Christmas day and I've still haven't got to mail that letter. I hope you understand and forgive me. Darling, did you and Larry have a good Christmas and New Year? Mine was all ruined. There was so much activity I couldn't enjoy it much, but I was thinking of you and Larry every moment. Is Larry walking yet? Maybe our prayers will help him a lot. It's okay to tell you I'm in Belgium now so you can probably guess where I have been. It's been pretty rugged around here for the last few days but everything seems to be going in our favor now. It's pretty cold now and the ground is really frozen hard. It's a lot better than all the mud we had early in the winter, but wait till it starts thawing. You should have seen what just happened! A Jerry plane just came over and I think our guns hit him all over. The plane was spitting flames to beat heck all the way down. That makes several I've seen go down today. Hitler seems to be losing everything he sends up. Maybe he'll give up someday. Please excuse this writing. I'm in a very unhandy position to write.

1/2/45
I still haven't received any mail. Maybe it'll get here someday. I'm still fine and in the best of health. It's pretty rugged now but that can be expected. It was pretty damn cold today and snowed some more. Later it got so foggy a person couldn't see much of anything. The cigarette situation is getting worse over here instead of better. I've only got 1/2 can of tobacco to last me till the next ration and its hard telling when that will be. If you can, buy and send me some cigarettes or even some tobacco. Honey, has Tom got home yet? I sure wish I could be there with you, but maybe I can next year. Keep your chin up high and try not to worry.

1/16/45

Some mail came in today, but none was for me. I'm feeling fine now. For a while, I could hardly breathe because the cold in my chest was so tight and I couldn't cough it up. It warmed up quite a bit today, but not enough to melt the ice and snow. I'll sure be glad when spring comes, then maybe we can get this war over with in a hurry. It'll sure be a great day when that time comes. Darling, I was 20 years old when you and I started going together. Boy we sure had swell times then, didn't we? Those swell times will be back again someday and we'll be just as young as ever.
PS. A Jerry just flew over, but he didn't stay long.

1/18/45

No mail again today, but I haven't given up hope yet. I'm feeling good now. I've been using the Watson's foot powder a lot and it sure helps. It seems to help my feet from sweating so much. There is so much trench foot over here and it pays to be careful. Honey, remember how I'd get in the bathtub and you'd have to wait on me to get ready to go somewhere? That's the only time I ever heard tell of a woman waiting on a man. Boy, I'd love to get in that old bathtub right now and soak for about eight hours. If the Russians keep moving along like they are now, this war will be over before long. We're not doing so bad ourselves. I'm sending you a letter of commendation each of us received for service we did on December 24 and 25, so you can imagine how we spent our Christmas, but it's all about over now.

Hitler's last offensive Hail Mary ended in defeat. American forces pushed the Nazi bulge backward to where the attack started. The Battle of the Bulge was over. It ended on January 25, 1945. It had lasted six weeks.

A grateful Churchill addressed the British House of Commons after the battle. In part, he said, "This is undoubtedly the greatest American battle of the war and will, I believe, be regarded as an ever famous American victory."

The cost of victory during the Battle of the Bulge was devastating for the Americans. 10,419 soldiers died. 43,554 were wounded. 20,815 soldiers were listed as missing. December, 1944 became the worst month for American casualties since the Normandy invasion.

THE FINAL PUSH TO BERLIN

Karl took a picture of guarded German POWs.
He wrote on the back of this picture: "A group of those
so called Super Men. What do you think of them?
They don't look so super human to me, do they to you?
Those boys wouldn't hesitate a minute
to stab one of us in the back."

The Battle of the Bulge victory excited Americans. An Allied victory in Europe seemed inevitable. Soldiers kept tallying their points. The folks back home allowed themselves to dream that their boys might be coming home soon. To dampen such enthusiasm, the government felt compelled to remind soldiers and citizens there was still a war in the Pacific that had to be won.

The *Republican* reported the military's plan for troop movement after the European war was over. The plan would move up a Japanese mainland invasion by three months. Some of the plan's benchmarks were:

- Most of the war tested troops in Europe would be moved to the Pacific once the European war was over.
- Equipment and weapons in Europe would stay in Europe.
- Soldiers would be re-armed when they arrived in the Pacific.
- Most soldiers would go east through Asia, not west through America.

American families couldn't believe what they read. Talk about letting the air out of a balloon.

After the Bulge, Karl's 983rd Ordnance Depot Company moved its headquarters from Rennes, France to Brussels, Belgium. Brussels was much more comfortable for the brass, but not so much for the grunts doing the work. There were no barracks to house the troops. Pup tents in a mud pit of a field were the only protection the hardened soldiers had from the winter cold. The food supply chain seemed to bypass Brussels so "K" rations were all the soldiers had to eat. The citizens of Brussels saved the day. They offered American soldiers food and spare bedrooms to use. They felt it was the least they could do for the troops who had liberated them from the Nazi terrors.

Karl and a buddy spent some comfortable nights with a Belgium family. He did not mention this in his letters to Evie.

1/27/45
No mail again today, but I haven't given up hope yet. It'll all get here someday, or at least I hope it does. If it wasn't for letters, our morale would drop down to nothing. I don't know how I'd get along sometimes if it wasn't for you and Larry back home and knowing someday we'll be together again. I'm feeling pretty good now. My cold is lots better. Boy, I'm really getting my share of colds this winter. Honey, I can tell you now that I broke my toe in Sudbury, England before the invasion, close to Darby. I dropped a little wagon and the corner of the wagon struck the toe next to the big one and broke it. I didn't know it was broken till the next day. It really got sore. My forefinger on my right hand has got a scar on it from where I cut it so badly. I think I told you about that. It happened when Floyd Rowlett and I were lifting a Jeep motor off the tailgate of a van. The goddam thing slipped and caught my finger between it and a hand truck. It very nearly tore my finger off! It's okay now, except a nerve which isn't healed over right and

it hurts when I touch it. Honey, I'm aiming to send some money home this month but I don't know how much yet. I loaned some out to a guy in my unit, so that's why I didn't send any. I also paid the 1000 francs I owe a guy on the Notre Dame and Navy football game and I paid half on a mandolin me and another boy bought. I saw in tonight's paper where it's really cold back home. We're having a little warmer weather now, or at least we did today. I don't know how long it will last though. Does Larry still call my picture 'pappy'? If he does, it's perfectly okay with me as anything he does is alright. The Russians are right close to Berlin now. I'm anxious to find out what happens when they get there. Surely the Germans will give up then. They should know there isn't any hope and many more people will be killed if they continue.

Hitler's only option after the Bulge was to prolong the fighting. The longer the Allied march to Berlin lasted, the greater the chance he had to have a new weapon at his disposal. His scientists had been working on such a weapon. They called it a dirty nuclear device. There was one problem. The scientists needed time to make the device into a bomb to use against the Allies. The question was how much destruction of his country Hitler would allow. All he had left between him and defeat were land, soldiers and civilians. He did not hesitate to sacrifice any of them.

2/5/45
I'm feeling just fine yet. Honey, in the last three days, I've got sixty-one letters and cards. I have read them over twice. I finally got a letter from Tom. I also got a very mean letter from my brother. You know which one. He really blew up at me for some reason. When I was younger, I remember him doing the same thing to me and he always dared me to say anything to Mom or Dad. Well, I'm big enough now to take that dare. I sent some of the pictures from England home to you, but I got several of them back because I wasn't supposed to send such ones. I don't know why. Other boys have sent the same ones. Well honey, in a few more days I'll be 25 years old. Right now, I feel 75 but once I get back to the states I'll sure feel younger than 25. It's getting so I almost forget what the states are like. In a couple weeks, I'll have 18 months overseas and I still can't see me home in the near future. I may pass Tom and Ronald's record of 33 months, but I hope not. I sure don't know what Hitler wanted with any of these

countries. Over here, a person can't buy anything and it seems impossible because we know Americans have about everything. A person doesn't realize how lucky we are to have a place like the states to live in instead of a beat up country like this. Germany itself was pretty well off before the war and was up to date, but that was before the war. It certainly has changed now. PS. Hitler surely hasn't run out of buzz bombs yet. They're still coming.

Buzz bombs, or doodlebugs, were primitive missiles used by the Germans starting in June, 1944. The Nazis called them Vengeance Weapons. A missile was twenty-seven feet long and carried a 1,870 pound warhead. The engine was so noisy that it could be heard for great distances. Missiles were initially launched from the European continent towards Britain from mobile truck launchers. They were not aimed at a specific target, but just in a certain direction. They had enough fuel to get over the English Channel and hopefully enough to get to London, but that was not always the case. It really did not matter. When out of fuel, wherever it was, the missile fell to the ground. Its warhead exploded when it hit the ground. Now the Nazis were using buzz bombs on the continent. Citizens and soldiers learned to listen to the sound of the engine. If it stopped, they sought the nearest shelter and waited for the explosion.

Those missiles would have been used to drop the dirty nuclear devices. The last buzz bomb was launched on March 29, 1945.

2/7/45
I didn't get any letters today. If you get some letters with the date way behind time, don't pay any attention to it. I've almost lost track of the days. Last night I found myself putting the month of January down instead of February. I'm still feeling fine, except the cold in my chest isn't gone yet. Has Larry been putting anything else down the commode? I still don't think I could ever spank him for anything, but I may change my mind. It's warmed up a lot over here in the last few days and I certainly hope it continues. I saw some civilians over here trimming trees so it must be going to get warmer, or they may have been nuts. You ask me what No Compree meant. It's French. It means I don't understand. When I get home, I'll say No Compree whenever you ask me anything.

The noose was tightening around the Nazi neck, but the killing was not over. From 1939 to June, 1944, the Nazi soldiers had been on the offensive as they devoured countries. After D-Day, they defended territory they had conquered, but the Allied movement into Germany changed everything. German soldiers were now were defending their motherland. They fought ferociously as they retreated toward Berlin. The War Department reminded Americans, "We must still fight the battle for inner Germany. There have been other periods when the enemy has reorganized and found a new line on which to fight."

Allied progress slowed to a crawl. The fighting was now house to house, street to street, and town to town. The *Republican* reported the Allies were throwing everything into the assault but horse cavalry in a bid for a quick ending of the war. A confident Winston Churchill predicted in March, 1945 that the decisive Allied victory in Europe was near.

Karl's letters also displayed enthusiasm. He allowed himself to bring good memories out of storage.

3/19/45
Monday. It's a beautiful spring day. I'm still in the best of health and feeling fine. Honey, I had a wonderful dream last night and, boy, how I wished it was real. You, Larry, and I were all home together and we sure had fun. It's been such a long time since I've seen the old homestead. Darling, it must be getting near the spring of the year back home. I'll be glad when you, Larry, and I can take off and go fishing, hunting, and swimming together. He should be walking a little by himself now, isn't he? Have you ever sent those pictures you and I had taken at home before I left? If I remember right, those pictures were really good. I would love to see what we looked like in civilian life. I guess it gets pretty warm over here in the summer time so there's something I wish you'd do, darling. Send me a military sun-tan shirt. I think you'll be able to get one at one of the men shops downtown. The Army doesn't issue us any over here and these wool shirts get pretty hot. Be sure and get a good one. It'll probably cost around $4.00 or $4.50. My size is 14 ½" neck by 33" sleeve. This war surely can't last much longer. We're doing everything we can do to finish it, but the Germans hang on. It looks to me like the Germans should have a revolution and that would surely end the war. Boy, I wish you could see what's going on above my head right now. It sure is a

good sight to see. Our Air Force is hitting the Jerries with everything but the kitchen sink.

In his next letter, Karl either did not know where he was or could not say.

3/22/45
Somewhere
I sure love you a lot. I'm still feeling okay and in the best of health. It's really been pretty out today again. If this weather keeps on Germany will sure keep paying for everything as she's taking a beating right now. Maybe it'll pound the war out of their people's heads. Honey, I was thinking. Remember on the warm nights we'd go out for a long ride? This reminds me of the nights when you and I would take those nice rides in the country, but it's still a lot different. Right now the moon is about 2/3rds full and it's really shining. Perhaps you are looking at the same moon tonight. 18 months is a long time to be separated from you and the states, but it will be a lot longer before we get back. I hope not, but it looks like the long way home for most of us. If we do have to go to the Pacific, I wish at least I could have a 30 day furlough at home. Then it wouldn't be so bad, but maybe it would be harder to leave again after knowing what home is. Darling, is Larry taking any steps by himself yet?

American casualties from all fronts by late March, 1945 were 150,310 Americans killed, 464,732 wounded, and 88,209 missing. 64,430 American soldiers were listed as prisoners of war.

4/2/45
I'm still feeling fine and in the best of health. I got several letters today, and I got the two pictures you sent of us on the morning I left for the Army two years ago. I really think they were pretty good. When I get that new suntan shirt I sent for, I'll have my picture taken again.

The first few weeks of April, 1945 were crucial for the Allies. Nazi resistance in the German countryside had nearly collapsed. The new, and last, front was the outskirts of Berlin.

The American journey through the occupied countries and Germany took a nauseating turn on April 11, 1945. The first of several concentration camps was discovered by Allied soldiers. Human beings had been subjected to unimaginable horrors in the camps. The Nazi goal was to eliminate entire populations of people from the face of the earth. They had imprisoned, starved, tortured and executed millions of Jews, gypsies, and other "undesirables". The numbers were unbelievable. One camp in Poland, by itself, had killed and incinerated 1,200,000 men, women, and children. 800,000 of the victims were Jews. A reporter who saw the carnage wrote that the site was so horrible as to be almost unbelievable. Apparently no one other than the Nazis knew the camps existed.

Another momentous event happened that month.

The war was progressing well for America. Roosevelt wanted to see it to its conclusion, so he had run for a fourth term in 1944. His health was a time bomb waiting to go off. The public was not told during the campaign that he had high blood pressure, hardening of the arteries, and heart disease. Despite Roosevelt's worrisome health issues, the Democrats chose to select an inexperienced, unknown senator from Missouri, Harry Truman, to be the President's running mate. Roosevelt and Truman won the election. They were sworn into office on January 20, 1945.

Once he was Vice President, Truman was ignored by Roosevelt and his inner circle. He spent his eleven weeks as Vice President dithering in the background. He did not receive war briefings. He was not included in war strategy or political meetings. He was not briefed on secret weapon development. He was such a minor figure that many Americans did not know his name. Needless to say, Truman was not adequately prepared to step into the role of Commander in Chief of the American military.

America learned more of the cost of the huge burdens the war required of the President. On the morning of April 12, 1945, sixty-three year old President Franklin D. Roosevelt suffered a massive stroke. He died later that day. As directed by the Constitution, Vice President Harry S. Truman was sworn in as President. Prepared or not, Truman found himself as the President of the United States of America.

Despite the country's shock, there was a war going on. There was no time to grieve the man who had guided America through the Great Depression and World War Two. Roosevelt did not get a lavish ceremonial farewell. American flags were not flown at half-staff in his honor until the European war was over. His body did not lie in state. His last rites were "majestic in their simplicity." His burial was three days after his death. He had been President of the United States for over twelve years.

A newspaper reporter watched the new President at Roosevelt's burial. He wrote of what he observed, "President Truman stood with dim eyes and lowered head. There was a hush. Then, in a moment of supreme grief, he squared his shoulders as if to assume completely and finally the enormous burden left by the death of Mr. Roosevelt."

One of Truman's first tasks was to convince America he was up to the task of leading the country. The day after Roosevelt's funeral, he promised the war would remain "unchanged and unhampered" by his accession to the presidency. Using the firm and determined voice the country needed to hear, he vowed America would join in punishing those guilty for the war with these words, "Lasting peace can never be secured if we permit our dangerous opponents to plot future wars with impunity at any mountain retreat, however distant. Tragic fate has thrust upon us grave responsibilities. We must carry on. Our devoted leader never looked backward. He looked forward and moved forward. That is what he would want us to do. That is what America will do."

President Truman succeeded. He had convinced America he could lead. The public's resolve to win the war hardly skipped a beat.

Truman received a crash course in both the European and Pacific conflicts. The military advised him of the horrendous price if American forces invaded Japan. The prediction was upwards of one million American casualties. This was over the one million casualties the United States had suffered so far.

Truman was informed that he might have another option available. The military briefed him about a very top secret weapon he had not been aware of when he was the Vice-President. Early in the war, Roosevelt had approved what was called the Manhattan Project. The Manhattan Project's scientists had been working a new weapon since 1942. The weapon was an implosion-type nuclear bomb. It was given the name Atomic Bomb. Its destructive power might prevent another costly invasion. The new President was told the weapon was developed to the point that a test of it could be possible by mid-summer 1945.

Good news from Europe continued. Berlin was completely surrounded. The press couldn't contain its excitement on April 27, "A symbolic historic junction occurred which guaranteed the defeat of the Nazis." American forces and the Russian army met at the outskirts of Berlin on the banks of the Elbe River. The news story continued, "The whole day was almost too fantastic to believe. Never before have our American troops looked on scenes which showed so clearly Germany's defeat. The darkness faced by the German people accentuated the joyful meeting of Allied troops. Berlin's inner defense core appeared cracking today under a massive Soviet squeeze operation."

On Monday, April 30, 1945 the *Republican's* headline read:

Complete German Collapse May Come At Any Moment

The *Republican* reported on Saturday, May 5 that Rushville would enjoy warmer fair weather that evening. It was a perfect night for the Courthouse Curbside Court re-convene. There was much to debate. The day's headline was **It is Senseless To Fight On**. All members of the court put a quarter in the pot. Whichever member picked the correct date of Germany's surrender would win the kitty.

There was more news for the court to debate. The point system was about to become public. The *Republican* printed an article that read, "The army plans to discharge 2,000,000 men beginning with the fall of Germany. It will send 6,000,000 picked troops against Japan. The discharged men will be those with the most dependents, the longest service, and most active service record. The weight given each of the factors in determining priority discharges has been a closely guarded secret."

Most members of the Courthouse Curbside Court had a relative in the service. They debated who would get discharged and who wouldn't. It was an intense and spirited discussion, to say the least.

VICTORY IN EUROPE

Victory so close you could taste it. The Nazis were now an afterthought. Politics prevented a swifter end to the European hostilities. The spoils of the inevitable victory were huge. Land, natural resources, and laborers were up for grabs.

The English, American, and Russian alliance was awkward from the beginning. It was formed to fight the Nazi threat. The unlikely coalition was doomed from the beginning and the fragile Allied partnership was now falling apart. Each country wanted something that the other members also wanted. The result was the soon to be former Allies raced each other to occupy Berlin.

The Russians arrived first from the east. From Berlin's outskirts, they foraged and bombed Berlin before forging ahead to the center of the city. In the meantime, American and British field commanders waited for orders to advance into Berlin. They could not enter the city from the west until their politicians and generals quit bickering.

Hitler was trapped like a rat in a bunker in central Berlin. He used the Allies' disarray for one more win. It was a big victory for him. He denied the victors the pleasure of capturing him. He and his mistress committed suicide on April 30, 1945. Loyal Nazis burned their bodies beyond recognition.

Karl kept telling Evie what he was up to in Europe.

5/2/45
Darling, in a few days it will be Mother's Day. I'm so sorry I won't be able to be there. I'm in the best of health. I sure don't like this European weather. We're still having really bad weather over here. Every day we have sunshine, rain, snow, and hail, or anything else that's possible. Either yesterday or today was when you were supposed to have taken Larry back to the hospital. I sure hope the doctors find him a lot improved. It was better news to me to hear he is, at last, walking a little than to hear that the war will soon be over. We have been hearing rumors every day about the war being nearly finished, but we don't pay any attention to it. We know there is still one more war in the Pacific to finish before we're through. Oh yes, we also heard Hitler is dead. That's an easy way out for him because they think he'll be safe if we all believe he's dead. Try not to worry.

On Monday, May 7, 1945, the *Republican* printed the news everyone had been waiting for:

WAR IN EUROPE IS ENDED

"The end of the European warfare is over. It has been the greatest, bloodiest, and costliest war in human history and has claimed at least 40,000,000 casualties on both sides in killed, wounded, and captured. Hitler's arrogant armies invaded Poland on September 1, 1939, beginning the agony that convulsed the world for 2,075 days."

The newspaper article went on to remind the public the war against Japan needed to be finished. Soberly, it said many more casualties were yet to come.

This picture was taken in Belgium
after the Germans surrendered.
Karl is the first on the left, top row

Karl wrote a letter the day the European war ended.

5/7/45
My Dearest Evelyn and Larry, Well honey, this is the day we have been waiting for. The unconditional surrender was signed today by the Allies and the Germans. It will take effect tomorrow. Boy, it sure makes us all happy, but we haven't forgotten that there's still a war in the Pacific to win, but maybe it won't take too long. Let's hope that in two more years everyone is home again. I don't know how this discharge point system is going to work, but I'm sure I don't have enough. I've got 20 months overseas, 3 battle stars, and one baby to figure, but I don't think that is enough. Darling, I still love you and Larry more than anyone in the world and I'm longing for the day when I can be there with you all to prove it. We three will really have a big time when we do get together again. My heart is always with you and I know yours is with me. Honey, it sure is good news about Larry. I'm sure it won't be long till he'll be walking and talking real good. What did you think when the news came out that the war was over in Europe? I guess you already heard a rumor it was about over. Well, darling, I'm going to close for tonight. I'm so excited I can

hardly write. Always remember I love you and Larry more and more every day. There never will be anyone else. Our motto will be true and I'll never forget it. Give Larry a big kiss for me and tell him to be a good boy for daddy. Take the best of care of yourselves and I'll do the same. Keep your chin up high. Try not to worry. I'll remain as ever, Karl

The Allies formally accepted Germany's unconditional surrender on May 8, 1945. It was officially called V-E Day ($\underline{V}$ictory in $\underline{E}$urope).

May 8 happened to be President Truman's 61st birthday. He addressed the nation at 9 am that morning, "This is a solemn but a glorious hour. I only wish that Franklin D. Roosevelt had lived to witness this day. General Eisenhower informs me that the forces of Germany have surrendered to the United Nations. The flags of freedom fly over all Europe. The Allied Armies, through sacrifice and devotion and with God's help, have wrung from Germany a final and unconditional surrender. I call upon the people of the United States, whatever their faith, to unite in offering joyful thanks to God for the victory we have won, and to pray that He will support us to the end of our present struggle and guide us into the ways of peace. I also call upon my countrymen to dedicate the day of prayer to the memory of those who have given their lives to make possible our victory."

Rushville's fire whistle blew for two minutes. A concert of church bells, factory whistles, and automobiles horns joined in. Businesses and factories closed for the day. All of Rushville's churches gathered together in a show of unity at Main Street Christian Church. The gathered Christians said a prayer of thankfulness. Music from the church's tower played for one-half hour before the service began.

The *Republican* took "the edge off any planned jollification." It reported, "There were no excited street demonstrations, no shooting of firearms, and no whoop-la of any kind. Japan still must be whipped." To keep a lid on the celebration, Rushville's mayor promised, "Wait until Japan is licked. Then we'll all celebrate in big style."

Also on the May 8 front page of the *Republican*, next to the church celebration article, was a sad reminder of the consequences of war. Another soldier with local connections had died. William Kincaid was killed in Germany. His wife resided in Rushville. He was like most of the soldiers who died in the war. He did not get to come home. His body was buried in Germany.

Karl had survived the European war. He felt like a man freed from a two year prison term. His letters were no longer read by censors. He could say whatever he damn well pleased. He had been careful during the war to not let Evie know how much danger he faced. Now he could tell her everything. He wanted to tell Evie what he had been doing, where he had been, and what he had seen. He had a hell of a lot to tell her. His next letters were two of his best. He wrote like she was hunkered down next to him.

May 11, 1945
Darling, it sure does seem wonderful to know the war in Europe is over, but we still have lots of work to do yet before we go anywhere. The Army has lifted the censorship a little so now I can tell you everywhere I've been and all about our different experiences. First, I left Camp Perry, Ohio on August 11, 1943 and arrived at Camp Patrick Henry which is located at New Port News, Virginia on the afternoon of August 12, 1943. That was my Port of Embarkation. We sailed from there on a brand new troop transfer ship, General J.C. Pope, on September 5, 1943 on a real hot Sunday afternoon. We spent 8 days at sea. After three days out, we hit a storm which lasted three days and two nights. It was a pretty bad storm and we lost several of our lifeboats. We came by way of the north Atlantic, almost to the coast of Iceland and landed at Greenwich, Scotland on the Thames River, 25 miles from Glasgow. From there, we went by train to Sudbury, England which is a few miles from Darby. Then we had a lot of training in operating a depot while we stocked up stock and supplies for the invasion of France. I got lots of chances to see some of the old sites in England. I traveled England almost all over. It has some pretty scenery, but it's never clear long enough to see it because of fog. From Sudbury, we went to New Brighton, England which is across the river from Liverpool. That was the best place in England, or at least I think so. There we got more training in operating a field depot which I liked. From Liverpool, we came to southern England at New Hampton. I came to France on June 15, 1944. We landed on the Omaha Beach. I'd rather forget the things that happened at that beach and the things I saw. When we landed, we went in to Isigny and Carentan. From Carentan, we went to Cherbourg. It would take too long to write everything

about Cherbourg so it can wait till later. From Cherbourg, we went to Rennes, France where the Americans broke through the German lines on July 25, 1944. We stayed at Rennes for a while and then moved to Brussels, Belgium when the Germans broke through at the Ardennes forest. A lot of things will be easier to tell when I'm safe at home, but I've seen lots of bad sights. Also, the German buzz bombs have been over my head many times. Many nights we were in our bunks and the bombs came almost roof top high right over our heads. One night, Johnnie and I were in a restaurant and one landed half a block away. The shattered glass cut Johnnie's face. All it did to me was shake me up, but it certainly put cold chills up my spine. A guy never gets used to it.

PS. The Army has announced the point system and I've got a total of 72 points. I have three battle stars which include the invasion of France, the battle of northern France, and the battle of Germany. I need 85 to get out of the Army, so it looks like I stay in for a while.

May 19, 1945

Just a few lines to let you know I love you both more and more every day. Honey, I got a letter from you and one from Mom yesterday. I'll be glad when we won't have to write letters anymore, but can talk instead. Someday we'll be together again and then we'll really be happy. I'm still feeling fine and in the best of health. I hope and pray these few lines find you the same. I told you the other day that I look forward to being in the States around November. Now it looks like a little longer. We have about six to eight months of work over here and then maybe we can get back. Honey, several times you've asked me what Army I was with and several different questions, but at that time I was unable to answer them because our officers said it was against the censor's rules. I knew different, but I had to abide by them. Now I can tell you. When I came to France on June 15th, 1944 or nine days after the invasion of France, I was attached to the American 1st Army at the time. I think I told you we came in on Omaha Beach, which was the worst of the two American Beaches. Omaha Beach is where I saw thousands of American dead piled up. It was a very hard sight to look at. The papers stated there were just a couple thousand causalities on those beaches. Well, right now there are three American cemeteries which hold about 12,000 each. We were an Automotive Field Depot. That's a pretty rugged life, but not as bad as the Infantry. The first time I was under fire was at Carentan. A German 88 blew up a bridge right in the middle of our convoy and the semi-trailer I was driving had just passed over that bridge. The second truck behind me was partly torn up, but no one was killed. Later that day, a Major and an MP were killed there when an 88 hit in the fox hole with them. The Army's plan was to take the Normandy peninsula in a hurry, but the battle was a little tougher than expected. We helped out on the final drive on Cherbourg which fell on June 27, 1944. That is where I saw the U.S.S. Texas come in close to shore with two other battleships. At that time, we didn't know what ships they were but found out later. The Texas was hit, but I couldn't tell how badly. From Cherbourg, we moved back toward St. Lo where we had lots of fun shooting at German planes that would come over every night and sometimes during the day. We never hit any because we were using 50 caliber machine guns that couldn't hit a cow in the ass with a scoop shovel. Ha Ha. It was lots of fun trying though. Before the breakthrough at St. Lo, we were assigned to the U.S. Third Army under General Patton. The breakthrough came on July 25, 1944 and we followed Patton to Rennes, France, then we halted for a long rest. Next, we went with the 29th Division and helped them at Brest, which was one of the toughest battles of France. We supplied ammo to the artillery. Those Krauts (Germans) just wouldn't give up at Brest, but after Brest finally fell, we came back to Rennes for another long rest. We set up a depot just to keep us doing something. On December 16, 1944, the German breakthrough came in the Ardennes. That was in Cuttie's (a friend from Rushville) territory. He was located at Leige at the time. Well, there were some pockets of Jerries on the French coast which the 94th Division was keeping under control, but the Jerries started a fight on December 24, 1944. On Christmas Eve Day, we got orders to prepare 100 Armored Scout Cars and mount 50 caliber Machine guns on them all so that's what we did on Christmas Eve night and Christmas Day. Then we went out and helped check that minor German offensive. It wasn't much, but we did it in almost zero weather. Some of the boys froze their ears, feet, and noses, but I was lucky again. That is why we got the commendation I sent you. We came back to Rennes the day after Christmas and got orders to move to Belgium to take part in the battle of the bulge, so we left France on December 27, 1944. We got in Belgium on December 29, 1944. It was colder than hell there. We had no place to sleep but the cold ground, but we were pretty rugged by then. We crossed over into Germany for a while and then came back to Brussels where we set up a depot by the code of O-686. About everyone in Europe knows it as one of the largest. Brussels is where Johnnie and I were so damn hungry and cold that a Belgium family named Freson helped us out. They fed us and gave us a bed to sleep in till we got set up. After we got the depot operating, we worked very hard so we could all make the final drive across the Rhine into Germany. We worked day and night, but no one cared because we knew the end for Germany was near. We all thought Germany would collapse, but we were wrong. After the infantry crossed the Rhine, I made several trips into Germany and have taken some pretty interesting pictures which I'm putting in an album. Well, darling, I thought you would want to know and this is the first time I could tell you. I've been with the First Army, the Third Army and two different Divisions who weren't assigned to an Army at that time. When the war ended, a boy and I were in Brussels. We had just seen the movie "Hollywood Canteen". We sure had a good time for a couple of days, but all the time I was wondering what you and Larry were doing. I knew you both were really happy to know the war with Germany was over. Yes honey, it's over, but I wonder if the peace will be worth the price paid in blood. Us boys that actually have seen it can't even imagine how brutal it was. Thousands on top of thousands of American boys will never see home again, yet we have to face another enemy in the Pacific. I don't know if I'll go there or not, but before I do, I at least want to spend a few days with you and Larry and the folks at home. Our job right now is to fix and ship all available material we can to the Pacific. It should take from six to eight months. From there I don't know what. I'll let you know later.

    Remember, I love you both more than anyone in the world and I'll prove it to you when I get home again. Our motto will always be true and I'll never forget it. Give Larry a big kiss for me and tell him to be a good boy till I get home. Keep your chin up and try not to worry. I'll remain yours and Larry's Forever, Karl

Karl sent this picture home of an American cemetery in Europe
There were no names on the crosses.

Karl wrote on the back of this picture:
"Near Mastriche, Holland. All German paratroopers"

THE HORRIBLE END OF WORLD WAR TWO

"Little Boy"

- First Atomic Bomb Used – Uranium
- Detonated over Hiroshima Aug. 6, 1945
- Weighs 9,000 pounds
- 20,000 tons of TNT explosive capacity (2,000 B-29s w/ standard bombs)

A chain of islands to be used for supplies and airbases in the Pacific was essential for an American invasion of Japan. Those islands served to make up the supply route needed to support an American invasion of Japan. For over three years, the Allies conducted a process called island hopping. In the spring of 1945, the American military prepared to invade the next island it needed before a Japanese mainland invasion could successfully occur. That island was Okinawa. It was a small 466 square mile island 70 miles long and 7 miles at its widest. Okinawa was 340 miles from Japan's mainland. The Americans stormed ashore Okinawa on April 1, 1945.

So much for the soldiers who whipped the Nazis getting to enjoy the victory celebration. There was still much work for them to do. The May 11 *Republican*, three days after V-E Day, reported troops in Europe were already moving to French ports. They were going to the Pacific to prepare for the invasion of Japan. There was no mention of these soldiers getting a furlough at home.

Back home, the paper printed some encouraging news. The military announced it planned to proceed with the discharge of up to two million soldiers over the next year. As a result, the Selective Service publicized the discharge point system which had been cloaked in veil of secrecy. The military re-emphasized that the scoring system did not guarantee a soldier would be discharged. It only established the minimum point total a soldier needed to be eligible. The magic number was 85.

The *Republican* published how to calculate a soldier's score:
- One credit for each month of army service since September 18, 1940.
- One credit for each month served overseas since September 18, 1940.
- Five credits for each award of combat decoration since September 18, 1940.
- Twelve credits for each child less than 18 years of age.

The newspaper article ended with, "There seems to be only a few local soldiers who are eligible for speedy releases."

Evie calculated Karl had 75 points. Karl figured he had 72. Either way, his point total did not matter. He was not even close to 85. He needed at least five more months in the military plus five more months overseas before he would be eligible. The invasion of Japan would likely happen before Karl reached 85 points. He would not be discharged until the Japs were whipped.

Evie was mentally and emotionally fatigued. She was on the brink of collapse. Karl, however, was a battle tested soldier who was accustomed to the military's nonsense. He treated the disappointment like water on a duck's back. It just rolled off. He prepared Evie that he likely wasn't coming home soon. They would have to endure an enemy more brutal than the Germans.

May 13, 1945
Outskirts of Brussels, Belgium.
This is Sunday afternoon and it's really hot over here. The place where I'm at is like a desert. It's all fine sand and the wind is blowing it around to beat heck. Darling, I expect to be in the States around November or a little sooner, but if I'm not, don't feel disappointed. In other words don't build up too much hope. We have lots of work to do over here getting material ready for the Pacific. We're still working every day including Sunday, but a few of us get off one day a week now. I got my suntan shirt and it was swell. I wonder if you could send me a brown pair of shoes and some good dress socks but if you're short on money, don't get them. If you do, send them right away. Get the plain toe type shoes. (As fragile as Evie was by this time, this request certainly didn't help. She couldn't help but wonder, why did he need to dress up?) **I think I'll have some pictures made and I'll send them to you. I've also got some other things to send home too. I'm so glad Larry is now walking a little. By the time I get home, he'll sure be walking good and should be talking pretty good. I'm sure proud of you both and I show your pictures to everyone I see. This Belgium family that John and I stayed with made Larry a little summer suit and they sent it to me. I'll send it on home. They say that way I won't forget them. They're really swell people. They helped John and me out a lot this winter when it was so cold. Honey, have you ever made up your mind where you want to spend our vacation when the war is over? Myself, I'd like to get another couple and go somewhere where it's quiet, for instance, the lakes or the mountains. By the time I get home, I'll probably have seen enough of the sea. I think Ronald gets out of the Army on this point system and I'm sure glad he is. He may be home by now. If he is, ask him how civilian life feels. I don't think Tom gets out yet. According to my figures he should have 74 points. I've got 72. There's a rumor that all troops going to the Pacific and have been overseas more than a year will get at least a 30 day furlough in the states. I hope it's true.**

May 15, 1945
I'm still just fine. Though the war with Germany is over, we have a big job ahead of us in the Pacific. I still don't know if I'm going there or not. It seems like there's enough work right here to last for a long time. It's really pretty over here today and it reminds me

so much like home. A couple of the boys and I went into town today and bought a few souvenirs of Belgium. I'll send them to you and Larry when I find time. Darling, those two pictures you sent of Larry are really cute. I can hardly wait to get back there to see you and him. Keep your chin up high and try not to worry. It can't be much longer till we can see each other again.

May 18, 1945
It is Friday and it's pretty hot here today. I'd rather see it like this than cold and rainy. I got letters from you and Mom yesterday that were written on May 7, 1945. That was the day the peace treaty was signed, but became official on the 8th. Honey, is Larry walking any better now? Have you ever got his special new shoes from Indianapolis yet? I hope he'll be able to wear ordinary shoes after his arches are better. I still don't know if we're going to the Pacific. The rumor is we're staying here for six to eight months. That's better than the Pacific, isn't it? I haven't got any envelopes, but I will have in a couple days. Till then, I'm writing V-mail.

The War claimed another casualty. Winston Churchill, the man most responsible for stopping the Nazi juggernaut, faced serious opposition in the British Parliament after the European war ended. He was unpopular not only with the opposing Labor Party, but some in his own Conservative Party had grown weary of him. Churchill sent a letter of resignation to the King on May 22, 1945. The King of England accepted the resignation, then he immediately appointed Churchill to continue leading the British government until an election could be conducted.

The election was held on July 5, 1945. Most observers thought Churchill's Conservative party would win, in which case Churchill would continue to be the Prime Minister. Not so. The Labor Party won. Its leader, Clement Atlee, was elected as the new British Prime Minister. Atlee was sworn in on July 26, 1945.

May 22, 1945
Darling, I love you and Larry more and more every day. I can hardly wait till we can be together once again. It may be some time yet, but when it does come, we will have fun together. I imagine Ronald is coming home now with the point system, isn't he? (Not yet. Ronald received his honorable discharge from the

army on July 16, 1945.) **I got a letter from John** (a classmate at Woodbury College). **He is going home and then on to the Pacific. He's in the Infantry now. That's a rugged detail. We'll see him when the war is finished. Darling, give Larry a big kiss for me and have him to give you one in return. I'll bet he'll be a lady killer when he gets older, just like his Dad.**

The *Republican* ran stories for the folks back home to digest. On May 24, it reported U.S. casualties during the war. Most distressing was the fact that 181,739 soldiers had been killed. Also in the May 24 paper was a story about American bombing of Tokyo. Destruction was reported to be so intense that smoke was visible 200 miles away. On May 25, Tokyo was reported to be in flames. Nonetheless, B-29 Superfort bombers continued to bomb the Japanese capital daily.

May 27, 1945
I imagine you and Larry are in Sunday school right now. I sure wish I could be there with you. Maybe it won't be so much longer. Let's hope we've been separated better than half the time now. I really look to be going toward home during this fall or winter. I could be wrong so don't build up any hopes. Honey, you were wondering what I was doing on May 8th. Well, Bob and I were off on May 7 so we had gone to Brussels. We heard the news over a loudspeaker. We sure had a good time. I sure wish you could have been with us. On May 8, I worked till 3:00 in the afternoon, then I had to dress and we had a parade at 5:30. It was so darn hot we almost melted. The night of May 8, Sam and I took a 2 1/2 ton truck into town. The crowd was so thick it took us about 1 1/2 hours to go one block. Boy, it was awful. We got home about 10:30 and went to bed. We worked the next day, but the Limeys and Belgium people had a holiday. In fact, I think the Limeys have a holiday every day. I bet I will see a big difference in the yard when I get home. Have you got grass planted on the side yard yet? I'm going to either plant grass in the back or use it for a garden. I'm sure Dad and Mom will sell us the place if we want to buy it or they just may give it to us if we would finish paying for it. That would be better, wouldn't it? Honey, I think Larry should be walking pretty good by himself now. Is he? I'm so glad he's getting so much better. I'm sure he'll lead me on a merry chase when I get home but I'll be able to take it. Tell Dad I can picture Tom and me sitting around the stove on a cold winter night

swapping stories with him. Tom and I used to come pretty well neck and neck with Dad's stories. I think I could now tell some tales that would make the Old Man's hair stand on end if I wanted to. I'd rather forget them if that is possible.

June 2, 1945
I got a letter from you today. It had Larry's picture of him standing up. I'm still okay and enjoying the best of health. I'm sending a box to you that contains some pictures. Some are what you have sent me. I thought I'd send them home so I wouldn't lose them. Besides, my pocket book (his wallet) was getting too full. You remember me telling you about the bridge at Carentan, France that was so rugged? Well, a picture of it is in today's paper. I had just crossed that bridge when a German 88 shell blew it to kingdom come. The Jerries blew it up about every day for a while till some Jerries in a church steeple who were giving information to the German gunners were captured. Right across the road from the bridge is where a MP (Military Policeman) and Major were killed in a foxhole when an 88 came in to give them company.

88 millimeter gun shell being loaded by a German

The Okinawa battle lasted 82 days before the Americans finally claimed control of the island. The American cost for this small island in the Pacific was a nightmare. There were 75,000 American casualties, including 12,500 killed in action or missing.

The long, costly battle for Okinawa showed American citizens what was in store for them. Okinawa was a small island, but nearly three months of savage fighting were needed for it to be occupied.

The battle revealed more chilling news. There were no Japanese soldier survivors at Okinawa. When faced with inevitable defeat, all remaining soldiers had committed suicide. 90,000 Japanese soldiers died defending that **one little Pacific island**!

June 18, 1945
Honey, when I came to work on Saturday morning, guess who was waiting? No one else but Cuttie. (Cuttie was a friend from Rushville.) **Boy, was I glad to see him. It's the first time I'd seen him since January, 1943. We sure had a lot to talk about. He came to France on June 30th, fifteen days after I did. He came on the Omaha beach. That's the same one I was on. He stayed all day Saturday, Saturday night, and yesterday till 12 noon. We really had a good visit, just like old times. He's been here in Brussels three different times on pass and he's coming back if he gets another. If you see his mother or father, tell them he is looking good and getting along fine. He's still in the best of health. Is Larry still getting along as good as ever?**

The saber rattling, fighting, and bombing escalated throughout the summer of 1945. Japan and America did attempt to negotiate a peaceful settlement to end the war. Japanese leaders tried to play the victim. They told the world that they had proposed ending of the war with only one condition. The Japanese emperor would remain in power. They predicted Truman would not agree to their one request.

The Japanese leaders were correct. Harry, "the buck stops here, Truman did indeed say NO. He did offer a counter proposal. A peaceful conclusion was possible, but there would be absolutely no concessions from the United States. He stressed, once again, for the citizens of the world to hear; the loss of life would stop only if the Japanese agreed to unconditional surrender. To add salt to the wound, he emphasized the destruction of Japanese cities would worsen if they did not agree to unconditional surrender.

Negotiations went nowhere. Everyone knew an American invasion of Japan was inevitable. It was just a matter of when.

Clara and Ott were starting to wear down from age, constant worry, and never having enough money. The evening routine at this stage of their lives was to sit in their rocking chairs on the front porch. While Ott sucked on a big wad of Red Man Chewing Tobacco, Clara read the newspaper to him since he could not read. One evening, she read another in a long line of stories that the invasion of Japan was getting closer to reality. Ott couldn't help but notice the worried look on Clara's wrinkled face. He was not sure what to do to comfort her, but he tried. The tough old man threw his used wad of tobacco into the yard. He wiped the tobacco juice off his chin with the handkerchief he always carried in his back pocket. He put a new wad into his mouth, then looked Clara in the eye. He reached out and touched her knee. He then modified his favorite expression, "Clarie, listen to me. The shit's gonna hit the fan again. Remember, Karl is a goddam Floyd. He'll be fine." Inside the Old Man's head, he was not sure he was right.

The Japanese Premier warned his nation after Okinawa was lost that an Allied invasion of the mainland of Japan was impending. He did reveal comforting news to the Japanese citizens, "A new kind of underground warfare is now being prepared. It is so different from anything used in Europe. It will mark a new epoch in military history. It is time the entire nation burned its bridges. Make the fullest preparations for this imminent development. The outcome will decide the rise or fall of our country for centuries to come."

He was bluffing.

The Emperor began to sound much like Hitler before the Normandy invasion. He told his people Japan faced a crisis "unprecedented in scope in her national history." He promised defensive planning for the upcoming invasion was nearly complete. He bragged that Japanese suicide bombers were "crippling" Allied ships. On June 28, he droned on, "I request the entire nation to endure mounting hardships and difficulties with utmost perseverance and with the defiance of death characteristic of the Japanese. The enemy's arrogant counteroffensive, in sole reliance on superiority of resources, is expected to be further intensified and will lead eventually to an invasion of our mainland."

June 30, 1945
Honey, Guess what? Mohawk showed up last weekend and we went out on a boat. (Mohawk was another colorful friend from Rushville. Evie didn't care much for him. He liked to drink and womanize. Word around town was that he fathered some children during his time in Europe.) **I've got a slight cold caused from the fan on the boat, but it is worth it. We had a good time. Thanks for the pictures of Larry. I can hardly imagine him being so big. He's**

the cutest baby I've seen, but why wouldn't I think so? It's a shame that he turned his face when the picture was taken. Mom and Dad both look like they've aged a lot in the two years I've been gone. Maybe it's the way the camera took their pictures. Dory and Madge look the same. As for you, honey, you're getting prettier every day. You're swell and I'll certainly be glad to get back to you. I'll keep the pictures for now but if I go straight to the Pacific, I'll send them home. So the preacher's wife died? The donation the church got for her funeral should really come in handy. It probably cost him a lot to ship her clear back to Illinois. Honey, the name of the family here in Belgium who made the little suit for Larry is Frison. Send me the letter you wrote and I'll give it to them. To get mail to civilians over here from the states is almost impossible. I'm sure glad the new shoes have helped Larry's feet out. Maybe in a few years his feet will be okay. Let's hope and pray so.

July 4, 1945
I'm on CQ tonight. (CQ meant Charge of Quarters. He was guarding the front door of the barracks.) **It's something I hate. There's nothing to it, only you have to stay awake most of the night. We're off tomorrow, though, so that makes it better. I don't know what I'll do yet, but probably will go into town with some of the boys and see a show at a GI theater. I started typing this letter, but found out I've lost a lot of my speed on a typewriter so I'm writing instead. I saw in today's paper where some admiral guessed the war with Japan will be over within six months to a year. Darling, how are you and Larry getting along? Sometimes, I lie in my cot and wonder what you're doing at the same time. Just think, when we're home together we'll get to do whatever we want and then we can really look into the future. I'll do my best to make you the best husband. My goal is making you and Larry happy.**

The American bombing of Japan continued. On July 14, United States Navy battleships anchored ten miles from the Japanese shore started bombing the mainland. The devastation was such that forty-six Japanese cities were left "charred." One American general bragged that Japan was being "bombed into a nation without cities."

July 16, 1945
I got one letter from you today. It was written July 2, 1945. I hope the mail gets straightened out one of these days. I'm still feeling fine and in the best of health. The weather is still good and hot over here and I'm glad. I certainly don't like the cold rain they have here nine tenths of the time. Surely we'll be on our way somewhere else soon. I got a letter from Johnnie. He's leaving Antwerp for the states. His new outfit has just been here a year so we'll surely get to go to the states too, but the Army does foolish things sometimes. All we can do is keep our fingers crossed. How much perfume have you got left from what I sent you for Christmas? That was awful good perfume I sent you. At least they told me it was. Yes, I'd like to have another baby some of these days, but as long as I'm in the Army, I don't. Honey, it would sure be swell if we could be together and enjoy the good times like we used to have. Here's hoping I see you all soon.

The American military made a big announcement. Some Army units in Europe would travel to the states before going to the Pacific. Evie prayed that Karl's unit was one of those coming home. Evie read the newspaper article three times. She did not see the 983rd Ordnance Company in the list.

She had been alone for over two years. She had done everything in her power to make her handicapped son better. She had worried Karl would die on every single one of those days. He hadn't told her anything before he shipped to England. Now, for all she knew, he was already on his way to the Pacific. The thought kept ringing in her mind, "Karl is not coming home… Karl is not coming home…Karl is not coming home…."

Italy and Germany had already been soundly defeated. Japan was the lone remaining member of the Axis. There was a difference in the three members; Germany and Italy fought for economic and political reasons while Japan fought to defend a several centuries old culture.

The Japanese Emperor was a god in Japan. He had convinced the citizens that their island nation's very existence was at stake. To that end, the Japanese justified their military's savagery and tenacity. Its military taught soldiers to be vicious and brutal against the enemy. The death of a Japanese soldier for the Emperor was an honor. Surrender was never an option.

The American's continued preparations for an invasion. Despite his bluster, Truman wasn't certain his country had the stomach to pay such a high cost. He wasn't certain he did either. To his relief, the military gave Truman and his advisors a briefing on another alternative at their disposal.

America and Germany had competed during the European war to develop a nuclear bomb. Germany failed. America did not. The Manhattan Project successfully detonated a test atomic bomb in the New Mexico desert on July 16, 1945. President Truman was immediately informed of the successful test. He was told one more secret. There were only two atomic bombs, but they were ready to go. Their nicknames were Little Boy and Fat Man.

Truman faced an appalling and most difficult decision in his life. The atomic bombs could shorten the war. They would likely save thousands of American lives. There was a flip side that he had to consider. Using the bomb would unleash the most terrible weapon ever. The world would change forever if he approved the use of an atomic bomb. Truman discussed the conundrum with his advisors.

He ultimately said it was an easy decision. He had no choice. America would use the atomic bomb. He gave Japan one more chance for an unconditional surrender. Japan rejected the offer.

On July 25, 1945, only nine days after the successful atomic bomb test, Truman signed the order to drop an atomic bomb on Japan. The order said in part, "The 509 Composite Group, 20th Air Force will deliver its first special bomb as soon as weather will permit visual bombing after or about 3 August 1945 on one of these targets: Hiroshima, Kokura, Niigata or Nagasaki."

Little Boy dropped from a plane on August 6, 1945. The bomb with its unimaginable power exploded over Hiroshima, Japan. The *Republican* headline filled the front page:

NEW ATOMIC BOMB, CARRYING GREATEST DESTRUCTION YET KNOWN, FALLS UPON JAPS

Little Boy's unbelievable destructive power was enormous. It was 2,000 times more powerful than the largest bomb ever used before. It destroyed sixty percent of Hiroshima. 66,000 people died from the detonation. 69,000 others were injured. The *Republican* article concluded, "Those outdoors burned to death. Those indoors died by indescribable pressure and heat."

Japanese leaders remained defiant. They told their citizens after Hiroshima to remain calm and to remember they had trained for such an occasion as this. They pledged to fight until the last American was dead.

In response, "Give 'em Hell" Harry Truman warned of more devastation unless Japan surrendered immediately. He said the bomb would be a tremendous aid in shortening the war. He made a pledge to Japan, "Expect a rain of ruin from the air, the likes of which has never been seen on this earth. We shall completely destroy Japan's power to make war."

Truman and a few military leaders kept the closely guarded secret to themselves. America had only one more atomic bomb.

Truman waited two days for a Japanese surrender. He did not get one. He then approved the use of his last atomic bomb. Fat Man exploded over Nagasaki on August 9, 1945. 39,000 human beings died. 25,000 others were injured.

After Nagasaki, Japan offered to surrender before more of its cities evaporated. There was a catch to the offer. The Emperor was Japan's living god. Some of his War Council argued that he must remain Japan's sovereign leader. American leaders suspected the offer was a delay tactic. They hoped Japan did not know there were no more atomic bombs. The Americans did what they had to do. They lied. They told Japan the bombs would keep falling until ordered to stop by Truman.

Japanese Emperor Hirohito, in reality was only a puppet to his War Council, but he was ready to surrender.

Truman was war weary. He knew the Japanese were done. He was burdened by the devastation and suffering his decisions had caused. He did not want the Japanese people to suffer any more pain "especially to all those kids" in Japan. A ceremonial emperor was harmless. He could live with that.

The two sides worked out an agreement understanding on August 10. Japan would surrender unconditionally, but the Emperor would maintain the hereditary and traditional role of emperor in Japan. In other words, the emperor would stay in a ceremonial role, but he would have to "subject himself to the orders of the Supreme Allied Commander."

President Truman ordered a halt to any more atomic bombs being dropped on Japan. The Japanese agreed to the unconditional surrender terms on the morning of August 15, 1945 (Japan time). World War Two ended nine days after the first atomic bomb detonated. The dastardly wars that consumed the entire planet were over. They had been a dispute over geography, politics, economics, and tradition.

A representative of the Japanese government gave a radio address to its citizens that morning. About the same time, President Truman gave a radio address to America at 7 pm (United States time). The date in America was Tuesday, August 14, 1945. He announced that Japan had agreed to surrender. The formal signing would take place on September 2nd. He proclaimed September 2 would be V-J Day.

Three years, eight months, and seven days after Pearl Harbor, the world was finally at peace.

The *Republican* reported the events in Rushville after Truman's announcement, "A crowd like on a Saturday night turned out for the unorganized celebration seconds after the radio flashed the official word of Japan's surrender. Bells and whistles throughout the city started a din that signaled a general whooping it up by hundreds of the local citizenry. A rainstorm failed to dampen the mood. Car horns were in full blast. Car owners soon found some things to tie to their cars to make more noise. Firecrackers were set off."

The Rush County Courthouse Curbside Court convened in special session that wonderful historic Tuesday evening. There was no debate. Lots of laughter was heard. More than a few tears were shed.

Unlike the German surrender, Rushville's mayor encouraged citizens to celebrate. He declared August 15 and 16 to be holidays. He ordered "all businesses but food stores and essential services" to close. He ended gas rationing "immediately."

Rush County held a parade on August 16. The *Republican* reported, "Thousands lined the streets of Rushville. Every musical organization in the county participated. First, a minister gave an invocation. The high school band played the national anthem. The assembled crowd sang *America the Beautiful*. Next, everyone went silent. The Mayor stood on the Courthouse lawn next to 46 white crosses. He read the names of the Rush County soldiers who had died. Grown men and women cried and sobbed while a lone trumpeter played *Taps*. Finally, the crowd erupted. Rushville enjoyed its first parade in four years. Scores of novel floats and decorated vehicles were featured. Veterans of World War One and World War Two marched the length of the town. The parade ended at the park where Willkie, four long years ago, had given stirring speeches.

World War Two left rivers of tears in its aftermath. The numbers were shocking. Up to 70 million people died worldwide. For America, there were 417,000 dead and 671,000 wounded from the 16 million, five hundred thousand who served in the military.

The obliteration Japan suffered defied imagination. The two atomic bombs dropped on Japan left 480,000 people dead, injured, or homeless. For weeks after the bombs detonated, people died from burns. Many who received what appeared to be minor burns looked quite healthy at first. They became ill days later for some unknown reason. They often died. The atomic bombs produced other mysterious effects on the human body. Survivors suffered and died for years after.

Rush County Courthouse lawn
The crosses bore the names of lost Rush County soldiers

Evie got a telephone call a few days after Japan surrendered. The caller was a woman who lived a few blocks away. What she said stunned Evie beyond words. Evie dropped the phone. There was nothing left.

August 21, 1945
I didn't get any letters from you again today, but I did get one from Mom. She said you haven't been leaving the house. I can't understand why I never get any from you unless you're sick. If I could only be there with you and help you out, I know you'd feel a lot better and so would I. I'm on C.Q. again tonight and that's the detail I dread. There's nothing to it but sit and try not to sleep, but it gets tiresome. Boy, I had my first treat tonight for supper that I've had for a long time. Believe it or not, I had one whole banana. It's the first I've had since I came to the Army and it sure tasted good. I'll be glad when I can be able to eat your banana pies. How is Larry making out? Does he still call you Susie? I've forgotten how I nicknamed you that. Just how did that come about? It shouldn't be too long till we three can be together again since I heard an awful good rumor today. All guys with 76 points are supposed to be in the marshalling area by September 15. I should then be next on the list as I've got 72 points. I should be home before Christmas. It would be so good to celebrate and spend Christmas at home. Boy, that's hard to believe. It'll be a happy day to get back in civilian life again and work and get paid every week, but I don't think I'll start to work right away. We'll take a vacation first, then I'll lay around at home and rest up a bit before I go back. Remember honey, my heart will always belong to you and Larry and no one else. Our motto will always be true and I'll never forget it. It can't be much longer till we're together again

DARKNESS BEFORE THE LIGHT

At first glance, the two sexes should not be attracted to each other. The survival of the human race, however, dictates that one can't live without the other.

Conflict is the fuel that powers a man's soul. He is wired to protect and provide for those he loves. He will leave home for long periods of time when he senses danger. He'll beat on his chest and make noise while he defends his family. He respects strength. He prefers to run in a pack. The struggle fulfills him. He doesn't need to understand how much damage he generates. If he dies, so be it.

Conflict is the sword that pierces a woman's heart. Her nature is to nurture and be patient. Her love of family is bottomless. She sees the madness of fighting. She knows the pain which is required to give life. She wishes to ease suffering, not cause it. Her family's very existence is her reward for the misery she suffers when childbearing. She cherishes every day there is joy and no pain. The male's unsheathed sword is a burden she cannot escape. Hers is a lifetime of worry.

Nature gave the advantage to women. A man cannot exist without a woman's love. He needs to return when his battles are over to the inviting, safe home she has maintained. She welcomes him with love. She cuddles him until the next fight calls.

The cycle never ends.

August 30, 1945
Just a few lines to say I love you both more and more every day. Honey, I didn't get any letters from you again today, but I did get another one from Mom. She hadn't seen you for three days. If my presence at home would make you better, go to the doctor and have him go to the Red Cross and have them send a request for an emergency furlough home. If the doctor thinks it's necessary, he'll do it and I can come home that way. I'll be home in November or December anyway I think, and maybe discharged from the army by Christmas. When the peace treaty is finally signed by the Japs, we've been told we'll get some more credit for our overseas points which will give me 80 points. 80 points is what will entitle me to get discharged. Darling, I know you've kept your chin up a long time without me. Honey, I'm really proud of you for it. I love you so much I can't put it in writing. Someday in the near future, I'll be there with you and we won't get out of each other's sight. It'll be so good to hold you and Larry in my arms again and know you're both mine forever and ever. I dream at nights about a lot of the good times we've had together. I know it won't be long till those good times will return and we'll be the happiest family in the world. I'll make you the best husband and Larry the best father possible. All during the war with Germany the thoughts of you and Larry, knowing someday I'd be with you again, kept me going. I

didn't mind it so much on the Normandy beach when the Jerries would fly over strafing us or the buzz bombs when they'd hit close by because I knew your heart was with me and it would carry me through okay, but all I want now is for you to get well quick and me to hurry home to you and Larry. Remember, if the doctor thinks it is necessary, have him contact the Red Cross. The Red Cross will then notify me to get an emergency furlough home. I'll see my CO (Commanding Officer)**, he'll send it to HQ** (Headquarters)**, and HQ will okay it and send it back to me. Then I'd be able to leave immediately, but by the time all of that could take place, I'll probably be home. Please ask the doctor and see what he says. I'll close for now, darling. Good night, sweet dreams, and God bless you both.**

Karl's Floyd bullheadedness sometimes drove Evie to tears, but it was also one of the reasons she loved him. He was man full of stubborn pride. He had told her it was his duty to fight for his country. He told Evie that Ott and Clara raised him to do what was right. Evie was not able to change his mind. In reality, she didn't want to. She was forced to let him go. Then she awaited his return.

Evie tried to do everything right. She wrote encouraging letters while he was gone. She went to church. She prayed every day for the war to end. She begged God make Larry normal. She couldn't find the strength to tell Karl the truth. She told him Larry was improving. She knew it was wrong. She had lied to her husband to protect him. She repeatedly asked God to forgive her.

The war was now over. Evie needed Karl to come home. Over twenty-eight months, a five day furlough and a bus trip to Ohio were all she had been with him. He was in Europe almost two years. She had to endure the European invasion and the long battle to defeat Germany. The possibility that Karl might go to the Pacific tortured her. By her way of thinking, he should have been at the head of the line to come home.

Evie wasn't alone. Everyone wanted their soldier to come home. Now! Evie suspected the process would be unfair. She remembered how the selection process worked. Some men were drafted into the military that shouldn't have. Others that should have gone, for some reason, didn't.

Some Congressmen played political games after the war. They insisted that the military discharge five million soldiers immediately. Their reasoning made some sense. The great American system of individual initiative and private enterprise needed them home. The military responded to the outcry for rapid demobilization. It changed the point system for discharge eligibility. Nonetheless, it insisted it could only discharge two million men soon.

August 31, 1945
Honey, if you're not well, it's okay if you don't write. I understand. I haven't got a letter from you now for more some time, but I know you'll write after you start feeling better. I love you so much, honey. I'm longing for the day when I can hold you in my arms again and call you mine. It's been a long time, but we'll make up for all the lost time. I can hardly wait till I get home to you and Larry. I'll make the best husband and father I can and I know you'll be the same with me. I'm still feeling fine and in the best of health. All I want is for you to take good care of yourself and get well quick. Oh, I wish I was there with you right now. I know that would make you feel a lot better. Just be patient though. I'll be there someday. I hope soon. So far, you've been the best wife a guy could ever wish for and, darling, you're tops in this world. Mom said Larry is really getting big and boy, am I glad. Let's hope and pray he's okay now. I'm awfully sorry I wasn't there to help, but I can't help some things. He was just getting into the cute stage when I left. It's been cold and cloudy over here all day and I'd certainly welcome some Indiana sunshine right now. Honey, I saw in The *Stars and Stripes* that the Rush County draft board resigned. That's awful generous of them, the crooks! They should have resigned before they started. Well, that's about all I can think of right now, so I will close. Remember, I love you and Larry more and more every day and when I get home I'll prove it to you. Our motto will always be true and I'll never forget it. Your mine, I'm yours and Larry's ours. Honey, try and get well quick for me, will you?

War experiences haunted returning soldiers. They couldn't forget what they had smelled, seen, heard, and done. Bad dreams frequently invaded their sleep. They missed their fellow soldiers. They had visited Hell together and could understand the lingering torment.

When they returned home, the freedoms of civilian life confused them. They got angry at the littlest things. The doldrums of daily living bored them. Some couldn't accept the responsibilities of being husbands and fathers again.

In some ways, it had been easier on Evie while Karl was gone. Her mind now was consumed with a multitude of worries. Would God punish her for the lies she told Karl about Larry? Her young husband two years earlier didn't have to shave every day. Would he still have that boyish look? How different would he be after seeing the world? Would he still sing love songs to her? Would she still love him if he had changed? Would he still love her if she had changed? Could he accept a handicapped son? Would he blame her when he realized Larry would never be normal? Would he get angry when he realized that she had not told him that Larry had Cerebral Palsy? He had traveled all over America, England, and the European continent. Could he adjust to coming home in Rushville? Worst of all, would he abandon her like her father had?

There was a dirty little secret that everybody knew. An American in uniform attracted English, French, Belgian, and German women. Rumors back home ran rampant of soldiers' shenanigans. The Courthouse Curbside Court debated the topic one Saturday evening. One member argued, "What happened in Europe stays in Europe." The final verdict was along the line that boys will be boys. The court soon regretted their conclusion. The "boys will be boys" ruling was not popular with their wives.

Evie watched other soldiers come home. One such soldier was her brother, Ronald. He was discharged in July. She remembered how he and his wife were so very much in love before the war. They had difficulty adjusting to each other now that they were together again. It was like they didn't know or even like each other.

The postwar divorce rate jumped. The *Republican* ran a regular listing of divorce filings in Rush County.

There was more distressing news. Growing numbers of American soldiers were marrying European women before they came home. An oblivious Catholic priest increased anxiety levels of American wives. He foolishly said he knew of married American soldiers who wanted to divorce their wives. They wanted stay in Germany. This chaplain then twisted the knife he had stabbed into many wives with horrible words, "If a marriage between an American boy and a German girl represents true love, then it is natural law." To further intensify Evie's fears, the *Republican* ran a story about a returning local soldier who divorced his wife for a girl from France.

Evie wanted to believe she and Karl could avoid those problems. She told herself that Karl was different than other men. She also was aware, as one high school friend told her, Karl had those "bedroom eyes." She reminded herself that he had written to her regularly. He repeatedly wrote "I love you" and that he missed her. No matter, being together for only five days in over two years haunted her. Evie feared, in fact dreamed about, receiving the dreaded "I have found someone in Europe." letter.

That is not how it happened.

The message came in a phone call. It was a hot August evening. Japan had recently surrendered and Rushville was alive with merriment and relief. Evie had spent the day cleaning the house. She was ironing and folding clothes when the telephone rang. When she answered, the voice on the other end was that of a woman. She had worked with Karl at the furniture factory. She was a war widow. Her husband was killed early in the war. The call was short and to the point. She informed Evie that Karl had been writing letters to her since her husband died. She said Karl recently wrote that he loved her and was anxious to see her when he came home. The call was short. The caller didn't say goodbye. She just hung up.

Evie dropped the phone receiver. She started screaming which made Larry cry. Stunned to her soul, she couldn't move to pick up Larry. It was hard for her to catch her breath. Those words bounced around in her head. Karl must not have been telling her all the truth during those long, lonely months. She had been lying to him about Larry. Now she knew he had been lying to her. It never crossed her mind that the caller might also have been lying to her

Evie couldn't help but believe that Karl was going to desert her like her dad had dumped Madge. She got mad for him leaving to join the army. He could have found a way to avoid the military like many "stay-at-homers" did. For goodness sakes, he had a handicapped child! Larry could have kept him out of harm's way. What was she thinking when she married this guy and had a baby for him?

She felt betrayed. She lost interest in living. She wanted to run away, but she had no place to go. She quit eating. She couldn't sleep.

It was all she could do to care for Larry. She couldn't get over the idea she might have lost Karl.

Karl's letters kept coming. She cried when she read them. She tore several of them into small pieces. Her gosh dang world was falling apart and he was writing of the fun he was having. Her blood boiled when he wrote how he was anxious to come home.

She couldn't take any more. She stopped writing to him. She was done with Karl Floyd.

While he was busting his butt to complete his army obligations in Europe, Karl sensed something was wrong. Evie always answered his letters. Now he was getting nothing from her. He didn't know what the hell was going on. He usually wrote letters to Evie at bedtime or after mail call. The day before America and Japan signed the Japanese surrender documents, he wrote a letter before mail call. Completely clueless, he tried to cheer her up. His words only sank the dagger deeper into Evie's heart.

September 1, 1945
I'm still not getting any mail from you. Honey, are you feeling any better, or are you worse, or what? I'd certainly like to know, but I guess I'll have to wait till I get home. Honey, it can't be too much longer now. I can't wait till I get home so I can love you and hold you in my arms again. My heart is always with you both and it belongs to you. I'm sure I've got yours here with me. Oh darling, no one will ever know how lonely these years apart have been for us. I've dreamed of being with you and Larry time and time again, but would wake up to find myself wrapped in a G.I. blanket in a hole in the ground or lying on a cot somewhere. Boy, it was cold this morning, but it warmed up and has become a beautiful day. It reminded me of a fall day back home when it's frosty in the morning and turns out to be warm. Honey, it won't be long till our 4th wedding anniversary. I'd sure love to be back home to spend it with you. Just think, our boy will be three years old. It'll certainly be swell to be back in our home. I'll stick to you like a leech. Surely, someday soon, I'll have a discharge from this Army. It can't be much longer now. Honey, try to hurry and get well for me. I hope and pray you're better now. Darling, give Larry a big kiss for me.

Mail call was the highlight of a soldier's day. It did not matter where they were, or how dangerous the situation. They gathered outside of the officer quarters after word spread that a bag of mail had arrived. Karl worked his way to the front of the group on September 1, 1945. It was as if being closer would reward him with a letter from Evie.

He did receive one letter that day. He hoped to see Evie's beautiful cursive handwriting on the envelope. Instead, he saw Clara's fragmented writing. He tore open on the stamp end of the letter like he always did. He unfolded the cheap yellow tablet paper. He read the letter his mother had written to him almost two weeks earlier. Her letter started with the three words she always used, "My Darling Son."

Clara's letter informed her youngest son about the phone call Evie had received. She wrote she had been worried when she had not heard from or seen Evie for several days. She had her brother, Omer, take her out to Madge and Dory's farm where Evie was staying. With Madge sitting at her side, Evie told Clara what had happened.

Clara's written words gave Karl a verbal spanking as only a mother can give. She told him that he had better get home before he lost his family. He cried like a baby while he read.

Karl always felt he had an angel protecting him. He always envisioned his angel as an invisible spirit. The letter he read that day revealed to him that his angel was made of flesh and blood. His angel was his mom, Clara Vansickle Floyd. She saved his and Evie's marriage.

After reading his mom's letter, Karl wrote Evie a long second letter of that day. He felt better when he finished it. He was fearful that it was too late.

September 1, 1945
My Dearest Evelyn and Larry, Just a few lines to let you know I love you more and more every day, and darling, I will forever. I got a letter from Mom today. I've been crying my eyes out ever since I got her letter. Honey, I can't help it. I love you so much. She didn't say how you were, but said you were still out to the farm. She also told me the doctor said the best medicine you could have was for me to come to you. I've prayed to be home with you before, but never like I've been praying tonight. I've prayed for you

when I was in danger and I knew I was safe because your heart was with me. I just sent a cablegram to notify our Red Cross at home to send a message to the Red Cross here in Brussels so I can get an emergency furlough home. I also had the Red Cross here send a cablegram to the Rushville Red Cross. There should be an answer in about two weeks. If they give me a furlough home, I'll be there for you, honey, and I'll be coming as fast as I can. As long as I've been gone, I've got my first girl to go out with as my heart has always been there with you. The only enjoyment I have is when the boys and I go to town for a show. I know you've been the truest girl ever and I'm certainly proud of you for it. I may as well tell you about the details. The reason I never told you I was writing (the other woman) was I knew you were jealous. Please know that no one means anything to me but you and Larry. Since her husband was killed in the Pacific, we've been writing back and forth. I thought all my letters to her were friend to friend. I was an awful good friend of hers from work and she had to turn to someone for help. It almost got the best of her. I tried to cheer her up by telling her everything probably turned out for the best and God knew what was right. If he never thought it best, it would never have happened. I try to be friends with everybody but, honey, I can be mixed up more than any person in the world. She never wrote me any letters like the one I wrote her, and I wouldn't have done that if my mind wasn't on you. In fact I think there was only one I ever wrote her with stuff like that in it. I'm trying to tell you the whole story. Darling, it's you I love. Please believe me. Honey, please try to understand what I mean in this letter. I really don't know why I ever wrote a letter like that. I must have been meant it for you or I wouldn't have put such things in it and above all, I'm not in the habit of doing such things. In other words, a guy's mind wonders sometimes. If I wrote a letter like that, and I must have, well, I must have thought it was to you instead of (her). I don't go around telling different people I love them unless I mean it and, darling, it's you who I love. I've got one more letter to write her and that is to tell her not to send any Christmas packages as I won't be here. I'll either be home by that time or on my way. I don't know if she was aiming to or not, but we were told to write everyone so there wouldn't be a mix up in the mail. Darling, I have tried to be the best husband and father a man could be, but sometimes I've failed. I'm no good at letter writing so I can't really say to you what I want. I would tell you the whole story if I could talk to you. Maybe I will soon get to. I love you so much, darling, but I can't be perfect. That's impossible. Please believe me. Darling, I hope and pray you understand what I mean in this letter. It's you I love. There is no one else. My heart and soul is continually with you. I'm asking God right now for you to believe me. If you don't want to write, it's okay. It's up to you. I've suffered plenty before and I guess I can still suffer some more. Remember honey, this letter is being written from the bottom of my heart. I've loved you ever since I met you and I will until my dying day. Honey, before I came in and started writing this letter, I was watching the sun sink in the west. It was a beautiful sight, but I couldn't help thinking in a few more hours you'll be watching the same sunset and how much prettier they are at home. I guess it's because that's the place I want to be. It would be so good to be with you and Larry right now and hold you both in my arms. Darling, no one knows how much I miss those good times we've had together. I tried to forget a lot of that while I've been gone. If a guy didn't, he'd go nuts. Sometimes a guy does things he shouldn't, but honey, anything to relieve the strain of what I've been through is better than nothing. I've been as faithful to you since I been in the Army as anyone could be except for letter writing, and darling, I assure you she means nothing to me. I still don't drink, chew, or gamble. I hate all three as bad as ever. I'll close for now. Remember darling, I love you more and more every day and I will forever. Our motto will always be true and I'll never forget it. Give our boy a big kiss for me. Tell him his daddy will be home soon. We'll all three have those romps like we had before I came to the Army. Remember? That was lots of fun, wasn't it? Honey, again I hope and pray you and Larry are in the best of health. I'm okay except for a sore throat. As ever I'll remain: Yours and Larry's with All My Love, Karl**

Evie had her best cry ever after she read Karl's letter about a week later. Her fear for Karl's life and the burden of raising their handicapped son alone the past three years gushed out. The tears poured until there were none left.

There is something therapeutic about a good cry. Evie's head was clear for the first time in months. She realized she was acting like a little school girl. Karl meant more to her than anything on earth. He had gone off to war to protect her and his country. Now someone else wanted her husband. Evie's whining and pouting was encouraging him to seek comfort from the other woman.

The only other people who knew about the phone call were Madge and Clara. Evie expected them to be mad, too. To her relief, they weren't. They each assured her Karl was a good man. Madge talked of the power of forgiveness. She told Evie to search her soul for God's grace to forgive Karl. Clara, on the other hand, said she would spank Karl with a switch when he got home, but only after she held him in her arms for about an hour.

Evie decided to fight back. She drove Tom's car the few blocks to the other woman's house. She didn't just knock. She pounded on the door. The surprised look on the woman's face gave Evie strength and more than a little pleasure.

The visit was short. Evie did all the talking. In no uncertain terms (One of Ott's goddams may have slipped out.), she told the old rip that Karl was a married man with a son. She yelled at the hussy to stay away from Karl when he came home. Evie didn't wait for a response. She strutted back to the car.

Evie's war was over. She had survived and won. She was safe. Karl still loved her. Karl was coming home. He was coming home to her. She was now full of excitement for the first time over two years. With Larry on her lap, she wrote Karl her first letter in over a month.

Karl started working on getting home as soon as he read his mom's letter. Her letter also let Karl know the war, the worry for his safety, and the stress of being a single mom had taken a toll on Evie's health. He wrote Evie another letter the next day.

September 2, 1945
Honey, in three more days it'll be two years since I left the states. In six more days, it will be 25 months since you and I last seen each other at Camp Perry, Ohio. These past 25 months have been the loneliest of my life. Without you and Larry, my life is incomplete. I hope and pray we can soon be together again. This is Sunday and I'd certainly like to be there to go to church with you and Larry tonight. Honey, I've longed to get back to our home with you and Larry, and now that time is near. I told you I sent a cablegram to the Red Cross about your condition. I also had the Red Cross here send one to the Red Cross Chapter at home. After the Red Cross okays it, then the Army over here has to okay it. That's the only way I know to get home right away and they have

been doing it a lot for other guys since the war ended. Oh Darling, I'm hoping and praying I can be with you and Larry soon. I'd sure like to know how you are right now, but we're so far apart. Mom wrote me about your back. What is the doctor giving you for your back and to help you sleep? Is it helping you out? Why didn't you let me know sooner? By now, I could have been home with you. I'm praying day and night for you. Please take good care of yourself and don't worry about me. I'll be there holding you and Larry in my arms before we know it. We didn't work today and we don't work tomorrow on account of Labor Day. Today, Bob and I sang while we played the guitar and fiddle. I also did my washing, which was a lot. Tomorrow, I'll do my ironing. By the time I get out of this Army I should be pretty good at it. I'd better close for now, honey. Remember, I love you and Larry with all my heart. Our motto will always be true. We've got lots to look forward to and we'll take a good vacation wherever you want to go. Keep your chin up high, darling. I'm praying to get home to you soon.

September 5, 1945
Two years ago today, our boat left Newport News and headed out toward the north Atlantic. I never will forget that day. I never dreamed it would be two years before I got back home to you and Larry. It's been a long and lonely time for me. No one will ever know how lonely it has been, but I know it can't be much longer until I'm home. Our Army paper yesterday said everyone with 70 points or above would either be home or on their way home by Christmas. I've got 80 now so I'll surely be there unless something goes snafu somewhere which is easily done in this Army. I'm sending home a cigar box containing some pictures and a present for you. I'm also going to send another box with a rifle and an old French broadsword in it. When you get the box with the rifle and sword, put the things away somewhere. They're not much, just some souvenirs. Another thing, I'd like to teach you to swim next summer. Remember when we all used to take our picnic out and eat? We're bound to be together soon. All I can do is hope and pray.

September 6, 1945
I'm still in Belgium. I'm still waiting on word from the Red Cross. I'd sure love to get home in time for our wedding anniversary, but, honey, that's almost impossible unless a miracle happens. I'm almost sure I'll be home for Christmas, so don't send any

packages. I may even be discharged by then since I've got 80 points now and that's enough for discharge. My heart and soul has always been with you and Larry ever since I've been gone and I've always tried my best. I love you so much, honey. Tell Larry to be ready for a rough romp. His daddy is coming home soon.

September 10, 1945
Honey, are you feeling any better now? I'd certainly like to know but will have to wait on the answer from the Red Cross. I don't know if it will be approved or disapproved but I'll let you know as soon as possible. Here I am again on a cold foggy Monday evening. The darn fog is so thick a person can hardly see anything out doors. I just brought our truck up here and it was awful driving. How is our boy getting along nowadays? Is he still as mischievous as ever? We have almost completed evacuating all this stuff and in three weeks we should be pretty well finished. It can't be long now before I get out of here. Honey, won't it be wonderful for all three of us to be together again? It will seem almost like a new life for me to be a civilian again after being in this Army.

September 12, 1945
I hope and pray these few lines find you much better. The mail over here is all messed up so I don't know how things are back home. All I know is what Mom's letter said. I've sent in the request for an emergency return to the states. All I can do now is wait. As soon as I find out, I'll let you know if it was approved or disapproved. If it's approved, I should leave right away for Paris and either come home by boat or plane. I wish I could be there with you and Larry right now and then we'd all feel better. It's been so long since we've seen each other, but the time has made me love you that much more. I'll make you the best husband and father that is possible. I'd love to be there for our wedding anniversary, but that's impossible now, I think. I don't understand why, but now that the war is all over they have started feeding us K rations again, as if we never got enough B, C, and K garbage during the war. I guess they're trying to help out the food shortage and making the soldiers suffer, as usual. What makes me burn up is this damn black market is selling our meat to the civilians over here. That don't make sense to me.

September 13, 1945
Honey, I hope and pray these few lines find you in the best of health. I'd love to know how you and Larry are. You haven't written since early August and it's a long time not hearing from you. Honey, you don't realize how much I miss you. I hope you love me more than anyone in the world and, darling, I do you. I haven't written xxxxxxxx since Mom wrote and told me about what had happened. Immediately, I went to the Red Cross and sent in for an emergency return to the states. I should be hearing if I get it or not in a few days. Earlier in the evening the boy from Oregon and I were playing songs like Coleman (one of Karl's brothers) **and I used to. Well, darling, I'm telling you my heart and soul is with you and Larry right now and it always has been. Get well and I'm praying you, Larry, and I can be together soon.**

Saturday, September 15, 1945 started out like any other monotonous day in the army. Word spread about noon that the mail had arrived. Karl waited while the sergeant read names. He expected another disappointment. Then he heard his name. The cursive writing he loved was on the envelope. He read it immediately. He quickly wrote back.

September 15, 1945
I got the shock of my life today. I got a letter. It's been a long time since I'd heard from you and, darling, I sure was glad to get this letter. Honey, I know you think of me all the time and I do you the same. It's okay with me if you spent every cent we've got if it will help you get well. Your health means more to me than all the money in the world. So Ronald and his wife are out staying at Madge and Dory's farm too? I'm pretty sure my job at the factory will give us a steady paycheck, but no one knows what will happen. I really look for a pretty tough time for a few years so it wouldn't hurt a bit to save and plan ahead some. Larry must be getting pretty rugged if he's letting the chickens peck him on the hand. I can picture him running from them. What do the roosters do to him? Larry must be like me if he likes to be outdoors a lot. I hope I'm back there before rabbit hunting season is over as Tom and I will have some fun then. Is my shotgun at home or does Dad have it? Larry is too small to go hunting, but it won't be long till he'll be able to go. I want to teach him as much as I can about sports and hunting which will come in handy when he grows up.

We have tomorrow off. It would be so good to be there with you and Larry.

September 21, 1945
I'm a happy boy tonight. I got another letter from you. I'm sure glad you're a lot better and glad the doctor is helping your back. Darling, be sure and tell me just how bad you have been and are right now. I want you to get well so bad but honey, I also want to know how bad you really are. It will surely be wonderful when we can be together again. Darling, I doubt if I'll know how to act, but I'll have you to teach me how to be a civilian again. You said Mom and Dad have some pretty big worries. I know everyone has worries, but I didn't know they had many. That's the first I've heard about this. In fact I thought everyone was getting along pretty good. I guess I'm not up on my home news. You said Larry was standing beside you while you were writing. I sure would have liked to have walked in about that time. Mom told me Dad put a new roof on our house. It probably needed it. Darling, we could buy it from them in no time, have it all paid for and fixed up really nice. I'd like to fix the yard up real pretty and put a rock garden in the front yard if we could. I don't see why we couldn't, do you?

September 22, 1945
I'm still in Belgium. I haven't heard anything yet about the emergency return, but hopefully I will one of these days. I'll let you know as soon as I hear. I saw *Duffy's Tavern* last night at the Metropole Theater and it was pretty good. I'm out of envelopes so I had to write a V-mail. There's not much room on them so I will have to close. I love you. I am fine.

I'M ON MY WAY HOME

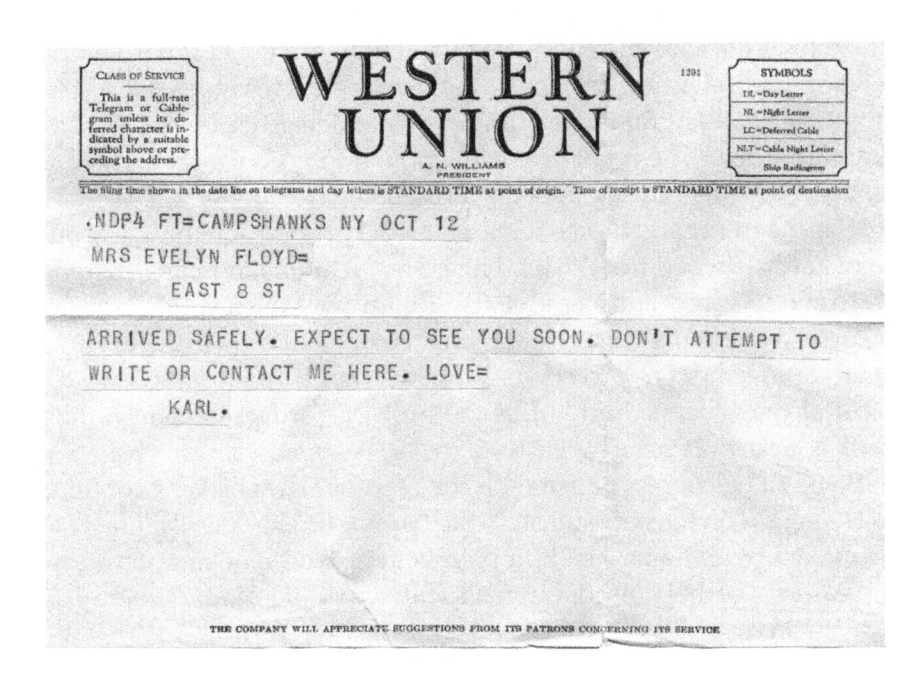

```
.NDP4 FT=CAMPSHANKS NY OCT 12
MRS EVELYN FLOYD=
    EAST 8 ST

ARRIVED SAFELY. EXPECT TO SEE YOU SOON. DON'T ATTEMPT TO
WRITE OR CONTACT ME HERE. LOVE=
    KARL.
```

Karl wrote his last letter of the war to Evie.

September 25, 1945
Paris, France. My Dearest Evelyn and Larry, Darling, don't write anymore. I'm on my way home. I left Brussels yesterday afternoon by plane and flew to Paris. I was supposed to fly from Paris to New York, but the plane service was discontinued so we'll leave here in three days for La Havre, France and get a boat there. I'm traveling on #1 priority and should be home on furlough in anywhere from 10 to 15 days or maybe a couple days longer. After that, I should get a discharge at Camp Atterbury. I can tell more about how that will go when I get home. Darling, I'm hoping and praying I'll be there with you and Larry for our wedding anniversary and his birthday, but if I'm not, I'll be thinking every minute of you both. I've got a present for you and will try and get Larry

something in the states before I get home. Darling, our motto will always be true.
PS. Tell Madge I'm dreaming about fried chicken.

October was the perfect month for Karl to come home. It is Mother Nature's gift to the hardworking folks of Indiana. An Indiana autumn invigorates the soul and sharpens the mind. It is a time for hard work, reward, and reflection before the long, cold gray winter invades. The stifling heat and humidity of summer surrenders to clean, dry air. The days are warm. The nights are cool enough to need a jacket. There is no better weather during the year for sleeping.

The magnificent sunsets serve as a background for the gorgeous colors of hardwood trees' fall foliage. They paint a landscape creating a sense of comfort and peace. Ears of corn bow toward the earth on their gold colored stalks. A hazy dust cloud settles over the evening landscape as the corn pickers harvest the grain. The substantial, sweet scent of the harvested grain fills the nostrils. Farmers replenish their bank accounts after the harvest.

Some things don't change with the seasons. The chickens continue to lay eggs. The roosters still stalk the barnyard. The cows still have to be milked twice daily. The Bull patrols the pasture looking for a cow in season. The hogs need water to wallow in the mud. If there is a heaven on earth, October in Indiana is it.

A Victory ship

Karl sailed 3,100 miles across the Atlantic on a Victory ship, the SS William and Mary. The troopship was as packed as the one he traveled to Europe on. The bunks were still uncomfortable. The sweaty odor of the now battle tested soldiers was the same. No one cared if the seas were calm or not. The troops were coming home, not going to war.

The destination was Camp Shanks, New York. The William and Mary entered New York Harbor on the cool, misty morning of October 12, 1945. Screaming soldiers packed its deck. They could not help but cheer and weep. The Statue of Liberty appeared before the troopship entered the Hudson River. Many of the returning soldiers had seen Lady Liberty when they were young, raw, scared GIs going to fight a war they did not understand. They were now hardened, crusty war veterans trying to put the war memories behind them. After the ship docked, Karl was eager to get American soil under his feet for the first time in over two years He was still in the army, which meant he had to wait in a long line before descending the ship's gangplank. After what seemed like an eternity, he got to walk down to a concrete covered shipyard. It did not matter. He kissed the ground.

Each returning soldier was handed a sheet of paper titled INFORMATION FOR ALL RETURNEES. The goal of the paper was to assist returning soldiers in the transition back to civilian life. Some of its mundane information included:

- Returning soldiers were reminded they could relax. They were no longer in danger.
- Soldiers with any hand grenades or other possible explosives still in their possession needed to take those items to the Ordnance Officer.
- Ammunition or cartridges were not to be put in trash cans.
- Every soldier had to meet with a re-enlistment officer. The officer would ask if a returnee wished to sign up for a new tour of duty. Karl gave a simple answer to that question, "Hell No."

Karl couldn't keep from running to the Telegraph Center after he made it through the Disposition Area headquarters. As usual, there was a long line ahead of him. He got in line and like he had done for two and a half years, he waited. Finally, it was his turn. Karl wrote a message on a small piece of paper. The clerk asked him the name and address to whom the telegram was being sent. Karl paid the fee. The army had taught him to trust no one so he watched the telegraph operator type the address and message. He did not leave until he knew the clerk had sent the message.

Saturday, October 13, 1945 was two days after Karl and Evie's fourth anniversary. A Western Union messenger delivered a telegram addressed to Evelyn Floyd, 714 East 8th Street, Rushville, Indiana. Clara anxiously opened the door. It had seldom been good news during the war when such a messenger appeared at the door. Life itself and the war had turned her into an old, worn out woman. She didn't know how much longer she could pretend to be strong. She felt the same dryness in her mouth she had felt when two of her young children died in one year during a flu epidemic. Her hands shook when she took the envelope. She wished this message would end the nightmare. She hoped her youngest son was coming home.

Neither Ott nor Clara could drive an auto. As luck would have it, Tom had received his honorable discharge from the army on October 9. His bus arrived at the Rushville station the day before the telegram arrived. He had been in the army almost four years. There was no welcoming committee. He walked home from the bus station, but he couldn't resist stopping first at the Greek's to enjoy an ice cream cone and coca cola.

Tom after his discharge from the army

Tom drove the four miles to Madge and Dory's farm. As usual, Dory's old dog with a limp, Pepper, barked when the auto rounded the bend in the road that led to the farm house. Autos seldom came down the isolated road, so Dory stuck his head out of the barn where he was shoveling cow manure to see what was going on Evie, Madge, Ronald, and his wife were down in the basement helping Madge make apple cider. They went out on the front porch to see what was making Pepper bark. They were surprised to see Tom. Ott was riding shotgun and Clara, no more than five feet tall, was in the back seat. Clara jumped out before Tom could completely stop the auto. She excitedly shuffled toward Evie and said, "Evie, you got a telegram. I think it's from Karl."

The seven people in the barnyard on that beautiful autumn day were so different from each other. Two kids who fell in love had created the common bond for the two families. They circled around Evie, each hoping the tears, grief, and worry were about to be swept away. She opened the envelope and removed the message.

Karl sent his last message of the war to his childhood home because he knew his mom would get it to Evie. With her voice breaking and tears pouring down her face, twenty-one year old Evie read every word out loud:

Mrs. Evelyn Floyd East 8th St,
Arrived safely. Expect to see you soon.
Don't attempt to write or contact me here. Love, Karl

Everyone had been waiting for this moment. They hadn't allowed themselves to be happy for two and a half years. Everyone but Ott cried. He complained about a goddam splinter in his eye.

Evie moved back to their home on Benjamin Street to prepare for Karl's homecoming. His guitar was still leaning in the corner of the living room exactly where he had left it 2 1/2 years earlier. She moved it to clean the dust that had accumulated. She put the breadbox that held their letters in the bedroom closet. She asked Ott to clean Karl's 12 gauge shotgun. He oiled it up real nice. He even brought along a couple of boxes of 12 gauge shotgun shells. After all, rabbit season wasn't too far off. Ott went further. He found Karl's hatchet and sharpened it so a guy could shave with it.

The house cleaning was done. There was food in the refrigerator. She took Larry to get a haircut. She bought her first pair of nylon stockings since 1942. The sheets on the bed were clean. She was now ready to pounce on her man like a duck who finds a June bug.

She now had no option but to wait for a call.

The phone call came four days after the Western Union message arrived. She almost fell flat on her face racing to answer it. Karl was on the other end. The first words she heard were, "Honey, I love you. I'm so close to home I can taste it." He was at Camp Atterbury, Indiana. He told her he had been waiting in line to call her for over an hour in what he hoped was his last army line ever. His discharge was scheduled for the next day, October 18. He didn't know what time. From what he was hearing, it should be before noon. Could she find someone to pick him up?

Tom volunteered to drive Evie on the forty-two mile trip to Camp Atterbury. Gas rationing had stopped and the thirty-five mph speed limit was history, so he calculated it would take an hour and a half to get there. He and Evie agreed to leave about 7 am.

Excited as she was, Evie had the fear of Jesus in her soul. Karl would soon discover her secret about Larry's problem. She and Clara had a good talk. Clara suggested that Larry stay with her and Ott. That way, the two women who meant the most to Karl would be with him when he saw his son for the first time in over two years. Together, they would help him see how much of a blessing Larry was.

Ott listened while Evie and Clara plotted. He waited until he thought they had finished. He cleared his throat. He spit some tobacco juice into the can Clara made him carry when he was in the house. He wiped his mouth with his red bandana handkerchief. He then said, "Don't worry, Evie. Karl's a Floyd. He can take whatever goddam thing that's thrown at him. If he gets out of line, I'm still his old man. I'll whip his ass." Problem solved.

Karl didn't need an alarm clock on the morning of his last sleep on an army bunk. He was up before six. He decided he didn't need to tuck in the bunk's sheets. He showered and shaved. He spit polished his shoes. He put on his dress uniform. The thought crossed his mind that he would never have to wear a uniform again which caused a little sadness. Not much, though. He realized he might have to wear it for a few more days since he had no civilian clothes. He packed his few possessions in his duffel bag.

Karl and several other eager soldiers waited to hear their name called. The army took one more opportunity to torment the GIs. The process was slower than molasses. The next few hours seemed like an eternity. After two and a half years of doing things the army way, Karl took the nonsense in stride.

When his turn came, he reviewed his discharge paper for errors or omissions. A clerk explained any benefits he might have coming. He was asked if he had any questions. He answered, "Only one. How do I get to the front gate?" The clerk handed him his honorable discharge papers. Karl expected a salute. Instead, the clerk reached over and shook his hand. He was free to go. Corporal Floyd was a civilian again.

Karl Richard Floyd was back.

Tom and Evie arrived at Camp Atterbury by nine that morning. Though the war was over, the military did not let civilians inside the grounds. The guards at the gate weren't the least bit helpful. Army rules dictated that families wait in a parking lot at the front gate. They waited with many other excited people. Tom told Evie he would go up to the gate and would come get her when he saw Karl.

Karl walked out of the building where the discharge process took place. He made a beeline toward where he thought the gate was. By now, Tom had befriended the guards. He was trading war stories and a few lies with them when he saw a familiar face approaching the gate. He ran to get Evie. They made it back to the gate just as the guards gave Karl permission to leave.

Mr. and Mrs. Karl Floyd hugged and kissed like there was no tomorrow. Tom finally picked up Karl's duffel bag to get the show going and told the lovebirds to get moving to the automobile. Tom asked Karl if he wanted to drive home. Karl answered his nephew and best friend with, "Hell No."

Karl and Evie sat in the back seat. They talked. They kissed. They talked some more. They kissed even more. Tom adjusted the rear view mirror. He didn't care to watch the tomfoolery going on back there.

The trip back to Rushville flew by in a flash.

The road leading into Rushville is Indiana Highway 44. Like most everything else in Rush County, the road is flat as a pancake. About two miles out of town, Tom interrupted the activity in the back seat. He told Karl to look for the Courthouse clock tower. It was still where Karl had left it two and a half years ago.

Karl was wrong about civilian clothes. Evie had bought some duds for him she thought might fit. She put the wool dress uniform he wore home from Camp Atterbury away in a closet next to her wedding dress. On their first evening in their home, they popped popcorn. Karl played his guitar and sang songs to Evie. True to his word, he romped with Larry.

Thursday, October 18, 1945 had been a beautiful Indian summer day. Karl and Evie left the windows open that night. Ott's old rooster, most of its tail feathers gone from advanced age, crowed at the first flicker of sunlight the next morning. In response to the old cock's chatter, the goat the Old Man had bought for the grandkids started to bawl. Evie slept though the commotion, but Karl didn't. He decided to get up and go see Flatrock River.

He got out of bed hoping he wouldn't awaken Evie. He dressed fast. He looked for his hatchet. It was exactly where he had left it. Like he had done countless times over his nearly twenty-six years, he hung it inside his belt. He walked down the street to the old Indian trail leading to Flatrock River. He arrived at his favorite fishing spot. He stood frozen for a few minutes as all the memories of his past, packed in his mind for safekeeping, came flooding back. He never felt so great.

He remembered he had carved his initials into the trunk of the sycamore tree on the riverbank's edge the morning he left. He looked for his handiwork. All that remained was an area of discolored, thickened bark. As he knew would happen, Mother Nature had covered the wound. It was almost like his actions had never happened.

He did one more thing before leaving Flatrock River that morning. He locked his memories of the war into a small corner of his mind. He told himself to throw away the key. He never let them come out.

When he returned, Evie was making breakfast. Toast, bacon, and fried eggs sunny side up, just the way he liked them. He smiled and kissed her. She didn't ask where he had been. She figured he had gone to his mom's to have a cup of coffee.

The war was over. Karl had made it home. He kept his pledge to "take over where I left off with plenty of interest." Their family grew by five more children before their family was complete.

The captain of the SS William and Mary published a daily newsletter during the trip across the Atlantic to keep the returning soldiers informed and entertained. The day before docking at Camp Shanks, he included this cartoon for the soldiers to enjoy.

LIFE AFTER THE WAR

Karl fishing after returning from the war

Karl served his country for two and a half years. He never received the three bronze stars the Army awarded to him. He didn't want them. His reward for doing his duty was coming home.

The *Republican* listed the names of returning soldiers for months after the war ended. In every edition was a listing of discharged soldiers. Four returning soldiers were of particular interest to Evie:

- July 27, 1945, "Pfc. Ronald C. Yoder, who entered the service October 24, 1941, was released July 16 at Fort McPherson,

Georgia. He served in New Guinea and the Philippines. He was awarded the Asiatic-Pacific theater ribbon with two battle stars, the Philippines Liberation ribbon with one star, and the American Defense service ribbon."

- October 16, 1945, "T/Sgt. Thomas A. Beckner of 714 East 8th Street was discharged October 9 at Camp Crowder, Missouri. He was inducted December 1, 1941. He served in Asia. T/Sgt. Beckner received the Asiatic-Pacific theater ribbon and the Good Conduct ribbon."
- October 23, 1945, "T/5 Karl R. Floyd was discharged October 18 at Camp Atterbury, Indiana. He was inducted April 7, 1943 and served in the campaigns of Normandy, Northern France, and Rhineland. T/5 Floyd received the European-African-Middle Eastern ribbon with three battle stars, three bronze stars, and the Good Conduct ribbon."
- March 9, 1946, "Robert Lowell Brown of Rush County was discharged at Camp Atterbury, Indiana on March 1. He entered the service February 4, 1943 and is entitled to wear the American theater ribbon, Asiatic Pacific theater ribbon with one battle star, the Philippine ribbon, and the Good Conduct medal."

The adjustment to civilian life was not easy. Karl and Evie dealt with his emotional scars for years. For months after coming home, Karl instinctively dove to the ground when he heard a loud noise. Such a reaction concerned Evie. He told her to not worry. It was funny habit he picked up. He followed the unwritten code of silence for returning veterans. He would not talk of what he had seen and experienced. He got angry when people asked him questions about the war. He told people the men left behind were the real heroes. He wanted to let the past rest or the nightmares would return. He carried his memories, without bitterness, to his grave.

Karl and Evie dealt with Larry's handicap with ferocious determination. They kept him out of school an extra year, and finally allowed him to start first grade at age seven. Public school for Larry lasted three months.

> **TEACHER'S COMMENTS**
>
> Date *Dec. 5, 1950.*
> The work is too difficult for Larry to do.
>
> Jan. 19, 1951.
> Larry will have a special teacher next term Mrs. Jackson on Harrison st. I am sure this will be better for him.
> Larry has learned many things. He is a good little boy.

Larry was getting failing grades in every subject. His first grade teacher wrote to Karl and Evie on December 5, 1950, "The work is too difficult for Larry to do."

The school system's Superintendent asked Karl and Evie to meet for a consultation. He informed them school was a waste of time. Larry would never learn to read, write, or do arithmetic.

Karl, by 1950, was a man who smoked two packs of unfiltered Lucky Strike cigarettes a day. He was still having occasional flashback nightmares. He hadn't stepped inside a church since he had come home. He was well aware that his son was handicapped. He snapped at the idiot, "Go to hell, you son of a bitch!" as he stormed out of the room.

Evie was still adjusting to Karl's mood swings that came back with him. She apologized for Karl's outburst.

She was accustomed to rejection and, as a result, had learned the art of making lemonade out of lemons. She calmly responded, "You don't understand. You're going to help us find a way educate our son."

Her negotiating skills paid off. The Superintendent agreed to hire retired teachers to tutor Larry, one on one. He was tutored until he was eighteen. He learned to read, write, and do some math.

Karl and Evie kept few reminders of the war. There were two crystal swans Karl had sent from France. Child number two dropped one of the swans. Evie glued it back together. They shared the top of the chest of drawers in their bedroom. There was a picture of Karl looking young and proud in his dress uniform. His handsome features, cocky smile, and bedroom eyes were always fixed on their bed. The uniform and overcoat he wore returning home stayed hidden away in their closet. The breadbox that held their letters never saw the light of day again until after they both had died.

They didn't attend parades honoring veterans of the war. They did, however, need and want to pay respects to the war dead. On Decoration Day every May, they traveled downtown to the Courthouse lawn. Someone always read out loud the names of Rush County's soldiers who died during World War Two. Karl said nothing during those ceremonies. His mind was somewhere else.

East Hill Cemetery soldier section

They often visited the soldier section at East Hill Cemetery. It was as if they were visiting a holy place. They walked among the simple white headstones with their heads hung low. They paused to read the names on the markers. They spoke few words until they were on their way home. There were no dinner table stories about the war at their home.

When asked about the war, Karl and Evie momentarily seemed to go into their own separate world. They answered as if each had experienced a different nightmare. Evie would look down. Her eyes glazed over with tears, but she held back. She knew crying did no good. No words ever came out of her mouth. She…simply…slowly… sighed. Karl always looked away. It was if he were looking at something out of the corner of his eye. He would shrug his shoulders and answer, "There's really nothing to say." He did admit the army taught him to drink coffee because there were times he was so cold he needed the heat from the tin cup to thaw his frozen fingers.

Soldiers have that locked vault deep in their brains that only fellow combatants are allowed to enter. Non-combatants did try to unlock the vault. A kid once asked Karl if he killed anyone during the war. Karl's eyes hardened. He stared directly into the eyes of his inquisitor and answered, "No decent soldier would ever answer that goddam stupid question. Don't you dare ask me again!"

Despite the code of silence, Karl needed people to know there were times he had been scared for his life with, "It's easy as hell to dig a foxhole when someone is shooting at you." He also divulged that he learned a foxhole exposed a man's character. "I'd share a goddam foxhole with that guy." was Karl's greatest compliment while, "I wouldn't let that sonofabitch in my foxhole." was his ultimate damning assessment.

Karl was still working on his cussing. He did until his dying days.

Nine years after he returned home, Karl's routine was to have a cup of coffee after work at his folk's home. One day at the dinner table, Clara's eyes went into a blank stare and she collapsed. Karl caught her before she hit the floor. She turned blue until he swept food from her mouth so she could breathe again. He lifted her into his arms and carried her to bed. She didn't recover from the stroke she suffered, but she was never alone. Her daughters and daughters-in-law took turns attending her for over a year. Karl visited her daily.

Ott, now needing a walker, spent his days sitting next to her. He talked to her constantly. She never answered him. Her partially paralyzed body only allowed her to weakly blink her eyes, and sip water and soup. She laid in that bed until she was granted her well-earned angel's wings on January 15, 1956.

After Clara's death, Ott continued to suck on Red Man Chewing Tobacco and he cussed like a sailor until he also suffered a stroke. Mother Nature was nice to him. He lay in the same bed Clara died in for only a few days. He passed away on January 8, 1959.

The anguish and tragedy in Evie's life continued. Ten years after Karl was discharged from the army, October 9, 1955, Madge and Dory were returning home from church on a sunny, warm Indiana Indian summer Sunday morning. One mile from their farmhouse, Dory approached a railroad track that he had crossed countless times, the same track Karl traveled on when he left home for the army in 1943. Dory apparently didn't see the approaching train coming from Rushville. He drove his Plymouth onto the track, right in front of the train. Madge and Dory died that morning. Their time on earth was up.

Karl learned to rely upon others when he lost his eyesight in his mid-fifties. He carried the confidence and swagger learned as a child to his dying day. A visitor asked him how he was doing shortly before he died. Karl, his voice down to a whisper answered, " I'm fine. Don't worry about me. Just make sure Evie is okay." The cigarettes won. He died from lung cancer on September 28, 1981.

Larry learned to walk without a walker by his fifth birthday. Karl and Evie never abandoned him. He spent his entire life under their care and supervision. He never worried about his safety. He never lost his big grin. He had many friends. Thanks to his handicap, Larry never judged others. He accepted all people as God presented them. He died on May 20, 2003 at the age of 60.

Evie buried Karl and Larry before she was relieved of her burdens. All through her life, she never ceased to give God the glory for the good things she enjoyed. Dementia in her final years erased the rejections, disappointments, fears, and tears she had endured during her life. The nightmare of the war vanished as her memory washed away. She joined Karl and Larry in death on May 27, 2007. If there is a heaven, she is walking its streets of gold.

Someone decided long ago to place East Hill Cemetery on a rolling bluff just east of Rushville. East Hill welcomes the rising sun to Rushville casting its loving shadow over the town where Karl and Evelyn met, fell in love, married, raised six children, and died.

East Hill Cemetery is a peaceful place. It overlooks the banks of the Flatrock River where Karl learned to swim, fish, and hunt. Anyone who grew up in Rushville knows a trip home is incomplete without a visit to East Hill. Generations of families rest there. Wendell Willkie is buried there. So are the remains of Civil War veterans, World War One and World War Two soldiers, paupers, distinguished citizens, and thousands of other souls who are long forgotten but to God.

One travels through a large, arched, gothic gate to enter East Hill. It is an odd entry into the final resting place of the citizens of a small rural town like Rushville. At first glance, it resembles to grieving families a giant orifice about to devour their loved one. Once the grief lessens, the structure is seen as a sentry protecting the dead from the worries of the living. Thousands of mourners have transported a loved one through that gateway. It gives comfort the departed are safe. East Hill reminds every one of the cycle of life all must travel.

There is a tombstone on planet Earth at 39 degrees 36'14.85"N longitude, 85 degrees 26'03.16"W latitude. Under the heading of FLOYD are the names KARL EVELYN LARRY. Evie is in the middle. Karl and Larry are on each side protecting her. Interlocking wedding bands are between Evie and Karl's names. The pledge they made to each other when Karl left for the war, "I'm yours, You're mine, and Larry is ours" will last forever.

Evie, Karl, Larry, and the author in 1948

Thank you for reading my book. If you are inclined, I would appreciate your review of this book on Amazon.com. The number of reviews a book accumulates on a daily basis has a direct impact on how the book sells. Just by leaving a review increases the chance of others becoming aware of this World War Two love story.

To submit a review:
- Go to **Amazon.com**
- Go to the product detail page for **Come Share My Foxhole**
- Click **Write a customer review** in the Customer Reviews section.
- Click **Submit** when you have completed writing your review.

Thank you. Ric Floyd

About the author

Richard D. Floyd, M.D. is Larry's younger brother and the first child born after World War Two to Karl and Evelyn Floyd. Mama Evelyn instilled in Ric the determination and desire to learn. Karl furnished the genetics for Ric's stubborn bullheadedness.

He is the first member of the Floyd family to earn a Doctor of Medicine degree from the Indiana University School of Medicine. He devoted himself to a wonderful thirty year Obstetrics and Gynecology career in Indianapolis.

When Ric was a boy, grandpa Ott, father Karl, and his cousin Tom taught him how to fish and hunt in order to provide food and money for the family. While doing so, they told him their colorful, sometimes unbelievable tales of growing up in Rush County. Those stories and the letters found in the old metal bread box Evelyn had hidden in her closet inspired him to write this memoir.

Ric still loves rural Indiana's corn and soybean fields, and the hardwood forests, but he no longer hunts or fishes. If you are one of his Hoosier friends or family, he will have your back and share a foxhole with you.

You can communicate with Ric at: sfloyd3252@aol.com

Made in the USA
Coppell, TX
17 March 2020